RAV DOVBER PINSON

ליבי ער

THE
MYSTERY
OF
SHABBOS

Shabbat
Rediscovered

סוד השבת

— חלק א' —

IYYUN PUBLISHING

Published by IYYUN Publishing
232 Bergen Street
Brooklyn, NY 11217

http:/www.iyyun.com

Iyyun Publishing books may be purchased for educational, business or sales promotional use. For information please contact: contact@IYYUN.com

Editor: Reb Matisyahu Brown

Editor: Reb Eden Pearlstein

Proofreading / Editing: Reb Simcha Finkelstein

Cover and book design: RP Design and Development

pb ISBN 978-1-7338130-7-5

Pinson, DovBer 1971-
The Mystery of Shabbos: Shabbat Rediscovered
1.Judaism 2. Jewish Spirituality 3. General Spirituality

THE MYSTERY OF SHABBOS

—

Shabbat Rediscovered

THIS BOOK IS DEDICATED
IN MEMORY OF

הרב ראובן
בן ר' שמואל יום טוב
שיינער ז"ל

Harav Reuvein
ben Reb Shmuel Yom Tov
Scheiner ז"ל

A humble man, loving father and devoted Rebbe;
Reb Reuvein dedicated his life to teaching Torah and raised
generations of upright, Torah committed Jews, united in
their love for Hashem.
It was his legacy of love for Shabbos burning brightly in his
children that inspired the writing of this book.
May it be a Zechus for his Neshama.

INTRODUCTION
THE LIGHT OF SHABBOS

S HABBOS IS ONE OF THE GREAT WONDERS OF THE WORLD. The weekly "day of rest" is a universally acknowledged phenomenon, but one that is not easily understood or explained. On the one hand, it appears that Shabbos is simply one day out of the seven-day weekly cycle dedicated for "down-time." This simple idea of an alternating rhythm of work and rest is nearly ubiquitous across cultures; in fact, all current civilizations celebrate, in one form or another, some type of rest during the course of the seven-day cycle of the week. (*Kuzari,* 1:57. *Even Ezra,* Shemos 16:1) And yet, there is an obvious but profound mystery in this. Why is there such a thing as a seven day cycle, punctuated by a period of rest, in the first place? Why do nomads in Mongolia, for example, who have little to no exposure to Torah's assertion that, "In six days Hashem created the world and then rested on the seventh," have a seven-day weekly cycle with one day of rest?

A solar calendar follows the objectively experienced cycle of seasons, while a lunar calendar follows the more subtle phases of the moon, which have no overt bearing on the seasons or weather. Both the concepts of years, defined by the solar circuit, and months, as determined by the waxing and waning of the moon, are innate to the mechanical rhythms of nature. They are each tied to astrological phenomena that all cultures observe, and all people experience. But where do weeks come from? Why does a week exist at all? And why specifically a seven day week, which seems to have no astrological nor seasonal reason behind it, nor any basis in a universally observable phenomenon?

The short answer is that the construct of weeks originates in a Divine mandate, based on a sacred view of time. It is the Torah, in the narrative of Creation, which reveals the existence of that which we call a week. In fact, the only possible reason and purpose for a specifically seven-day weekly cycle is a meta-physical, Torah-based reason and purpose. And yet, the seven day week is embedded in human consciousness to the point that all known civilizations measure time in this way.

By delving deeper into the spiritual nature of the weekly cycle, and through understanding Shabbos as the meta-root of the week, we will come to appreciate more deeply the power and magic that is Shabbos. We will then be able to open ourselves more fully in order to connect to the essence of this most simple yet profound and mysterious day.

THE BODY AND SOUL OF SHABBOS

Everything in life has both a 'body' and a 'soul.' The body is the 'what,' the thing itself in its objective and tangible reality. The soul is the 'how,' the inner and subjective experience of that thing, the quality of our relationship with it and the way in which we interact with it.

The same is true with Shabbos. The 'body' of Shabbos is the day itself, the seventh day of the week; the 'soul' of Shabbos is our *Penimi* / inner relationship to this utterly vibrant and alive construct.

The 'body' of Shabbos can also be said to be the laws and structures of Shabbos, which are like a skeleton or a canvas, upon which the soul of Shabbos reveals itself. The soul is the animating/enlivening essence and spirit of Shabbos, expressed through the way we experience, appreciate, and incorporate those laws and structures into our lives.

Similarly, there are also two dimensions in the way Shabbos was revealed to us: a) with great commotion, in public, at Mount Sinai, and b) quietly in a private way. On the one hand, Shabbos is part of the Ten *Dibros* / Commandments given at the Revelation of Sinai. At Sinai, "there were thunder claps and lightning flashes, and a thick cloud was upon the mountain, and a very powerful blast of Shofar" (Shemos, 19:16). When the Torah was (about to be) given, "the whole world shook and shuddered" (*Mechilta*, Yisro, 1). The revelation of Shabbos at Sinai was thus accompanied by much fanfare, and was, on some level, acknowledged by every root civilization in the world.

Yet, on the other hand, we learn (in *Beitza*, 16a) that, "Every Mitzvah which Hashem gave to the People of Israel, He gave them publicly — *except Shabbos*, which Hashem bestowed upon them in secret, for it is said, 'It is a sign between Me and the Children of Israel forever'" (Shemos, 31: 17). Shabbos is therefore an intimate sign that exists only between *HaKadosh Baruch Hu* / the Holy One, Blessed be He, and us, the Jewish people.

This is the dual nature of Shabbos, the body and the soul, the revealed and the secret, the public and the very private (See *Rabbeinu Bachya*, Shemos, 31:17. *Kad Kemach*, Shabbos). On an even deeper level, the display of lights and thunder and the trembling are actually not meant to reveal, but rather to conceal what is truly being transmitted: the secret inner soul of Shabbos and all other Mitzvos. The great commotion, flashing lights and sounds are all a smoke screen, as it were, so that Hashem could reveal to the heart of *Klal Yisrael* / the People of Israel the private "sign" of affection between them, like the whispering on the pillow that intimate lovers share.

This "sign" is the hidden soul, the *Ohr* / light of Shabbos. The body (the revealed laws) of Shabbos is the *K'li* / vessel which protects and preserves the secret contained therein. (However, with regards to Shabbos, even the 'laws' of Shabbos are hidden and shrouded in mystery (*Chagigah*, 10a), as they too are part of the secret of Shabbos.) The vessel, the law, is necessary, as a person needs a skeleton, sinews and fibers to support and sustain their vital life force. However, a vessel or body without a soul, without animating light, is dead, inert and pedestrian. The text you are reading is about the *Ohr* / light, the *Neshamah* / soul, the hidden and intimate "sign" of Shabbos.

There are, of course, copious amounts of laws connected to Shabbos, what is allowed and what is not, what is considered *Melachah* / work and what is not; this book does not deal with or explain those in detail. Rather, this book explores the inner dimension, the essential life-force of Shabbos; in other words, that which the body and laws are meant to support. Sometimes the inner dimensions of a particular law will be explored, as each law is rooted in a deeper secret (*Siddur Im Dach*, Derushim l'Chasunah, 128b), but the overall focus of this text is on the hidden light of Shabbos.

SHABBOS AS A TEMPLE IN TIME

"The gate of the Inner Court (of the *Beis haMikdash* / Temple)... shall remain closed during the six workdays, but on Shabbos it shall be opened" (Yechezkel, 46:1). On a meta-physical level, the 'Beis haMikdash' still exists; not 'publicly,' in space, but 'privately,' in time and in consciousness.* On every Shabbos the gate to its 'Inner Court' is opened for us to enter within. The question is then, how do we enter this gate; how can we enter into a meaningful and intimate relationship with Shabbos to the extent that we can sense being in the Inner Court, so-to-speak, of the Divine Presence? This book attempts to answer just that question.

---

* Everything exists on three levels: space, time and consciousness. Space is the most physical and revealed of these three. In the realm of space, the Beis haMikdash no longer exists, however in the more intangible inner worlds of time and consciousness, the Beis haMikdash still exists.

All the laws of 'do not do such and such...' on Shabbos, are there to create the proper context, the body, the outline, so that our inner state of being can be expressed freely and fully. Without an 'outer' structure, there would be no 'inner' chamber, certainly no gate by which to access it. In this way, the laws are not merely about what is allowed to be done or not done, rather they provide us with an entry point to the inner reality of Shabbos.

The inner reality of Shabbos is ultimately what we are, and to truly 'be' what we are, we need to stop 'doing.' Shabbos therefore brings us into this deepest state of being, beyond all doing, beyond all proactive manipulation of the physical world, into a realm of creative perfection.

Shabbos reflects the deepest place within us, and indeed within all of creation. Accordingly, Shabbos is referred to as the "Holy of Holies," the innermost chamber of the *Beis haMikdash* / Temple, and, as mentioned, just as there is a Temple in space there is a Temple in time (*Pri Tzadik*, Vayakhel. All Mitzvos are included within Shabbos and the Mikdash (*Ramban*, Vayikra, 26:1). The *Ohr* / light of Shabbos is like the Ohr of the Beis haMikdash. *Tikkunei Zohar*, Tikun 21). The Beis haMikdash in *Yerushalayim* / Jerusalem had three main chambers: the Outer Court, the Inner Court or "Holy" Chamber, and the deepest place, the "Holy of Holies." The same is also true with the Temple in Time. The Outer Chamber of time is the weekdays. The inner Holy Chamber is the Yomim Tovim / holidays of the year. The innermost chamber, the Holy of Holies of Time, is Shabbos. It is the *Nekudah* / essence of time, the perfect stillness within the rhythms and commotions of time.

We know that the First Beis haMikdash began to be destroyed on Saturday night, right after Shabbos (*Ta'anis. 29a, Erchin*, 11b). The Second Beis haMikdash was destroyed on Shabbos itself (according to the Yerushalmi (*Ta'anis*, 4:5), it was destroyed on Rosh Chodesh, and we know that the 9th of Av that year was on Sunday). Out of all the days of the week, we might think that Shabbos itself would be the least appropriate day for such destruction, as Shabbos is beyond the world of destruction (*Shem M'Shemuel*, Vayakhel), and it would seem that this special quality of Shabbos would protect the Beis haMikdash. However, the Temples were specifically destroyed within the light of Shabbos so that we would seek out and find Hashem's Presence, the light of the Shechinah, even within our exile (*Yearos Devash*, 1, Derush 13). The Shechinah is always with us in the temporal Beis haMikdash: Shabbos Kodesh. And that Temple can never be destroyed, although it may be concealed through our own neglect.

SHABBOS MEANS 'TO RETURN'

The word *Shabbos* shares a root with *Shev* / sit or settle. On Shabbos we *Shuv* / return (which also has the same letters) to a state of stillness, silence and calmness of spirit. It is not what we do on Shabbos that defines it, rather, it is in the non-doing; refraining from action reveals its true essence.[*]

---

[*] In fact, before reaching Mount Sinai, when Klal Yisrael was encamped in Marah, we received the 'positive dimensions,' the 'doings' of Shabbos, and only at Mount Sinai were we told what we're *not* allowed to do on Shabbos (Ramban, *Hasagas Sefer haMitzvos*, Shoresh 14). In other words, Klal Yisrael received the Kedushah of Shabbos, the *Cheftzah* / 'objective sanctity' of Shabbos, at Matan Torah (the Brisker Rav, *Hagadah*, Dayenu). (Although, already before Matan Torah it says שבת־קדש שבתון (Shemos, 16:23). This suggests that the

Time is movement, and weekdays are all about externalized processes and productions. Shabbos is the state of having arrived at the destination, allowing for increased inwardness and reflection. This stillness is the essential *Nekudah* / point within all movements. When we enter the innermost chamber, the Holy of Holies, in which the service was done in complete silence, there is no more room to move, nowhere else to go and nothing to do. In other words, when we enter into Shabbos, we have arrived.

Movement, creativity, and 'doing' generates sound and noise; 'being,' on the other hand, is still and silent. On Shabbos we let go of our striving to creatively manipulate the world, we release our incessant drive to accomplish, and we thereby settle into a perfect, inward silence. As mentioned, Shabbos means 'rest,' and the word *Shabbos* actually begins with the word *Sha* / hush; an allusion to the verbal command to silence all the chatter of the world.

In addition to silence, Shabbos is also characterized by stillness. As a matter of course, movement creates friction, and friction ultimately generates sparks, and then fire. On Shabbos we refrain from producing fire, both literally and metaphorically. Fire suggests productivity and progress; it transforms and 'completes' objects, as in cooking raw foods. The beginning of human civilization is Adam's domestication of fire, which led to the ability to prepare and

Kedushah of Shabbos was given prior to Matan Torah (See also *Oznayim l'Torah*, ad loc). Only at Sinai were they commanded to offer the special offerings for Shabbos (*KolBo*), as we say in the liturgy of Musaf on Shabbos, אז מסיני נצטוו עליה / then, at Sinai we were commanded to offer up offerings. The Brisker Rav, on the other hand, contends that the *Issurei Gavrah* / prohibitions upon the people were given at Marah. It is important to note that Rav Yosef Engel writes, according to the *Yerushalmi*, the *Issur* / prohibition on Shabbos is *only* on the *Gavrah* / Jewish person, who is not allowed to work on Shabbos, not on action or object itself, the Cheftzah. However, according to the Bavli (which is more connected to the 'below'), there is an Issur Cheftzah. *Asvan d'Oraisa*, Klal 10 preserve foods, as well as to meld and mold tools. Although this "technology" was attained only after eating from the Tree of Knowledge, post-Eden. Had Adam and *Chava* / Eve not eaten from the Tree of Knowledge, had they remained connected to the Tree of Life, then human creativity would have been Divine-like and we would be able to create new realities via mere intention and speech, much like the Creator, without the medium of fire and other implements.

Contrary to many world mythologies, in the post-Eden reality, human beings did not 'steal fire' from Heaven; quite the opposite, Hashem gave us the gift of fire. (Hashem gave Adam the wisdom to create fire (*Pesachim*, 54a). And Hashem placed in front of him two flintstones. *Yerushalmi, Berachos,* 8:5). Hashem presented us this gift so that we too could create, even in our post-Eden reality. Fire is one of the most fundamental and powerful tools we have at our disposal to creatively manipulate and advance the world around us for our benefit, and the benefit of all creation.

Weekdays are a 'fire' reality, where we are focused on materially moving forward and creating. On Shabbos, however, we are not allowed to perform *Melachah* / work. There are many forms of prohibited work on Shabbos. In fact, there are specifically 39 *Avos* / parent or primary prohibitions, and many more *Toldos* / offspring or derivative prohibitions that emerge from these original 39 activities. Yet, the Torah singles out for mention only the act of lighting a fire as prohibited on Shabbos: "Do not light a fire in any of your dwellings" (*Shemos*, 35:3). (Plowing and harvesting are also mentioned as prohibitions in *Shemos*, 34:21, as these represent the main forms of human livelihood. *Ramban*, ad loc). This is because fire is the most pronounced form of transformation, and, in a way, is the root of all human ingenuity and work (see *Ginas Egoz*, 2, 33:2).

Shabbos is the very antithesis of fire; it is freedom from the need to advance, alter, move, or create. On Shabbos we allow our drive for productivity to fall silent. Parenthetically, this is another reason why we endeavor to eat fish on Shabbos (*Magen Avraham*, Orach Chayim, 242:1. It is a special Mitzvah to eat fish on Shabbos, although it is not a law of the Torah. *Kuntres Acharon*, Ibid, 4), as fish are 'quiet' as they glide gently and without friction through the waters. They are one with the environment in which they live.

Throughout the week we stand outside of our environment, so-to-speak; in a sense we are necessarily separate from the world as we manipulate it. In fact, we often find ourselves at odds with nature, and sometimes even 'at war' with it. If we feel cold, we turn up the furnace; if it is dark, we turn on a light. This is the paradigm of the weekday, the element of fire, which changes things from one state to another.*

On Shabbos, however, we leave the world of fire (the fires of *Gehenom* / hell or separation are extinguished on Shabbos, yet another reason we do not light fire on Shabbos. *Tikkunei Zohar*, Tikun 24), and re-enter creation as fish in water, so to speak, with no separation or resistance between us and the world around us. On Shabbos we experience

---

* According to many, the definition of fire is the combustion of a substance, when the fire actually manipulates and destroys something (*Avnei Nezer*, Orach Chayim, 138). Although, the Alter Rebbe rules that fire is defined by merely being a fire (*Kuntras Acharon*, Orach Chayim, 495:2). The Rogatchover writes that the Rambam, as well, rules that it is the mere act of fire which constitutes Melachah on Shabbos (*Tzafnos Paneach*, Kelalei HaTorah vHaMitzvah, Havarah, 5).

seamless unity, similar to the seamlessness of water. (Shabbos is connected to water; הני שבע דשבתא כנגד מי? אמר רבי חלפתא בן שאול: כנגד שבעה קולות שאמר דוד על המים.*Berachos*, 29a)

"*Olam haBa* / the World-to-Come is like the sea" (*Koheles Rabbah*, 1:9). Shabbos is a glimmer of Olam haBa, and its unifying flow has the power to bring us into an effortless alignment with Hashem and with the world around us. As we enter Shabbos, a distinct sense of lightness, ease and delight washes over us; simply, we no longer experience friction with creation. We are home.

CREATING THE CONTEXT FOR TRUE JOY & EXPANSIVENESS

Although they are many, the prohibitions of Shabbos are not meant to stifle or suppress us. To the contrary, they are there to liberate us from the wheel of perpetual doing, and induce us into a deeper, higher, freer state of being. The intent of the 'non-doings' of Shabbos are thus designed to bring us ever greater joy and openness, and not, G-d forbid, feelings of stress, constriction or melancholy. In other words, observing Shabbos should expand our minds and hearts, not close them, it should ideally make us feel more fluidity and light in our lives.

Shabbos should even inspire a more playful disposition. In fact, on Shabbos, parents should naturally play a little more with their children. According to our sages, on Shabbos we do not teach our children new study material, "So that the fathers of the children will have time to fulfill the Mitzvah of Shabbos [which is rest]" /

דיפנו אבהתהון דינוקי למצוותא דשבתא (*Nedarin*, 37b). Without the stress of teaching new or difficult ideas, parents have more time and head-space to be at ease with their children (משתעשעין עם התינוקות *Ran*, ad loc. See also *Shabbos*, 145:b regarding Raba and his child). A balanced, whole-some playfulness is part of the posture and vibe of Shabbos. It is a natural expression of our relief from the world of striving and progress.

Interestingly, the entire *Mesechtah* / tracate of Shabbos ends with the following story: "Ullah happened to come upon the house of the Exilarch and he saw Rabba bar Rav Hunah sitting in a tub of water and measuring it. So he asked Rabba, 'Did not the Sages say that it is permitted to measure only with regards to a measurement of a Mitzvah? And this is not a Mitzvah.' Rabba answered him, 'I am just acting without awareness — not intending to measure.'" He was sitting in a tub, probably to cool himself from the heat (*Ben Yehoyda*, ad loc), and was passing the time by playfully measuring the water. This story of the great and illustrious sage Rabba can be read as an illustration of the relaxed, lighter state of mind that flows from the 'non-doing' of Shabbos; a kind of spontaneous playfulness that is often simply not available during the week.

TRANSITIONING INTO THE MODE OF SHABBOS

On Friday it is important to prepare your mindset for the ex-pansiveness of Shabbos. As the week comes to a close and Shabbos approaches, we should aspire to be detached more and more from the hustle and bustle of life and the 'noise' of the week. For example, in the hours leading up to Shabbos, you could refrain from looking at your bills. Especially if paying the bills is stressful to you, it would only cloud your mind with agitation when your goal is to begin settling into the clarity and stillness of non-doing.

Centuries ago there was a custom in many Jewish communities to blow six blasts of the Shofar over the course of Friday afternoon. The first blast, for example, was a warning to the farmers to put down their tools and start heading home. The second blast was for the shopkeepers to start closing up their stores, and so forth. The sixth and final blast indicated that Shabbos was about to begin (*Shabbos*, 35b. Although this is, for the most part, not practiced, it is still brought down in the Shulchan Aruch (*Orach Chayim*, 256). Rashi writes that it is still practiced. *Gittin*, 60b). This was a visceral reminder of the incremental transition into Shabbos. Certain communities today still sound a siren as Shabbos is approaching (see *Kaf haChayim*, ibid). Perhaps another reason for specifically six blasts is their correspondence to the six days of the week; with each blast one would take another 'step' out of their weekday consciousness.

In the next chapter, the idea of gradually transitioning from the six days of the week into Shabbos will be further explored.

PREPARING FOR SHABBOS

Shabbos is a gift from Above. By nature, people only give gifts to those who find favor in their eyes (*Baba Basra*, 156a); the desire to give the gift is aroused by the receiver of the gift. Although Hashem gives us the gift of Shabbos for free, nevertheless, we only receive this gift to the extent that we consciously desire it and give ourselves to it. We need to make ourselves proper receivers, and one way we do this is by taking the time to prepare for Shabbos and cultivating a sense of anticipation for the depths of what we can receive.

As in every experience in life that requires preparation, the more we put into it, the more we can get out of it. In the language of our sages, "He who toils before Shabbos will get to eat on Shabbos" (*Avodah Zarah*, 3a). We receive spiritual nourishment from Shabbos commensurate to the depth of our preparation. In fact, there is actually a Mitzvah from the Torah to prepare for Shabbos (*Shemos*, 16:5. *Shabbos*, 117b. Tur, *Shulchan Aruch*, Orach Chayim, 250), and thus we only receive from Shabbos as much as we put into it (*Likutei Torah*, Beshalach, p. 2c). The second volume in this series on Shabbos will explore in great detail how we prepare for and enter into Shabbos; for now, just a few remarks will suffice.

Shabbos is like a pure light that shines down into and through us. The more clear and transparent the vessel, the more light that can be seen. The more cloudy and opaque the vessel, the less light is perceived and received. The radiance of Shabbos illuminates each person according to the extent that they prepare and cleanse their vessel.

If a person enters Shabbos harried, stressed and in a frenzy, feeling that he is being pulled away from his occupation and his workweek, then he will inevitably pull his workweek and stress into Shabbos. If a person works until two minutes before Shabbos or arrives from a long drive just as Shabbos is about to start, he cannot enter Shabbos properly and his Shabbos will not be all that it could potentially be.

It is vital to enter Shabbos rested and with a settled mind, not feeling rushed or pressured. In the desert, the *Mon* / Manna was available as a double portion on Friday morning, enough for both Friday and Shabbos. We too, early in the day on Friday, need to begin preparing, at least our mindset, so that we have 'what to eat' both literally and metaphorically on Shabbos.

HOW TO TRANSITION INTO SHABBOS

To enter into any new 'space' you need to be able to transition out of where you are coming from before crossing the threshold into where you are going. Say, for example, you get home from a hard day's work, where you were utterly stressed and overwhelmed and now you must go to your best friend's wedding. You need to transition out of your work consciousness and enter into another head space, otherwise you will physically show up to the wedding but you will not at all be present, and as a result you will not truly be there for your friend on their most important day. You will be dragging the burden of your stress, your "baggage" so to speak, into what is supposed to be a joyous occasion. In order to transition out of your work mode, physical acts such as taking a shower and putting on new clothes will help you let go of the recent past and enter into a new 'space' with a clean slate. Similarly, to effectively leave the workweek behind and enter Shabbos with freshness and presence, we need a transition period in which we can take off our literal and figurative *garments*, cleanse ourselves, assume new *garments* appropriate for the occasion, and gradually shift into a Shabbos mode of being.

In fact, techniques of transition are especially important when it comes to Shabbos, because Shabbos starts in the 'middle' of the weekday, as it were, since 'day' begins with the onset of 'night.' If we would go to sleep on Friday night and wake up and it would be Shabbos, sleep itself would serve as the transitional passage-way. We would wake up fresh into the new day, and enter into the new state of being. (Perhaps, before Matan Torah, Shabbos actually began in the morning and extended into the night. See *Tzlach*, Pesachim, 116b, regarding Pesach in Egypt. Note, *Rashbam*, Bereishis, 1:5. Although see *Even Ezra*, Shemos, 16:25 — yet simply this could be talking about before Matan Torah.) However, Shabbos 'interrupts' the weekday experience by starting late Friday afternoon; in some areas of the world, in the depths of winter, Shabbos can begin as early as 3pm. In any case, to make the shift from weekday into Shabbos consciousness without any natural break or transition like sleep, we need to learn how to consciously transition into another state of being while we are still awake during the very same weekday.

What is even more striking is the following. Say Shabbos (or candle lighting) is at 3:34pm. In that case, 3:33pm is still a week-day, and then one minute later, as the clock changes to 3:34, we must have stopped all work. There is no in-between time, much less an intervening night of sleep; it is a completely new 'day' from one second to the next. Without learning the art of transitioning from one state to the next in a thoughtful, smooth, and sensitive way, we will simply crash into Shabbos with no tact or taste for what we are about to experience.

In truth, all *Yomim Tovim* / holidays are also like this because, as mentioned, according to Torah the 'day' starts as the sun sets.

Yet, Yom Tov is a little different than Shabbos, because according to Torah law, the day before some of the Yomim Tovim is a special day in itself, not a regular work day. There is thus a built-in transition into the holiday. For example, on Erev Pesach, the day before Pesach, we were commanded to bring an offering to the *Beis ha-Mikdash*, when it was still standing (or when possible). As a result, we were forbidden to eat Chametz from the time we brought that offering at midday; there was, and still is, thus an extended segue into Pesach. Similarly, on Erev Yom Kippur, there is a Biblical command to increase in eating before the fast starts. This creates an extended passageway from a halachically 'regular' day into Yom Kippur. Biblically, there is something unique about the 'day before' certain holy days.

On Erev Shabbos, however, Biblically speaking, there is nothing unique; there is no special Mitzvah that needs to be done on Erev Shabbos itself. Yet what *is* unique is the command *to prepare for Shabbos*. On Erev Shabbos there is a Mitzvah to prepare; we ourselves must create this segue, as there is no specification for what we must do, other than 'to prepare.'

Erev Shabbos is therefore all about preparing and learning the art of preparing. This is in contrast to the Yomim Tovim, where the preparation is basically utilitarian. On Erev Pesach we prepare by baking Matzah so that we can have Matzah to eat on Pesach. On Erev Sukkos we prepare by building a Sukkah so that we will have a Sukkah to sit in on Sukkos. But on Erev Shabbos the Biblical Mitzvah is simply to prepare (*Shemos*, 16:5. A Torah Mitzvah: see *Mishnah Berurah*, Bi'ur Halacha, 243). Most simply this means to prepare food so that we have something to eat on Shabbos, but theoretically, if we ate food that was prepared on Wednesday we could still fulfill the obligation of eating two proper meals on Shabbos. And yet, there is a Mitzvah to prepare, not merely for utilitarian reasons but for subtler reasons as well. We need to be prepared inwardly — emotionally, mentally, and spiritually. When the clock changes and we have crossed into Shabbos, we must have already opened ourselves to the radically different mode of being that is the essence of this unique day.

In the 'Temple of Space' the Kohen was required to prepare himself before leaving the 'mundane space' of the outside world and entering the 'sacred space' of the Temple. Specifically, he needed to wash his hands and feet with water, immerse himself in a Mikvah (*Yumah*, 30a), and don special garments (without the clothes he is not a 'full Kohen.' *Zevachim*, 17b). The same type of process applies to our transition into the 'Temple of Time.' We too need to wash ourselves, at least our hands and feet (*Shabbos*, 25b. *Shulchan Aruch*, Orach Chayim, 260:1), ideally immerse ourselves in a Mikvah, and put on special clothes for Shabbos (*Shabbos*, 113a. Tosefos, *Baba Kamah*, 37a, writes, from the Yerushalmi, that animals do not recognize people they 'know' when they are wearing different garments. לפי שראה אותם במלבושים נאים אחרים וחשובים בעיניו נכרים ואינו מכירם. When we put on special Shabbos clothes, we too fool the 'animal soul,' and can enter Shabbos in a deeper and higher level of being).

There are three dominant issues that hold us back from transitioning and experiencing any form of elevation. These are: money, food, and garments (as explained by the author of the *Kli Yakar*. See *Chemdas haYamim*, Shabbos Kodesh, 1. Note, *Igros Kodesh* 8 (from the Rebbe) Letter 2,469). If a person really wants to leave behind a certain state of consciousness and enter into a higher state, whether it is to have a transcendental Davening experience or to enter into the world of Shabbos, they must not be dragged down by these three issues. If you are preoccupied with monetary issues, mentally involved in a business deal, or just worried about your finances, you are currently bound to that level and area of experience. If you just ate a heavy meal, your body and even your mind will be, to some extent, absorbed in processing the food. If you are wearing your weekday clothes, you are tangibly connected to your weekday identity.

For this reason, as Shabbos is approaching, it is important to release your attachment to weekday activities. Do not pick up your mail an hour before Shabbos and go through your bills. Eat less so that your body feels light, but also not too hungry (*Orach Chayim*, 249:2. *Magen Avraham* (the Bach) ibid, 7). When you remove your weekday garments and put on your special Shabbos garments, it is a literal and metaphorical transformation that reverberates in your body and soul. If you are lighting Shabbos candles in your weekday clothes, or if you are running to Shul after just paying another bill, you will miss the subtle elevation of consciousness offered to you at this point of entrance to the Temple in Time.

These transitional tools — stopping work a good few hours before Shabbos, refraining from eating a big meal, cleansing oneself and donning special Shabbos garments, among many others — will be explored in greater detail in the second volume of this series, *How To Enter Shabbos*.

THE TRANSITION BEGINS ON WEDNESDAY

Thoughts, words and actions are the three 'garments' of the soul. They are the interface between our inner world, how we think and feel, and the outer world, just as our clothes are an interface between our inner self and the outer world. Our thoughts, words and actions are the means through which we express and reveal who we are. If you have a feeling of fondness towards another person, the garment or medium of expressing your inner feelings is the words you speak and the actions you do. If you need to summon up the courage to make a certain decision in life, you express yourself through the garment of thought, telling yourself that you are capable.

In order to fully prepare ourselves to enter into a Shabbos reality, we need to ensure that our thoughts, words and actions correspond with that numinous reality. We have to establish a *Shabbosdik /* Shabbos-like way of thinking, begin using Shabbosdik speech, and begin to act in a Shabbosdik way. The three days leading up to Shabbos, Wednesday, Thursday and Friday, are opportune times to begin preparing our actions, words and thoughts, respectively.

On Wednesday we should begin paying careful attention to our actions, ensuring that they are infused with a sense of Shabbos elevation. The meaning of this will be expanded upon later, but now it will suffice to say that on Wednesday we need to more consciously consider what we are 'doing' in this world. Even in the very middle of the week, our actions should become reflections of Shabbos light and holiness. This is not only with regards to 'what' we are doing, but 'how' we are doing it as well. In other words, the refinement of the garment of action is not only meant to ensure that we are doing the correct things, but also that we act in the world with Shabbos-dik refinement and spiritual sensitivity. Two people can each give a hundred dollar bill to a poor person, one gives with a smile and a sense of gentleness, and the other gives with a stiff reluctance and a groan. At the end, the recipient receives the same hundred dollars, yet the quality of the act of giving is completely different. As we refine our garment of action, we infuse the things we do with the integrity, harmony and joy of Shabbos.

On Thursday, special attention and intention is given to the garment of speech. We should make an effort to ensure that 'what' we say is permeated with the *Kedushah* / sanctity and gentleness of Shabbos, and also, of course, 'how' we say it. Our mode of verbal communication should be sensitive, noble and refined.

On Friday, as we enter the palpable aura of Shabbos, we ensure that our thoughts are more restful. We stop identifying ourselves with our ego-based thoughts and ideas of what we 'have to do.' Moreover, we must introduce a spirit of restfulness in the *way* we are thinking our thoughts; gradually taking on more and more of the clam and ease of Shabbos.

Focussing in this way, on gradually refining our mundane or self-centered thoughts, coarse words and abrasive actions, empowers our Shabbos preparations. We can then progressively acclimate ourselves to the Shabbos state of 'being' beyond 'doing,' in total rest from weekday thoughts, words and actions or manipulations. On Shabbos we need the ability to transcend thoughts that are related to 'work.' We don't even speak about business or activities that we would like to do after Shabbos, and we even attempt to not think about such thoughts throughout the day.

Then, when Shabbos arrives, you are ready to just *be*, without doing, speaking or even thinking of doing. You are now prepared to be the self beyond what you do, beyond what you say and even beyond what you think. On Shabbos you are gifted with the ability to reach the inner place of 'silence' that is beyond all the noise of the world and beyond all the chatter of the mind. Shabbos is the auratic crown above the head, the soul above the brain, the mouth, the hands. Immerse yourself completely in the glow of this delightful stillness, this absence of all friction, this ultimate silence of being.

THREE DAYS — EXTRA SOUL

As mentioned, preparing for something reveals a connection between the person preparing and that which they are preparing for. In the phraseology of our sages, *Hechsher Mitzvah* / the preparation for a Mitzvah actually becomes part of the Mitzvah itself. The three days in which we prepare for Shabbos not only serve as the final transition into Shabbos, but they themselves contain traces of the qualities of Shabbos; they are like the Hechsher Mitzvah that is part of the Mitzvah itself.

From Wednesday onward, the light and soul of Shabbos begins to approach incrementally. How this works and what exactly it means will be explored in greater detail further on, but for now, consider a few words on this subject and its relationship to consciously transitioning into a Shabbos mode of being.

On Shabbos, our sages tell us, we are gifted with an "extra soul" (*Beitza*, 16a). The great Spanish poet, philosopher and commentator, Rabbi Avraham Ibn Ezra (Even Ezra) (c.1089 - c.1167), writes

(*Bereishis*, 2:3) that it is not literally an 'extra' soul which is given on Shabbos, rather, since we are given rest from the toil and affairs of the world, our 'soul' has 'extra' time and can freely occupy itself with matters of wisdom and words of Torah. A later Spanish rabbi, the Mekubal, physician and commentator, Ramban (Nachmanides), Rabbi Moshe ben Nachman (1194-1270), writes (*Bereishis*, 2:3) that there *is* an actual additional soul gifted on Shabbos. Which is it? A metaphor or a literal extra soul? In the words of the Sages, "These and these are the words of the living G-d" (*Eiruvin*, 13b) — both opinions are true.

When we cease being preoccupied with the mundane world, shutting out the noise of conflict and commerce, more of our soul is expressed; 'extra' levels of our inner reality are revealed. The quieter we are outwardly, the more our inner self emerges and expresses itself. The less focused we are on striving and 'doing,' the more sensitivity, vulnerability, and openness of spirit we can experience in the moment.

On a deeper level, similar to the *Nekudah* / point of Shabbos that exists deep within every moment of the weekday, our 'extra soul' is always present. On Shabbos, as we take leave of our workweek, release our aggressive ambitiousness, and take on a slower, quieter, more inwardly-oriented posture, these higher levels of self become more and more revealed and substantiated.

Not only do we have 'extra soul,' extra inwardness and light, but Shabbos itself is called the "day of the soul" (*Zohar* 2, 205b. 3, 174a). A student of the Ramban writes that throughout the week our soul is like a guest, perhaps even a foreigner, in our home. On Shabbos, our soul — our inner self — is truly at home (*Rabbeinu Bachya*,

Bereishis, 2:3); 'we' have finally fully arrived from our travels. We are present, without struggle or tension, for there is nowhere else to go. We stop and settle into the ultimate state of being, without any need for outward activity. On Shabbos, creation is perfect.

Indeed, the 'soul' or 'being-ness' of the "Day of the Soul" is not reserved for once a week only, and, on some level, every day can be Shabbos-like. Our sages tell us that a *Talmid Chacham* / wholly wise person is called "Shabbos" (*Zohar* 3, p. 29a). The more we embody the soul of Shabbos, the more every day and every moment can have a Shabbos quality. The actual day of Shabbos, however, is the eternal headquarters, the wellspring, from which the quality of Shabbos can shine into the weekdays, irrigating every moment of our lives with its heavenly light. Since Shabbos is the nerve center for this level of consciousness, on Shabbos itself we are gifted with an influx of Shabbos energy and it is readily available to all; no matter how one had been living up until that day.

Deeper levels of the authentic internal self, become revealed as we quiet more and more of the externally imposed 'noise' of the week. The more we open the 'gate' of Shabbos peace, during any day of the week, the more our vessels are cleansed and the more our light and soul can manifest. Interestingly, the word רעש / noise or clamor has the same letters as the word שער / gate. When we respond to the noise of the weekdays by turning inward and preparing our 'garments' for Shabbos, that 'clamor' becomes a 'gate' into the sublime quiet of the upcoming Shabbos, the welcoming radiance of our extra soul.

EXPERIENCING SHABBOS

When we deeply enter Shabbos, we come to the realization that Shabbos is also deep within us. We are surrounded by Shabbos and we are filled with Shabbos; we dwell within the holiness of Shabbos and the holiness of Shabbos dwells within us. There is a cosmic *Nekudah* / point, a focal center of Shabbos, that is revealed in the world of time on Shabbos, and there is a Nekudah of Shabbos within our consciousness as well.

To truly understand and appreciate this special quality of Shabbos, we need to experience it, to enter it. In that way, Shabbos is like the emotion of love. One could talk about love endlessly, but if he was never actually in love then he will never know what love really is. It is something that must be experienced, not just intellectually understood. Shabbos is an intimate mystery beheld only by her beloved, hence, it is referred to as a 'secret.'

Once, a Roman official asked the sage Rabbi Yehoshua, "Why do foods cooked for Shabbos have such a wonderful aroma?" "There is a special Shabbos spice added," he replied. "Can I have some of that spice?" asked the Roman. Rebbe Yehoshua answered, "This spice is only beneficial for those who practice and keep Shabbos" (*Shabbos*, 119a). What this really means is that Shabbos itself has a special aroma, a special sensation and quality, but it only 'benefits' the person who truly enters the experience of Shabbos. You cannot explain to another person why the one you are in love with is so special. Only the person in love can truly feel the beauty and majesty of the other; it cannot be observed or understood from the outside.

The word for 'cooked food' is *Tavshil* / תבשיל. When rearranged, these letters spell the words *Li Shabbos* / לי שבת / Shabbos is mine. When Shabbos is 'mine,' when I am intimate with Shabbos, everything tastes, feels and is experienced differently, as alluded to in the story above.

Only when we fully enter Shabbos and experience *Deveikus* / oneness with it, can we experience the true Heavenly pleasure of Shabbos. "There is no unity without pleasure" (Rashi, *Sanhedrin*, 58b).

In our liturgy, Shabbos is referred to as *Techilah l'Mikra'ei Kodesh* / the first of holy convocations. This sentence can be homiletically translated as "(Shabbos is) the entry-way into holiness." Let us enter fully and faithfully into the world of Shabbos, so that Shabbos may enter into us. Then, we will be able to truly savor its special "spice" and experience its profound and holy *Oneg* / delight.

01

A CONSCIOUSNESS OF BEING

HASHEM'S SECRET

SIX DAYS A WEEK WE TOIL, WE ASPIRE TO ACHIEVE MORE, we use our creativity and ingenuity, our intelligence and endurance, to put food on the table and shelter over our heads. We work for the sake of ourselves, our families, and our communities. Perhaps, through this toil, we also merit to move the dial one step further towards making this world a more hospitable, more peaceful and hopefully more G-dly place. If we approach our work in such a way, no matter what our job is, the six work days are, to some extent, "*for* Hashem." Yet, Shabbos is, by definition, entirely a *Yom laHashem* / a day *to* Hashem (Devarim, 5:13).

"To Hashem," in this context, means that on Shabbos every-thing we do is meant to acknowledge and honor Hashem's role and presence in the world and in our lives. We do not engage in any activities that pertain to our own self-advancement or aggrandize-ment. Everything we do on Shabbos is essentially *L'Kavod Shabbos Kodesh* / for the glory of the holiness of Shabbos. However, this 'glory' and essential 'holiness' of Shabbos is not something we can achieve or even understand on our own. It is inherent to the day itself. All we can do is acknowledge and align ourselves with it. In this sense, Shabbos is a secret; divulged only to Hashem's intimates, who enter the inner chambers of the Holy of Holies. What's more, *Shabbos* is actually a Name of Hashem (*Zohar* 2, 88b). It is thus a 'sacred' word, treated with reverence and 'whispered in secret,' as it were. (The word *Shabbos* is not uttered in the bathroom and it is written as a Divine Name in amulets. *Bnei Yissachar*, Ma'amarei Shabbos, Ma'amar 7).

"The mystery of Shabbos is Shabbos," says the Zohar, the pre-eminent 'text' of the Torah's inner teachings. But what is the Di-vine secret of Shabbos? It is that Shabbos itself is the mystery of Creation. It is the inner secret that sustains the world and sustains us as a people. The inner Divine quality and intention whispered and breathed into all of Creation is Shabbos.

BREATHING A SOUL INTO THE WORLD

"Six days Hashem, the Creator, made the heavens and the earth, on the Seventh Day He rested and *Vayinofash* — was refreshed" (Shemos, 31:17). The Ein Sof, the Infinite Light of the Creator, is of course not a physical being which needs to rest from hard labor. The root of the word *VayiNofash* is *Nefesh* / soul, the spiritual dimension of a person. As such, a more accurate rendition of the above verse is as follows: "Six days Hashem made the heavens and the earth, on the Seventh Day He ceased working *and withdrew into the spiritual realm.*" As we are bidden to observe Shabbos, as did Hashem, we too set aside a full day during the week when we step back from our work and focus entirely on Hashem, holiness, spirituality, and Torah.

Additionally, the word *Nefesh* / soul, also means 'breath' (Rashi, *Shemos,* 31:17), alluding to Hashem's exhale, so-to-speak, breathing 'spirituality' into Creation. *VayiNofash* then implies that on Shabbos, Hashem in effect 'ensouls' the world through the infusion of His Breath of Life (Rashba, *Chidushei Agados,* Ta'anis, 27). Shabbos is the soul of the world, and in turn, the animating principle of our own inner world as well.

Indeed, as mentioned, on Shabbos we receive an extra dimension of Nefesh. There is a Supernal 'exhale' on Shabbos, which continually and forever (since the first Shabbos) fills the world, and us, with an extra measure of Soul. On Shabbos, Hashem exhales and we inhale an extra measure of spirit and infusion of Life-Force. As a result, on Shabbos we feel revived as we catch our breath from the rat-race of the week.

When Shabbos comes along we are happily forced to take a break from 'mastering' the world. We take a respite, and pause for about 25-26 hours, from manipulating the created world. During the week we are devoted to 'masculine' pursuits, as it were, 'conquering' the world around us, harnessing the elements of creation for our benefit. On Shabbos we stop mastering the world around us and settle into a more receptive, introspective or 'feminine' quality, thus Shabbos is called *haMalkah* / the Queen.

As Shabbos is a time to withdraw from the external, material, transient world and to settle into a more inner, spiritual, eternal world, it is a prime opportunity to return to ourselves, to reflect, reevaluate and refocus our lives.

Exhaling represents extending ourselves outwards to achieve our ambitions, desires and yearnings. Inhaling represents our turning inwards to receive and fill ourselves up. The extra deep inhale of life-force that we receive on Shabbos allows us to truly rest, to let go of all our 'exhaling,' our ambitions and insatiable yearnings for more.

Shabbos is a time of deep inhalation on every level — providing us with much needed physical, emotional, mental and existential rest. In this state of rest we let go of our need to feel in complete control of our lives and the physical world around us. This release allows us to enter the world of pure being, rather than incessant doing.

THE DAY OF NON-DOING

A quick glance at the laws of Shabbos in the *Shulchan Aruch* / the Code of Jewish Law, reveals that we are mostly told what *not* to do on Shabbos. Certainly, there are many more laws concerning what we are not to do on Shabbos than what we are to do. In fact, the Mitzvah that most characterizes Shabbos is *Tishbos* / to rest, to not do. There are also laws of 'remembering' Shabbos, but the quintessential Mitzvah of Shabbos is *Shabbos*, literally *resting*. Since the source of Shabbos is deeper than any realm of action or doing, the only way to tap into the mystery of Shabbos is Tishbos, non-doing.

When you truly like someone you can just sit with them, without doing or saying anything; just being in their presence is enough. The same is true with Shabbos. We do not actually need to do anything, we can just *be* — present, alert, conscious.

Shabbos is the day of Nefesh, soul, a day of deep inhalation and inspiration. The word *Nefesh*, in numeric value, is 430; this is represented in Hebrew by the letters Tav-Lamed (Tav/400, Lamed/30). Tav and Lamed spell *Tal* / dew, which is a life-giving refreshment, provided for the earth as a Divine gift. The letters Lamed and Tav are also an acronym for *Lo Te'aseh* / do not do; referring to the prohibitions of Shabbos. As dew quenches the thirst of the earth, Shabbos quenches the thirst of our soul. The Nefesh of a person is revealed more fully in the stillness of their 'not working.' By ceasing from a 'doing' paradigm, we enter into a state of 'being.' The *Lo* / *not* or *no* of Shabbos prohibitions allows us to connect with the deeper *yes* of our being that often gets drowned out by the noise of all our doing.

On the level of body and personality, skill, and accomplishment, everyone is different and excels in different things to different degrees. On a Shabbos level, however, and on the level of soul, we are all equal — still different, but equal. Shabbos is the day of soul, and access to soul is revealed by being, not doing. No one is any better at being than anyone else. On Shabbos, we are all equally and infinitely holy, just as we are. This is also the essence of dew. According to the Torah, rain is promised or withheld on account of our actions and efforts. Dew, on the other hand, is vital sustenance that just appears every morning without cause, other than sustaining what is. This is the type of refreshment Shabbos offers as well.

Doing exists in the *Alma d'Piruda* / world of separation. In the world of doing, people are distinct, separate and unequal. However, in the world of non-doing, everyone is unified, equal, and infinite. Even regarding the area of *Kavanah* / intention in spiritual acts such as prayer and Mitzvos, one person can have more intention than another. However, on Shabbos, Kavanah is not needed for the Mitzvos of non-doing.

Observing Shabbos rest reveals in us an inner freedom, a perfect inner state that is beyond work or accomplishment. Interestingly, non-working or non-doing can actually be understood as a type of doing. With regards to *Halanah* / leaving the blood of a Korban past its time, for example, non-doing is considered an action (*Me'ilah*, 4b). In the words of Rashi, דלגבי מחשבה דפיגול חשיב ללינה מעשה בידים / in comparison to mere thoughts of Pigul, not sprinkling the blood in its allotted time is considered an action with one's hands. "*La'asos Es haShabbos* / to 'make' or 'do' Shabbos" is not merely an extreme form of passivity or a kind of drifting off to sleep; it is in fact an active form of not-doing. Shabbos rest is an awake, dynamic stillness that expresses who and what we truly are — beyond the surface appearance of what we 'do.' In a restful, 'non-doing' way we can turn inward and be quietly alone with HaKadosh Baruch Hu, and we can pray with intensity, sing with joy, dance, feast, and enjoy our family or community. When dynamic activity is sourced in non-doing, it is an expression of that all-unifying experience of *Tishbos*.

THE HUMAN NATURE TO TOIL

It is, however, also true that "The nature of the human being is to toil" (Iyov, 5:7. *Sanhedrin*, 99b), to do, to work, to strive. Due to this inherent existential identification, it may be easier for us to feel the *Kedushah* / sanctity, and the *Ohr* / light of Shabbos when we are 'doing' Shabbos activities such as singing songs in honor of Shabbos, festively celebrating a Shabbos meal, and *Davening* / praying the special liturgy of Shabbos. From this perspective, it may even seem as if our refraining from work on Shabbos is merely a container or context within which these positive Mitzvos and activities of Shabbos can occur. As true as that may be, it is absolutely necessary that we fully understand and appreciate that the non-doings of Shabbos are not merely context, there is in fact great depth to Shabbos rest. The non-doing on Shabbos allows us to enter an inner world of Yichud, the state of *Deveikus* / sensing how close to Hashem we are in Essence, of taking leave of this world of *Piruda* / separation. This is the essence of Shabbos, which is only achievable by virtue of our non-doing; without it, no activity on Shabbos would be the same.

Shabbos Deveikus is a level of freedom that reveals the equality, the soul, the inner 'perfection' within every person — and ultimately within every action and every phenomenon. When this inner perfection is revealed, there is nothing else we need to do. We are already there, so to speak.

As Shabbos reveals the 'perfection' within us and the world around us, Shabbos is experienced as a glimmer of a redeemed and perfected world called *Olam haBa* / the World-to-Come, a world in which the 'destination' of history has been reached and there is nothing else to *do*. Work suggests a lack, implying that something is missing, imperfect, or broken and we need to manipulate, fix or improve it. But Shabbos reveals the potential of perfection that is already present, deep within the here and now of our current reality. *Shabbos* gives us a foretaste of a world in which no work is required, as everything is already in its *perfect state*.

In the "world of perfection" there is nothing anymore to make perfect. Therefore, as Shabbos is approaching we need to internally access a state of mind where we can honestly declare, "All (my) work is done" / כל מלאכתך עשויה / *Kol Melachtecha Asuyah* (Tur, *Orach Chayim* from *Mechilta d'Rebbe Yishmael*, Yisro, 7. Rashi, Shemos, 20:9). Not only is all my work from the past week done, there is also no future work to be done. All is complete, and there is no reason to even bring it to mind. In order to truly enter into Shabbos we need to assume this posture of total rest and acceptance of perfection.

On Shabbos we are invited to entirely let go of our past week and to even think about our future week or what we may need to do after Shabbos. On Shabbos, in fact, we are not allowed to prepare for the weekdays ahead. As a simple example, let's say you have a flight on Motzei Shabbos night. You cannot pack on Shabbos, as that would be preparing for the weekday. But on a deeper level, on Shabbos you are in a state of having nothing to do at all, neither regarding your past nor your future; everything is done, all is complete. Resting in the timeless present, there is simply no 'flight after Shabbos.'

In this spirit, during every Shabbos we should aspire to sense that there is no such thing as *Melachah* / work any longer. It is not merely that Melachah is forbidden for these 25 or so hours and it will again be permitted after Shabbos. Rather, you are eternally free from Melachah. You have left the world of Melachah and you will never go back; you now live in a different sphere of existence altogether. That is the Messianic potential available to each of us on every Shabbos.

FROM EXTERNAL MOVEMENT TO INTERNAL STILLNESS

Friction and movement, noise and vibration, effort and transformation, all define the physical world (as the Maharal writes, "(An) existence that has movement is [in the category of] physicality" / ההויה שיש בה תנועה הוא לגשם. *Tiferes Yisrael*, 40). All forms of movement and vibration suggest a here and a there, an inside and an outside; and thus, the physical world appears to be a world of *Pirud* / separation. Everything within this world is teeming with life, growth, vibration and movement. There is nothing fixed or stationary in it. On a subatomic level, all particles interact with all others and they are being created and destroyed continuously. Once these particles are created they do not remain static but continuously move rhythmically.

Beyond the world of Pirud (physicality) is the world of *Yichud* / Unity (spirituality). This is a realm or consciousness in which there is no *Tenuah* / movement. There is total and timeless stillness, as there is no "here" nor "there," "inside" nor "outside," "before" or "after." There is only One, Infinite, without-end and having no beginning. On Shabbos we enter this word of Yichud, beyond the sense of duality. We are then like fish in a world of water; there is no separation nor resistance between us and our environment, there is no other world; and thus, there is no place to go and nothing to do, just to be.

Work is doing something 'outside' oneself. It exists only within the realm of *Tenuah* / movement and *Pirud* / separation — this is the realm of *Chitzonius* / outside. Shabbos is the cosmic and microcosmic, it is the *Penimiyus* / inner center of being; and thus the absence of all Tenuah.

Resting on Shabbos is not simply resting from work as the culmination of a hard workweek, rather it is to enter another dimension entirely that is beyond work altogether. *Chazal* / our sages pick up on a subtle allusion in the Torah and infer that following the Six Days of Creation, "the world was חסר / *Cheser* / missing, lacking something." And then, "Shabbos entered and rest entered" בא שבת בא מנוחה / *Ba Shabbos Ba Menuchah* (Medrash, quoted in Rashi, *Bereishis*, 2:2). In other words, Menuchah is not merely a resting *from* work, rather it is a creation in itself, an 'entity' as it were, expressed only through the anti-work that is not-doing, which is Shabbos. Menuchah is therefore what is said by not-saying, what is done by not-doing, what is created by ceasing to create.

On Shabbos the Torah tells us the Creator "ceased from work and rested" / שבת וינפש / *Shovas vayiNofash* (Shemos, 31:17. Rashi and Targum, ad loc). As mentioned, *Nafash* alludes to the word *Nefesh* /

soul. *Nefesh* also means *Ratzon* / will, the power of desire (Bereishis, 23:8. *Nefesh* means desire לשון תאוה וקורת רוח. Rashi, *Chulin*, 120a. *Ratzon* comes from the word *Ratz* / running, moving. Also, a cognate of the word *Nefesh* is found in the Aramaic term, *Fushu* / multiply, *Unkelos*, Bereishis, 1:28). All of these etymological connections suggest that *Vayinofash* is not simply a passive cessation, but rather an active, even creative type of rest. It is therefore not merely an absence of work, a 'negative' state or void, rather it is a 'positive' presence that was missing from, and then added to, the world; allowing the world to more fully express and enjoy itself. On the Seventh Day then, we can say that Menuchah, a tangible and pleasurable calmness of spirit, was created (*Tosefos, Sanhedrin*, 38a). Shabbos and Menuchah thus give meaning to the other six days and all the work of Creation; without them, life and this world would be pointless toil without end, a form of self-imposed slavery. Shabbos sets us free from this endless loop of servitude Shabbos reframes What (and Who) our actions and efforts are actually in service to — Hashem.

Essentially, Shabbos Menuchah is the opposite of the 'goal-oriented' Tenu'ah of the work-week. Following the Six Days of Creation, on the Seventh Day a new reality, a higher dimension was revealed, a positive presence and purpose that came from, and connects us back to, the Ultimate World of Unity and Perfection.

AVODAH AND MELACHAH: TWO TYPES OF WORK

In Hebrew, hard labor, whether physical or otherwise, is called עבודה / *Avodah*. *Avodah* is related to the word עבד / *Eved* / slave. On

Shabbos we are asked to rest (Shemos, 23:12) and refrain *not* only from *Avodah* (see Tosefos, *Pesachim* 117b. לפי שבמצרים עבדו בהם בישראל בפרך ופר"ך בא"ת ב"ש וג"ל. שהם מלאכות ארבעים חסר אחת וכשנגאלו ממצרים הזהירם על השבת לשבות מאות' ל"ט מלאכות), but also to rest from *Melachah* (Shemos, 31:14). "Resting on the Seventh Day from Melachah is a positive Mitzvah."*On Shabbos the *Isur* / prohibition of Melachah is not necessarily defined by hard labor alone. Carrying a piece of paper in a public domain, for example, is certainly not *Avodah* / hard labor, yet, it is a prohibited act on Shabbos. (Indeed, carrying is called a מלאכה גרועה / *Melachah Geru'ah* / an inferior category of work (Tosefos, *Shabbos*, 2a.) And thus it needs a special source to be considered a Melachah. *Shabbos*, 96b. *Tosefos* and *Rabbeinu Chananel*, ad loc. Rambam, *Hilchos Shabbos*, 12:8). Conversely, moving a heavy chair within one's home from one room to the next can be a hard, intense activity, yet it is permitted.

So, the question arises: If it is not *labor*, what then defines Melachah? The simplest answer is that we know which Melachah is permitted and which is prohibited based on the Melachos (plural of *Melachah*) that were performed in the building and function of the *Mishkan* / the temporary Temple in the Desert. In other words, the Melachos that we are not allowed to do on Shabbos are the

---

* Rambam, *Hilchos Shabbos*, 1:1. Only resting from a real Melachah is a positive Mitzvah (Rashba, *Yevamos*, 6a). Although the Ramban writes that any form of rest, even if not from full Melachah, is a positive Mitzvah [on Shabbos]. אבל פירוש "שבתון" כך הוא שתהיה לנו מנוחה מן הטורח והעמל כמו שביארנו והוא ענין הגון וטוב מאד והנה הזהירו על המלאכות בשבת בלאו ועונש כרת ומיתה והטרחים והעמל בעשה (Ramban, *Vayikra*, 23:24. See also, Ritvah, *Rosh HaShanah*, 32b). אלא כך כך עיקרן של דברים כי שבות שבת של תורה לשבות ממלאכות יש לשבות מכל שבות דרך כלל שלא לעשות שבת. כחול אבל בכל פרט ופרט כי עביד לי' וזהיר באידך דלא שבת הוי כחול הוי שבות דרבנן See. ועדיין היה *Markeves haMishnah*, 21, Hilchos Shabbos, and *Magid Mishnah*, Hilchos Shabbos, 21 who posit that perhaps the Rambam is aligned with the opinion of the Ramban. אדם יכול להיות עמל בדברים שאינן מלאכות כל היום לכך אמרה תורה תשבות.

same Melachos that were done to construct the Mishkan* (*Shabbos,*
49b. And perhaps (besides the construction of the Mishkan), the 39 Melachos
of Shabbos are rooted in the 39 forms of work, services that were done in the
Mishkan (*Medrash haGadol.* See *Torah Sheleimah,* 23, Pekudei, pp.118-119). According to the
Yerushalmi, this includes all the Melachos performed when offering an actual
Korban. *Shabbos,* 10:3**). Simply, all the acts of work and skill needed
to build the Mishkan are precisely the actions that we are not allowed to do on Shabbos. This includes even forms of work, such as
plowing the field, that were only indirectly involved in building the
Mishkan, but which were needed in order to prepare the ingredi-
ents or materials required to serve and build the Mishkan (*Eglei Tal,*
Hakdamah 1). Interestingly, the word *Melachah* is used regarding the

---

* One way to divide the 39 Melachos is into the following six groups: 1) Eleven actions
connected to making bread, from planting until baking (food). 2) Thirteen actions connected to fashioning clothes, from shearing to sewing cloth. 3) Nine actions connected to
writing (on parchment), from trapping the animal (skin for parchment) to actual writing
(for commerce). 4) Three actions connected to building a building, from destroying to
building, to the 'final hammer blow' completing an action (shelter). 5) Two actions related
to fire: lighting a fire or putting it out. 6) The one basic principle of moving an object from
one domain to the next (which will be explained as the main Melachah of Shabbos). These
categories are also the basic necessities of man: food, clothes, shelter, trade, fire. They are
connected to all forms of work and engagement with the world. Transferring objects from
a 'private' domain to the 'public' domain is also a basic form of engagement with the world.

** In other words, whereas the Bavli makes a distinction between building or preparing
the Mishkan and the Avodah in the Mishkan itself, the Yerushalmi, does not make such
a distinction. Perhaps, this is aligned with the general view of the Yerushalmi, which
maintains that a Hechsher Mitzvah / preparation for a Mitzvah is one with the Mitzvah
itself — even to the extent that we could recite a Berachah / blessing on the building of
a Sukkah (Yerushalmi, Berachos, 9:3). In the more inner/higher world of the Yerushalmi
there is less of a distinction between 'inner' thoughts and 'outer' actions, and also between
the preparation and the actualization of a Mitzvah.

Ma'asei B'reishis / Acts of Creation (Bereishis, 2:2), as well as in the construction of the Mishkan, thus, any Melachah that was employed to construct the Mishkan is not permitted on Shabbos, the Seventh Day when the Creator ceased creating.

The Mishkan was a microcosm of Creation (*Tanchumah*, Pekudei 2), incorporating both the physical and the spiritual realms (*Ramban*, Shemos, 31:2). Its construction parallels the Creator's acts of Creation (*Zohar 2*, 152a). As our creation of the Mishkan mimicked the Creator's Creation of the world, whatever was a Melachah in the building of the Mishkan is a Melachah that the Creator also 'rested' from on the Seventh Day, and thus we refrain from it when we rest on Shabbos.

Now we know what types of Melachah are prohibited, but still, we need to understand more deeply what Melachah is. In other words: what is the essence of Melachah, as opposed to *Avodah* / hard labor?

Fundamentally, Melachah is not defined by the level of exertion used to perform an act, rather it is defined by intentionality. The work done in the Mishkan was called מלאכת מחשבת / *Meleches Mach'shaves* / "intentional actions" (Shemos, 35:33). This means intentionally, manipulating the fabric of the world, for a particular constructive benefit. (Destroying for the purpose of destroying is not considered a Melachah, as it is not a Maleches Mach'sheves דמקלקל דעלמא לא מיפטר אלא משום מלאכת מחשבת. *Tosefos*, Shabbos, 75a. To qualify as *Meleches Mach'shaves,* a person has to have intention for that particular action to occur, and that has to be the reason why he does it (see *Minchas Asher*, Shabbos, Siman 3, for a good definition of *Davar sheEino Miskavein* / action taken without [full] intention).

Melachah is essentially an action done with intention and for the purpose to create, improve or develop something.

Only מלאכת מחשבת / Meleches Mach'shaves is prohibited (according to Torah law) on Shabbos (Rambam, *Hilchos Shabbos*, 1:9. *Baba Kamah*, 27a. *Kerisus*, 19a). This means that a person is allowed to intentionally perform an act that is permitted on Shabbos, even if through his actions it is possible — but not inevitable — that a prohibited action will occur as a result. This is called a דבר שאינו מתכוין / Davar sheEino Miskaven / "an action without intention" (As the opinion of Rabbi Shimon in *Shabbos*, 41b. Rambam, *Hilchos Shabbos*, 1:5). For example, a person can walk over grass on Shabbos, although it is possible that some grass will be cut. Because cutting grass is not his intention and it is not an inevitability, only a possibility, that any cutting will occur.

However, if a person does a certain act with intention, although he has no need for the actual labor he performed, he is still liable to the effects and consequences of a violation of sacred law (Rambam, ibid, 1:7, as the opinion of Rabbi Yehudah. *Shabbos* 73b. Most Rishonim, and the Shulchan Aruch (*Orach Chayim*, 278), rule like Rabbi Shimon). This is called מלאכה שאינו צריך לגופה / Melachah Sh'eino Tzarich l'Gufah / an action with no need for the action itself. For example, if a person extinguishes a flame, which is a prohibited act, but not because he needs to put out the fire, rather, his intention is so that he can use the oil, he is still liable because he had intention in the act itself.

Here, the main point is that Melachah is not defined by the level of exertion, rather by the intentionality motivating the performance of the act itself.

FROM SLAVERY TO SHABBOS

When *Klal Yisrael* / the People of Israel were slaves in Egypt, they performed hard, difficult labor. Shabbos came along with a surprising message, 'You are free; you have the choice to work and also the choice to stop working.'

In contrasting Shabbos with the conditions of slavery in Egypt, there seems to be two types of labor or work. In Egypt, the slaves were compelled to perform *Avodas Perach* / harsh labor; on Shabbos we refrain from *Meleches Machasheves* / intentional acts of work. What is the difference?

Perach means an inappropriate allocation of work, for example, in Egypt the natural task of a woman was given to a man, and the natural task of a man was given to a woman (*Sotah*, 11b). If the issue was getting the work done, say constructing a building, the slaves most skilled in laying bricks would have been told to lay the bricks, and the stronger slaves, with less dexterity, would have been told to carry the bricks. The fact that the Egyptian slave owners gave men's work to women, and women's work to men, indicates that the objective was not that the work should be done, and utilizing maximum labor force. Rather, the objective was producing the maximum frustration and despair. Not only does *Perach* mean inappropriate allocation of labor, but it represents forced *purposeless* labor, labor for the sake of keeping slaves busy and beaten-down (Rambam, *Hilchos Avadim*, 1:6). In contrast to Perach, the Torah tells us that the building of the Mishkan required Meleches Mach'shaves, intentional, *purposeful* work; and what's more, the work could not be forced, it needed to be done voluntarily (*Shemos*, 25:2. 35:22).

We are free during the week to perform, by our own volition, all types of Meleches Machshaves, purposeful, creative actions. On Shabbos we have the freedom to voluntarily stop performing these sorts of actions and let the world around us just be. Through this conscious refraining from such work, we reveal that our work during the week was also done with choice and intention.

Melachah comes from the word *Hiluch* / to walk, go, to move along. *Melachah* is thus an act of furthering or bettering Creation. This type of work changes the status of an object. It is an act of *Tenuah* / movement, propelling a conceptual and concrete advance within the world. Cooking, for example, is a Melachah. If you roast a piece of meat, you 'better' it and cause the inedible piece to 'progress' and become edible.

Through cooking you change the status of the object of food. On Shabbos everything is seen as already perfect and complete — nothing in this world needs to be, or should be, changed. Shabbos is the *Nekudah* / point of perfection that exists within the imperfection of the world.

Melachah is a type of purposeful and intentional manipulation of the environment and all the world around us. It is a type of activity where we demonstrate our control over the world, as it were. The prohibition of Melachah on Shabbos refers to refraining from any work that is purposeful or productive, transforms an object into something useful or more useful, or transforms an object by moving it from one domain into another.

Physical exertion is, technically, not a Melachah on its own. According to strict Torah-law you can tire yourself out by jumping up and down the entire day, and it would not be considered a violation of Shabbos. Yet, if you manipulated, even with little to no exertion, just the slightest change in an object, you have done a Melachah.

Bodily prowess and physical exertion is something we humans share with the entire animal kingdom; it is part of our animal nature. Creativity, as production and transformation, transcends our animal nature; these are expressions of the human spirit and our fundamental ability to manipulate and shape the world. During the week we are invited to transcend the animal kingdom, by being creative and innovative. On Shabbos, we transcend even human nature, to a certain extent, as we enter a state in which there is no *Hiluch* / movement, or furthering of Creation. We just simply let it *be*, and we too, just need to *be*.

NOT LEAVING YOUR 'SPACE'

Shabbos is about non-movement, stillness, the inner world. Regarding Shabbos (and the *Mon* / Manna) the Torah says *Al Yetze Ish Mimkomo* / A person should not leave his *Makom* / space (Shemos, 16:29). Our sages understand "his space" to mean his extended space, his city. This refers to the laws of *Techum Shabbos* / the circumscribed boundary of our movements on Shabbos. On Shabbos we should not journey more than 2,000 cubits (a cubit is about a foot and a half) outside the city (*Eiruvin*, 51a. Knowing about the idea of Techum on Shabbos is considered 'knowing' about. Shabbos. *Shabbos*, 79a). In the words of the *Shulchan Aruch haRav*, "Up until 2,000 cubits is called *his space*" (*Orach Chayim*, Siman 396:1). On a deeper level, the inner understanding of, "Do not leave your space on Shabbos," means to stay conceptually, mentally and spiritually in a space and state of rest and stillness.

On Shabbos there is no transportational *Hiluch* / movement and thus we are at a standstill, as it were; there is no 'change of space.' Everything is perfect as it is. On the weekdays we travel about according to our will, but on Shabbos we enter a world where there is no longer any *Bechirah* / free choice; only the will of Hashem (*Ohr Yitzchak* [Rav Yitzchak of Radvill, son of the Maggid of Zlotchov], Bereishis, 2:3). Everything is perfect and there is nothing to change or move; there is no journey to take. We transcend our restless week-day nature by staying put.

This sense of stillness on Shabbos is beautifully illustrated with the laws of *Muktzah* / objects that are separated and 'set aside'; which cannot be used, or in some cases even moved on Shabbos. An example of a Muktzah object is a hammer, whose primary function is to perform work that is forbidden on Shabbos, or a tree branch, an object that is not usually used on Shabbos as it has no ordinary function in relation to Shabbos. We let go of using or moving such objects, even if not for the express purpose of Melachah.

A Muktzah status can also extend to an object that is supporting a Muktzah item, such as the table upon which the hammer is lying. The law is that if something was Muktzah when Shabbos began, it remains Muktzah throughout the entire Shabbos. Even if that situation changed during Shabbos, the Muktzah status does not change throughout the entire Shabbos. Say, for example, a person has a hammer on the table as Shabbos began, and as such the table became Muktzah, one is not allowed, in most cases, to move the table. And even if the hammer was somehow removed from the table during Shabbos, the table remains Muktzah throughout that entire Shabbos. This means there cannot be a status change of an object on Shabbos. On Shabbos there are no changes, no movement, and even objects do not change status.

In fact, even objects that are not Muktzah cannot be carried or moved from one domain to another, for example from a private home into the street. Interestingly, there is a principle called *Chai Nosei Es Atzmo* / a living organism carries itself (*Shabbos*, 94a). This means that since living beings — animals or people who can walk — carry their own weight, according to Torah law (although Rabbinically it is not allowed) one may technically carry an animal or person in a public domain. The obvious question is: how does the fact that living beings carry their own weight, exempt the carrier from the Torah prohibition of carrying in a public domain? Certainly the person carrying is picking up some weight (See *Tosefos* ad loc, for one explanation).

Rav Moshe Feinstein, the great contemporary *Posek* / decider of law (*Dibros Moshe*, ad loc), offers a very important understanding of this law and allows us to see deeper into its spiritual implications. Only lifeless objects fall under the strict prohibition of carrying, as the only way they could move location is through the act of human participation and manipulation. The position of a lifeless object is where it is at presently. And so the Torah tells us, on Shabbos we need to rest from trying to 'move' objects. If we moved it, it would be a change in its status as a stationary thing. This is not so with regard to living beings. The nature and status of a living being is to move about. As such, when we carry a person from one location to another, we are not *changing his status* by carrying him, as his space is not one particular space.

Although a person's movement is limited on Shabbos, his Shabbos 'space' is not limited to one location, as an object is. Technically, in the law that "a person should not leave his space," the term "space" means his boundary which was established before Shabbos began. On a deeper, spiritual and mental level, on Shabbos we need to let go of our need and want to change our space, and allow ourselves to let go, be still and rest. On Shabbos we are gifted with the ability to enter a state of purity, where there is no need for 'transportation,' and on a deeper level, where there is no *possibility* of transportation or movement. On Shabbos we are settled in our space, at home within our boundary.

Rebbe Yaakov Yitzchak of Peshischa (1766-1813), known as the *Yid haKodesh* / Holy Jew, once quipped, "On Shabbos we should not be allowed (and again on a deeper level, 'not allowed' means 'unable') to even move our fingers or toes, but if we would restrict ourselves to this extent, or even aspire to such a level, we would be found lacking the joy of Shabbos" (*Niflaos haYehudi*, p. 80. Or even open our mouth (*Be'eros HaMayim*, (Rebbe Mendel of Rimanov), Bereishis. Note also *Sefer haKana*, Dinei Shabbos). On Shabbos, we are in a state as if in front of the King, where even the slightest movement is not allowed — and more deeply, in a state of such Bitul, movement is not possible. *Siddur Im Dach*, p. 149b. Rebbe Rashab, *Yom Tov shel Rosh Hashanah*, Samach Vav, p. 22). In other words, on Shabbos we should, potentially, be in such a deep being-state that even our limbs are simply just 'being,' with no movement whatsoever.

Shabbos is rooted in the word *Shav* / return. On Shabbos we can all return to our deepest space, to the unmoving core of our being. When we refrain and let go of all forms of Melachah, we do not *need* to do anything or go anywhere.*

---

* In contrast, on *Yom Tov* / the three major biblical holidays, there is a Mitzvah to perform an *Oleh Regel* / to walk up (i.e. elevate our space) to the space of the Beis HaMikdash, by making a pilgrimage up to Yerushalayim / Jerusalem. On Yom Tov there is a Mitzvah to 'leave' one's space and status by elevating it; on Shabbos, by contrast, the Mitzvah is to transcend 'leaving' and to stay where we are. Macro-cosmically speaking, on Shabbos the *Kedushah* / sanctity "comes down" into our lives, into our space, whereas on Yom Tov we leave to "go up" to the space of Kedushah. The essence of Shabbos is rest, an absence of work. On Yom Tov we don't perform work due to the holiness of the day. However, we still must strive spiritually; Yom Tov is thus connected to *Regel* / movement.

Another illustration: on Yom Tov it is integral to have guests. The Rambam writes in the Laws of Yom Tov (*Hilchos Shevisas Yom Tov*, 6:18), "When a person eats and drinks (in celebration of a holiday), he is obligated to feed converts, orphans, widows, and others who are destitute and poor. In contrast, a person who locks the gates of his courtyard and eats and drinks with his children and his wife without feeding the poor and the embittered is not rejoicing in a Mitzvah, but rather is rejoicing in (the filling of) his gut. And with regard to such a person the verse (of Hoshea, 9:4) is applied, "Their sacrifices will be like the bread of mourners, all that partake thereof shall become impure, for they (kept) their bread for themselves alone." This happiness is a disgrace for them, as (implied by Malachi, 2:3), "I will spread dung on your faces, the dung of your festival celebrations." The Zohar explains that this refers to Yom Tov, not Shabbos (*Zohar* 2, 88b. ואי איהו בשבתא חדי, אף על גב דלא). On Shabbos we 'should' endeavor to have guests, but no such harsh words are expressed about not having guests. This is because Yom Tov is about *Regel* / movement, and thus there needs to be a movement to reach out and *Mekabel Orchim* / receive guests. Also, the word *Orchim* literally comes from the word *Orach* / path, as in *travelers on a path*. On Yom Tov we need to receive 'travelers,' as Yom Tov is a Regel, whereas Shabbos is Menuchah, stillness, presence, and by definition is not connected to travelers or movement.

Another way of saying this: on both Shabbos and Yom Tov we need to rest from work (although certain Melachah is allowed on Yom Tov, like cooking). Yet, there is a big distinction between not doing Melachah on Shabbos versus Yom Tov. The Yomim Tovim are referred to as מקראי קדש / *Mikra'ei Kodesh*, and during the times of the Beis haMikdash on days of מקראי קדש we needed to bring offerings. As the Pasuk says, אלה מועדי ה' אשר-תקראו אתם מקראי קדש להקריב אשה לה' עלה ומנחה / these are the *Moadim* (Yomim Tovim) which are called מקראי קדש, to bring Olah and Minchah offerings... Therefore, as the adjoining Pasuk states, מקרא-קדש יהיה לכם... כל-מלאכת עבדה לא תעשו / "It shall be to you a Mikra Kodesh... all forms of work you shall not do." Since Yom Tov is a מקרא קדש, we refrain from work so not

All our work is done; we have arrived in our space of perfection. We are home.

Shabbos allows us to let go of our attachment and dependency on the world of *Tenuah* / movement; to let go of the urge toward productivity; to leave be all the fuel, electricity, wheels and mechanics of life. On Shabbos we release any need for outwardness, and enter into the interior world of Yichud. In this way, we leave the world of *Cheser* / lack, and enter the world of *Shalom* / wholeness and completeness. From this perspective, we feel no obligation whatsoever to leave our *Techum* / boundary on Shabbos; we find perfection right where we are.

RELEASING OUTWARDNESS

On Shabbos we are meant to let go of all attachments and things that hold sway over us during the week.

We let go of all our weekday 'addictions' — our phones, computers, internet, and any tendency to be drawn into the fray of the outside world. We are therefore free from the bombardment of the outside world with its endless stimuli, and so we are even free of the effort to shield ourselves from its toxic influences. On Shabbos we are free to breathe peacefully, let go, and just be ourselves. We release all cosmetic artifice and any 'need' to gain approval or impress others with an outer appearance. We let down our guard, turn inward and live in total alignment with our un-modified *Penimiyus* / inner reality.

---

to be distracted from the sanctity of the day and its special offerings. Shabbos, however, is different. The very definition of Shabbos is *Menuchah* / rest from Melachah. We refrain from all Melachah on Shabbos not because Melachah is a 'distraction' from Shabbos, rather, because 'not doing Melachah' is the essence of Shabbos.

Shabbos is a time to be 'naked' and unashamed in the presence of the Creator. There is nothing we need to 'cover' or conceal — we can be who we really are. Shabbos is likened to *Gan Eden* / Paradise, a state prior to the eating from the Tree of Knowledge, in which Adam and Chava were naked and comfortable with themselves. In this state, there was simply no need for any external, and more importantly any mental or inner, garments/coverings. This 'garden-state' of pure being that we enter into on Shabbos is completely innocent, undisturbed and unafraid; we are thus able to be deeply present with the Divine Presence, without any intermediary.

In fact, even our clothing on Shabbos is a manifestation of the unity of Shabbos. From the perfected perspective of Shabbos, we come to realize that there is no separation between outer and inner, between garment and body and even soul. In the light of Shabbos, both vessel and light are revealed to be transparently one seamless spiritual unity. This is the consciousness of the Tree of Life.

THE WORLD OF THOUGHT / OLAM HABA

HaKadosh Baruch Hu creates the world through Divine speech, "And Elokim said, let there be light, and there was light." On Shabbos, HaKadosh Baruch Hu rests from the creation of *Dibbur* / speech, and the world is maintained from the World of *Machshavah* / Thought (*Likutei Torah*, Alter Rebbe, Shuva Yisrael).

All that exists begins, even before speech, with a Divine thought of creating that particular thing. HaKadosh Baruch Hu has an idea or a vision, so-to-speak, and then through speech that inner thought is externalized until the world is created.

Let us think about this in terms of our own desire to create. Imagine you have an idea in *Machshavah* / thought to build your ideal home. The way the home exists in your mind is perfect; your visualization is exquisite. Then, you speak to your architect and she draws up plans. After you verify the plans, you give orders to begin construction. The process begins in your mind, within you, so to speak, then it becomes expressed and externalized in speech and finally manifests in action.

The way the home exists in your mind is exactly how you desire it to be, 'perfect,' but the myriad ways the project evolves and the technical issues that arise are complicated and the building process is filled with ups and downs. Every once in a while, you recall your original image and visit the site to speak with the builders to ensure that all is unfolding according to plan. Finally, to your great satisfaction, the home is completed in a way that matches your ideal vision.

Within the Creator's 'Mind' the world is 'perfect,' yet there is a process of 'building' that must ensue until creation as a whole reaches that potential. The ultimate perfection of the world envisioned within the Mind of the Creator, is *Olam haBa* / the World-to-Come. Yet, *Olam haZeh* / this world, which is still in the process of Creation through Divine speech, has not yet reached its fullest crystallization. It is still in the process of being built, as it were, thus the seeming complications, 'technical issues' and chaos of the world in its present state.

Shabbos, in this sense, is Hashem resting from the unfolding process of Creation, as the project of Olam haZeh evolves and moves towards the fulfillment of His original vision, Olam haBa. The Creator 'stops' and recalls the world in its complete state as it exists in the original Machshavah. On Shabbos, we too stop to recall the original image and goal of all Creation — life perfected, united, illuminated. In this way, we are able to tap into the 'future' world-to-come that always-already exists deeply concealed within this world, in the form of Machshavah.

NOT STOPPING, BUT SLOWING DOWN

To be clear, practically speaking, on Shabbos we are of course not just simply sitting around in total stillness and silence contemplating the world as it was always meant to be — in fact, quite the opposite. On Shabbos we are fully engaged with our spiritual life in a way that is integrated with our physical life. In other words, we are actually living our life as if the future world had already arrived. And so, on Shabbos, we may eat more, sleep a little bit more, perhaps engage in marital intimacy; however, none of these physical actions are experienced as a distraction from the spiritual depths of shabbos, to the contrary, these activities all contribute to and are part of the Mitzvah of *Oneg* / pleasure on Shabbos. In fact, according to the sages, the Mitzvah of Oneg Shabbos is as weighty as the entire Torah.*

---

* See Mahara M'panu, *Assara Ma'amaros*, Ma'amar Chikur Din, 1:23. To say that Oneg on Shabbos is like all the Mitzvos is a big *Chidush* / novel idea. The idea that Shabbos is as weighty as the entire Torah (*Tanchumah*, Ki Tisa, 33), i.e., like all the 613 Mitzvos (*Yerushalmi, Nedarim*, 3:9), is generally understood in terms of the negative consequences of *Chilul Shabbos* / desecrating the Shabbos. Meaning, if someone desecrates the Shabbos openly, he is considered a *Mumar* / violator of the entire Torah. *Chulin*, 5a. Rambam, *Hilchos Shabbos*, 30:15.

We do therefore engage in numerous forms of 'doing,' and yet, Shabbos is fundamentally a state of being, and our doing effortlessly emanates from that serene place of stillness.

Whereas we delight in festive meals on Shabbos, we do not cook on Shabbos. Whereas we sleep a bit more on Shabbos, we do not make the bed on Shabbos. The idea behind these examples is that we should have Oneg in effortless activities. Our Shabbos 'doings' are focused entirely on the pleasure they provide us in the moment, rather than the responsibilities they burden us with in the future. They are thus meant to keep us rooted in a place of pure 'being' for the duration of Shabbos.

While Shabbos is a slowing down and even cessation from all of our restless seeking and striving, the weekday paradigm is defined by *Tenuah* / movement and the quest for constantly accelerating speed. Indeed, as a civilization we are becoming quicker and quicker as we 'evolve.' So much of our development is measured by the rubric of speed — from the wheel to the locomotive, to cars, jets and supersonic planes; from horseback postal services to telephones, email and 'instant messaging.' We relentlessly crave and expect tremendous speed in everything we do. We think we need to know everything that is going on in the outside world as it is happening. Shabbos, by contrast, allows us to access an inner place of stillness and contentment with what is physically present, by unequivocally letting go of this obsession with speed. On Shabbos, we therefore unplug, step back and slow down to the point where we can once again hear Hashem's "still small voice" echoing throughout all creation.

On an even deeper level, such physical and mental deceleration brings us to a state *beyond* the entire issue of speed, movement and doing altogether. On Shabbos we uncover the deeper inner stillness of soul that is always present. This spacious placidity within is the context of all our active celebrations on Shabbos. And from that inner place of stillness and contentment, we are able to reconnect to the original thought of creation that is still present, guiding and nourishing everything we do.

A WEEKLY REDEMPTION

No matter how absorbed or compulsively preoccupied with our activities we may be during the course of the week, Shabbos is an oasis of sacred, otherworldly time when we can just *be*, free from all our habitual, perhaps even addictive, behaviors of the week.

In a world without Shabbos, without a 'forced' break, we could very easily end up toiling, striving, working without end. In such a reality, we would ultimately become completely defined and enslaved by the burdens of our labors and possessions. By introducing a period of deep respite and release from our materialistic involvements and creative activities, we are able to immerse in spirit, the essential aspect of who we truly are, fundamentally deeper than what we do or have. As we enter the Shabbos state of *being*, we are liberated from our materialistic focus on *doing*. With such a firm and focused rededication to spirituality every week, we gradually and subtly shift into an ever more wholesome, integrated and holy life.

Going through life without Shabbos would be like trying to read a book without punctuation. We need pauses and time to comprehend the messages of life, otherwise it is just one run-on sentence, leaving us feeling more and more disoriented and lost the further we go.

Indeed, we would utterly lose our way without Shabbos. Life would devolve into a continuous and relentless attempt to gain more fulfilment, until one would forget what fulfilment even is in the first place. Acquiring things would become an end in itself. We would start to make more and more money only for the sake of having more money. Even an artist could get lost and begin to produce art only for the sake of producing something, losing their original drive for meaning, beauty or deeper truths.

From this perspective, Shabbos protects us from ourselves. It ensures that the world around us does not overwhelm and get the better of us, so to speak. It puts a break on the perpetual pressure to achieve, and says, 'Slow down my friend, see, you are not enslaved to your work, money, ambition, or egoic desires. You can let go and rest. You can just be.' This ability to let go on Shabbos is actually a way to gain control of your life, rather than the ceaseless demands and pressures of life constantly controlling you. Shabbos is the living expression of a free person who is ultimately in control of their own life and time.

In this way, your being is not enslaved to your doing, on the contrary, your doing *comes from* the core of your being. At any moment you can stop doing to be more in touch with your being. We become a master over our life and actions by pausing and letting go of our mindless doing in order to cultivate mindfulness rooted in the experience of pure being.

Throughout the week we mimic the Creator and co-create positive developments in the world. We become busy mastering the world around us and harnessing the powers of the universe to achieve benefits such as educating others, designing prosperous businesses, building, fixing and finding solutions for the needy. On Shabbos, we let go, we stop trying to master the outside world; and thus we show that we are not slaves, not even to ourselves.

True mastery is not over something outside of you, rather it is mastery over yourself, your urges, inclinations, desires and ambitions. By turning inward on Shabbos, we surrender our assumed mastery over the outside world and demonstrate mastery over programmed drives and unconscious urges. We thusly subvert our ego's incessant need to please, produce and project; thereby revealing our deepest being, our Infinite self, our soul.

SHABBOS AS TZIMTZUM, FROM CREATION TO COMPLETION

Our bodies are finite. Our power of 'doing' is finite. The physical work we do in this world, no matter how grand, is finite. The effects of your work may last tens, hundreds or even thousands of years; your actions may create benefit for many people, nonetheless, it is all still finite. On the other hand, we also have a Spark of the Infinite One within us, which is our Soul. This 'Infinity' is expressed precisely, by our ceasing from creation. Our portion of eternity is therefore expressed effortlessly on Shabbos.

To create and manifest a world of physical dimension and action, the Creator 'needed' to withdraw and withhold the Divine

Light in order to make space for something other than the Infinite One to exist. This necessary act of *Tzimtzum* / constriction can be likened to a Divine cosmic Inhale, as it were. Thus, in the space opened up by this self-limitation, Hashem was able to create finitude, and eventually a defined, bounded (albeit, perhaps expanding) world. On the Seventh Day, however, the Creator rested from this Tzimtzum (*VaYechal Elokim* / and *Elokim* [Tzimtzum] expired," *Likutei Torah*, Behar); meaning that Hashem stopped withdrawing, inhaling, and 'limiting' Himself to the involvement in finitude. Hashem then released a cosmic 'exhale,' re-introducing the Infinite Light and 'ensouling' the world by breathing the holy Shabbos into the fabric of creation.

We are created in the (inverted) Image of the Creator; thus, while we too express our finitude by creating and acting, we reveal our Infinity by practicing Tzimtzum, withdrawing and withholding our doing. In other words, the Creator *is* Infinity and in order to create finite reality He 'needs' to practice Tzimtzum. We, on the other hand, are finite beings, and in order to reveal our Infinite self — the Spark of the Infinite One within us — we need to practice Tzimtzum, to simply stop from all our finite pursuits, and enter boundless rest. Hashem's Tzimtzum creates the finite world, while our Tzimtzum completes our creation by reintroducing the Infinite back into the equation.

On Shabbos we practice a Tzimtzum from our 'doing' and outward manipulation of the world around us, and by doing so, we reveal our deeper self, our pure being, our Infinity.*

---

* The *Avnei Nezer* writes that before immersing in a Mikvah, a convert is not converted. A male convert is not fully converted until he is circumcised *and* goes into a Mikvah. Once

Our sages say, "Anyone who makes Shabbos a delight receives an inheritance without *Meitzarim* / bounds" / כל המענג את השבת נותנין לו נחלה בלי מצרים (*Shabbos*, 118a. See also *Medrash Rabbah*, Bereishis, 11:7). This is not some unconnected 'reward' for keeping Shabbos, rather, an "inheritance without bounds" is the direct corollary of keeping Shabbos. When we take delight and celebrate Shabbos meaningfully, we 'rest' from our finite self and thus, through this act of Tzimtzum, we contract our finitude and create space to reveal our boundless Infinity — which is in Itself an "inheritance without bounds."

Regarding the nature of Shabbos there seem to be two contradictory statements. On the one hand, the verse says, "And G-d completed on the Seventh Day... and He rested on the Seventh Day," and then the next verse continues, "And G-d blessed the Seventh Day" (Bereishis, 2:2-3). Resting suggests the absence of all movement and outwardness, whereas the very idea of blessing means to increase and proliferate a process of benefit (צאן גורן ויקב מיוחדים שישנן בכלל ברכה *Kidushin*, 17a. As Rashi explains, blessing means something that increases, צאן פרה ורבה וכן גידולי קרקע. And increases independently. Rambam, *Hilchos Avadim*, 3:14). This can be understood from our experience of Shabbos, as follows: when we cease and rest from activity, from outwardness, from doing, we connect to the Source of all Blessings and reveal the Infinity beyond and within ourselves. The

he is circumcised, however, even before the Mikvah, he is obligated to keep Shabbos (*Yoreh De'ah*, Siman 351. See also, *Shu't Binyan Tziyon*, 1, Siman 91. *Shu't Tzitz HaKodesh*, 1, Siman 34. Although see *Shu't Chelkas Yo'av*, Tanina, Siman 8; *Minchas Eliezer*, 3, Siman 8; see also *Tosefos*, Yevamos, 46b). This is how Klal Yisrael was obligated to keep Shabbos even before the Mikvah at Mount Sinai that preceded the Giving of the Torah (See also *Zohar* 2, 40a). Perhaps the inner reason for the Avnei Nezer's ruling (based on the inner teachings of the Zohar, *ibid*) is that once a person has truly practiced a real Tzimtzum on his physical body, circumcision, he becomes connected to the essence of Shabbos, and transcends the world of nature, where "nothing rests."

sequence is thus as such: a) we complete our work and rest, and then b) become hooked into the ultimate Source of Blessing, a dimension that is beyond all work, activity and finitude (as the Mittler Rebbe explains: *Sha'arei Teshuvah uTefilah*, p. 86-87), c) from which point we thereby 'increase' to a state of Infinity.

Finitude, by definition, is *Cheser* / lacking and existing in a perpetual state of need. It is, by design, never in a state of *Shalom* / completeness. (Although, "The world was created in completion" (*Medrash Rabbah*, Bereishis, 14:7). Then again, its 'completeness' is that it is a Cheser.) Everything within creation needs something else in order to exist, whether it is food, water or sunlight, for example. On a macrocosmic level, the entirety of Creation needs a Creator to exist. Infinity, on the other hand, is always complete and has no possibility of being anything other than Infinite (although it lacks being finite). On Shabbos, by stopping our doing and ceasing from being preoccupied with the material, finite world, we allow the Infinite dimension within ourselves to expand and be expressed, connecting us to the underlying wholeness and unity of Hashem and His Creation.

When the need to do or manipulate is not prevalent, a wholesomeness with a sense of perfection and Infinity sets in, which brings with it a sublime sense of inner peace. Shabbos is, at its core, a time of *Shalom* / peace. In fact, Shabbos is called *Shalom* (*Zohar* 3, 176b. *Ohr haChayim*, Vayikra, 19:2). Therefore, we greet each other on Shabbos, by saying, *Shabbat Shalom*. *Shalom* means both wholeness and peace; intrapersonal wholeness and interpersonal peace. Every day we ought to be extremely careful not to become angry by staying away from anger; but on Shabbos we need to be doubly careful (*Avodas haKodesh*, Moreh b'Etzbah, 152). On Shabbos there is a special prohibition "not to light fire," i.e., the fire of anger and strife (*Tikku-nei Zohar*, Tikun 48). The Shalom of Shabbos must extend inwardly as well; most importantly, Shalom means peace within oneself.

Shabbos is a time of *Sheleimus* / wholeness, fullness. It is a time when the Part of our-self that is a Part of the Creator (lacking nothing, without Cheser) is revealed and expressed. Shabbos itself is Perfect. Throughout the week we struggle, work hard, and perhaps even a little bit like a slave, pursue an elusive physical perfection that will forever be *Cheser* / lacking. On Shabbos that perfection is effortlessly achieved; all the peace, serenity, and sense of completeness that we so doggedly pursue during the week is revealed to be already present deep within the Infinite-Space of our soul, our Infinite, and the Soul of the Universe.

On Shabbos we reclaim our wholeness, our place within that is always Unified, Infinite and Complete.

One dimension of the human being is its integral part of the Six Days of Creation, the world of Cheser, and thus we labor to attain an unattainable perfection. This is how humans are as seekers — always lacking, yearning, dreaming and insatiably building. Man toils to achieve ever greater gains and attainments. This is the nature of Adam and Chava as created on Friday, the Sixth Day. Yet, although Adam was created on Friday, he did not become a full, erect, communicating human being until midday on Erev Shabbos (חמישית עמד על רגליו ששית קרא שמות שביעית נזדווגה לו חוה) *Sanhedrin*, 38b. *Pirkei d'Rebbe Eliezer*, 11). In other words, Adam became who he was within the penumbral glow of Shabbos; already wading into the proverbial waters of *Menuchah* / rest, with no need or desire to move or struggle. As Adam 'matured' within the light of Shabbos, the light of perfection, he naturally realized that he was already perfect and that the world is perfect as it is. He recognized that he was actually a reflection of how the world and humanity exist as one within the *Mach'shavah haKedumah* / the Primordial Thought of HaKadosh Baruch Hu, that "spiritual desire" to create a world other than Oneself. Shabbos reveals to all of us the level of self that is Eternally-Perfect; as we are but a true reflection and complete expression of Hashem's infinite creativity.

SHABBOS AS A BRIDGE BETWEEN YESH AND AYIN

Shabbos is like a reset button, giving us the ability to pause the relentless linear trajectory of *Yeshus* / egoic consciousness/striving; allowing us to re-orient ourselves within the limitless fountain of the Divine *Ayin* / no-thing-ness. In a state of Yesh, limited existence, ego, we are always existentially lacking, perpetually in Cheser. Whereas in the place of Ayin — endlessly one with the *Ein Sof* / Infinite One — we are always perfect.

Accordingly, Shabbos can be compared to a *Mikvah* / ritual pool, into which one dips and immerses oneself, letting go of any Yesh reality (as breathing is no longer possible), settles into a place-less place of Ayin (under the water, as it were), and then emerges transformed as a new Yesh, a new creation. Shabbos is therefore a Mikvah in time, a wellspring of Ayin, a pool of being, present within every seven day cycle.

Shabbos is composed of three Hebrew letters: *Shin, Beis, Tav.* This same combination of letters spells *Tashuv* / return. Shabbos invites us to return, again and again, into this Mikvah of Ayin; relieving us of the restless toil and burden of egoic life. Each week we are liberated from materialism and brought back to the essence of who we are, our soul. As we emerge from Shabbos, just as from a Mikvah, we recognize that we are always-already whole, perfect and free, a brilliant spark of the Creator.

MUCH MORE THAN REST FROM WORK

Upon learning that the people of Israel had a weekly cycle in which every seventh day was reserved for rest, many ancient philosophers promptly dismissed this notion as an indication of a lazy people. The Roman philosopher Seneca contended that spending every seventh day without doing anything squanders away a whopping one-seventh of a person's life. Others hypothesized that dedicating a day to rest once a week trains the body and mind to become inactive, lethargic and sluggish.

The Gemara tells a story that once there was a Roman decree against the Jewish People keeping Shabbos. Dressed up as a Roman, and speaking to Roman authorities, one of the sages of the *Gemara* / Talmud, using a strategic form of reverse psychology, argued that letting the Jewish People keep Shabbos will ensure that they are poorer than the rest of society. "If you have an enemy do you want to make him rich or poor?" "Poor of course," they responded. "Okay, so then allow them to keep Shabbos" (*Me'ilah*, 17a). The sage's argument was aimed at the Romans' erroneous conviction that keeping Shabbos makes a person poorer, and depletes them of energy and confines them to laziness.

This is also what the Greeks, and arguably all other ancient peoples, thought about Shabbos. Challenging this assertion, the first-century Jewish philosopher, Philo of Alexandria, countered that Shabbos is rather designed to 'free' people from their physical and manual labor. He suggested that this resting, instead of making a person more lazy, actually does the opposite. Shabbos allows the person to regain his strength and focus, freeing him up to work more energetically the following week.

Despite a more positive view of Shabbos, Philo's error was still interpreting the purpose of Shabbos from a Greek-Hellenist worldview. Resting only in order to energize further labor is still a slave-like materialist mentality, in which any sense of personal respite must be validated in terms of future utility; such as a lunch-break that only serves to rejuvenate strength for continued work. In this context, there is no value in rest, enjoyment or spiritual development, in and of themselves, but only as means to enhance productivity or success. This is still a prevalent selling-point for popular 'spirituality': perform rituals or meditate and you can achieve your dreams of becoming rich, successful, powerful, healthy, happy and loved. From that world-view, materialistic achievements are really all that matters.

This is actually how Moshe explained to Pharaoh, the ultimate slave-owner, why the Hebrews needed a "a day of rest." In order to convince him he argued using Pharaoh's own worldview. Our sages in the Medrash tell us that when Moshe saw the hardship of his brothers, he was deeply troubled and went to Pharaoh. He said,

"My master, the way of normal slave owners is that they want to keep their slaves healthy, but you seem to want to weaken them." "How so?" asked Pharaoh. "Since you work them relentlessly," replied Moshe, "they will weaken." "What should I do?" "Give them one day of rest so they can strengthen themselves and they can work harder." "Give them any day you choose," decided Pharoah. So Moshe said, "Let it be the seventh day, since on that day the celestial influence is Saturn and no one sees success from his work on this day, in any case." Once they left Egypt and the Mitzvah of Shabbos was given, Moshe was joyous that his plan was aligned with the Divine will (*Medrash Rabbah*, Shemos, 1:32. *Avudraham*, Seder Shachris Shel Shabbos).

Perhaps Moshe knew about the concept of Shabbos from his ancestors, or perhaps he was tapping into an unmediated flow of prophecy. Either way, he chose to explain Shabbos in a way that Pharaoh would understand and be motivated to allow Klal Israel to rest.

It should now be abundantly understood that Shabbos is much more than a rest from work. That kind of rest only perpetuates an even deeper slavery to 'doing' and 'achieving.' Shabbos is of an altogether different order; it is about 'being,' rather than 'doing' or 'not-doing.' As such, we refer to Shabbos as a *Zecher l'Yetziyas Mitzrayim* / a remembrance, or *making manifest in the present*, of our exodus from slavery and return from exile, both physically and spiritually.

SHABBOS OR SHABBOS-OF-SHABBOS

Many times when the Torah speaks about Shabbos it calls it שבת שבתון / *Shabbos Shabbaton* / Shabbos of Shabbos. This phrase is often translated as, "a Shabbos of complete rest," as in, "Six days: work may be done, but on the seventh day, *a Shabbos of complete rest*" / ששת ימים יעשה מלאכה וביום השביעי שבת שבתון (Shemos, 31:15). And, "Six days you shall do work, but on the seventh day, *a Shabbos of complete rest*" / ששת ימים תעשה מלאכה וביום השביעי שבת שבתון (Vayikra, 23:3).

Sometimes the Torah calls Shabbos simply *Shabbos*, as in, "Six days you shall work and perform all your labor...but on the seventh day, Shabbos...." / ששת ימים תעבד ועשית כל־מלאכתך ויום השביעי שבת (Shemos, 20:9-10).

What is the basis for this seeming discrepancy, and how is the quality of "Shabbos of Shabbos" distinct from just "Shabbos"?

Upon closer inspection, this discrepancy is easily resolved. When the Torah uses the term "Shabbos of Shabbos" it also uses the words תעשה / "work shall be performed," or יעשה / "work may be done." Linguistically, these two words suggest *Ma'aseh* / an action-based work, yet a work that is 'passive' or somehow done on its own. On the other hand, when the Torah uses the singular term *Shabbos*, it also uses the word תעבד / labor, which suggests 'hard labor' as it is similar to the word *Eved* / slave.

When a person's work during the week is 'labor-intensive,' whether physically, emotionally or mentally, then when Shabbos comes along it is *Shabbos*, a respite from hard labor. However, we can have a healthy sense of emotional and mental detachment from our work, even as we are performing it, as the Chassidic Yiddish saying, *Men Ligt Nisht In Gashmiyus* / "We are not immersed or wrapped up in the material world." When we have this *Shabbosdike* detachment throughout the week, our work itself is more restful and joyful, and perhaps it is seemingly done 'on its own.' This posture towards one's work implies a Shabbos energy present even in the midst of the Six Days of the week. Then, when the actual day of Shabbos comes along, it is called "Shabbos of Shabbos," a 'rest of rest,' an inner rest that is beyond any relationship to work or toil at all. This idea will now be explored in greater detail below.

OUTSIDE THE RHYTHM OF TIME AND WORK

Shabbos was given to the Nation of Israel when we were still sojourning in the Wilderness. Neither working the land nor going to the city to engage in trade were part of their nomadic reality. And yet, they were still given the gift of Shabbos.* Why? Originally, Shabbos was not merely a day off from demanding labor or even a way of deepening creativity by taking a break from it, as it is commonly understood. The various restrictions of Shabbos are there to create a context for the experience of real existential, not just utilitarian, freedom and *Deveikus* / uniting with HaKadosh Baruch Hu, revealing an altogether deeper way of being in and of itself.

---

* This is also the reason why Shabbos is called a *Chok* / statute, as in, "There He gave them a statute" (*Shemos*, 15:25), referring to Shabbos (*Mechilta*, ad loc, *Sanhedrin*, 56b, *Kad Kemach*, Shabbos). In essence, Shabbos is not a rational Mitzvah, a logical "day off from work," rather in its root it is a decree, unrelated to taking time off from work. *Chok* can also refer to a boundary, as Shabbos sets a boundary to the work and creative involvement of man in the world. Maharal, *Gur Aryeh*, Shemos, 15:25.

Shabbos is the anti-instrumentalization of our lives.

Shabbos is the transcendent *Ayin* / emptiness beyond all *Tenuah* / movement, within the rhythm of time and movement. Shabbos is a day that stands completely apart from the week and its wheel of productive and coercive movement and 'progress.' It is from, and alerts us to, another dimension entirely. Shabbos, our sages tell us, was created before the Creation of the world (*Pirkei d'Rebbe Eliezer*, chap 3). It comes from a place that is completely beyond the weekday reality, prior to the Six Days of Creation. This is the inner reason why during the afternoon prayers (Minchah) on Shabbos we proclaim, "You are One and Your Name is One… A day of rest and holiness You have given Your nation… *May Your children recognize and know that from You is their rest.*" Why this latter affirmation? We do not say this regarding any other day or Mitzvah, though it may be true. On Sukkos, for example, we do not say, "A day of Sukkos You have given them; may Your children recognize and know that from You is their Sukkah." This is because unlike Sukkos, which is clearly a Mitzvah, rest *can* be quite mundane, as in napping or simply taking a vacation. As such, we declare, 'Our Shabbos rest is from You,' articulating our awareness of your profound presence and *Kedushah* / holiness, even within an aspect of our lives that on the surface registers as completely quotidian. This Divinne attribution elevates and transforms our rest on Shabbos into a higher, deeper, more transcendent form of rest (See, Tosefos, *Chagigah*, שלשה מעידין זה על זה על זה ישראל ושבת והקדוש ב"ה... ועל זה סמכינן לומר אתה אחד במנחה בשבת .3b אע"פ שאינו מדבר מעניינא דיומא דשבת). Indeed, our Shabbos rest is an extension of the Creator's own rest on the Seventh Day; it is thus quite literally "from" Hashem.

This Nekudah of Shabbos, this Divine silence, stillness, inner calmness and delightful rest, actually exists deeply within every moment of time, within every place, and within every soul. There is an aspect of Shabbos within the depths of all movement and even within all work. The Nekudah of Shabbos within multi-dimensional space is manifest in the *Makom haMikdash* / Place of the Holy Temple, and thus Yaakov is upset with himself after sleeping on that spot, since sleep suggests tiredness, and fatigue comes from motion —which is contrary to the quality of Shabbos. Yaakov had already discovered this Nekudah within his own being, but in this instance 'failed' to recognize it within the realms of space and time.

Within ourselves as well, there is a point of soul that is timelessly whole and perfect, and never needs to strive or become fatigued, as will be explored later. Although it is beyond the confines of time, we are gifted with a more clear channel of access to this Nekudah — that, again, always exists — throughout the 25 to 26 hours of Shabbos.

And, although the actual day of Shabbos is transcendent of Tenuah, work and weekday, Shabbos is also the depth of time itself, the multi-dimensional field upon which time reveals and recycles the fruits of its labor. Due to this foundational function of Shabbos within the mechanism of time, the sanctity of Shabbos irrigates and blesses the workweek that precedes and follows. Our immersion in holiness during Shabbos gives meaning and purpose to our six preceding days and imbues our six following days with spirituality and blessing (*Zohar* 2, 63b). Shabbos is the culmination of the past week and the foundation of the week to come, setting a higher tone for the week's mundane activities. On a deeper, paradoxical level, Shabbos is simultaneously beyond time and is the essence of all time.

To illustrate this point, our sages discuss and describe a scenario in which someone is traveling in the desert, loses track of time, and thus does not know when Shabbos is, when should they keep Shabbos? According to one opinion, they should observe today as Shabbos and then count six days until the next Shabbos. On a deeper level this means that if someone is lost in the 'desert' of life, cannot find their footing or place, and in general feels discombobulated, unfocused, and perhaps even ridden with anxiety, they can claim today as Shabbos; and Halachically, if they are literally lost (i.e. not just existentially), the day they confirm as Shabbos is in fact actually Shabbos (for them). This is because Shabbos, as the seventh day of creation, is a macro-cosmic truth and reality that enters and infuses each locale on the planet according to its conception of when the seventh day is; as it can be Shabbos in one part of the world and Sunday or Friday in another. The Kedusha / holiness of Shabbos is Transcendent of time, emanating from a world beyond, and yet, it permeates each place on the planet according to that time particular zone. (*Teshuvas haRadbaz*, 1, Siman 76. "For the sanctity of Shabbos and the festivals — all transcend the limits of space and time, though they radiate "downward" into the physical realms to each and every place at the time appropriate for it." Alter Rebbe, *Shulchan Aruch*, Orach Chayim, (second version) 1:8). And on the deepest level, the Nekudah of Shabbos is the essence of all time, and is therefore manifest to each individual person, whenever or wherever he or she is, so long as they open themselves up to this Nekudah.

THE OPPORTUNITY OF SHABBOS

Hashem tells Moshe, "I have a precious gift in My treasure house, and its name is Shabbos. I want to give it to Israel. Go and tell them" (*Beitzah*, 16a). Why does Hashem tell Moshe, "Go tell them"?

Once a poor man came to the home of the legendary *Tzadik* / righteous holy man, Rebbe Shmelke of Nikolsburg, and poured out his heart, saying how he was in a desperate situation with no money to feed his young family. The Rebbe, who had very little money himself but felt deep compassion for this poor man, looked around his room and noticed a small, nice-looking lamp. He assumed it was worth a few rubles, and so he gave him the lamp, telling him, "Sell this, and with the money, buy food for your family."

As the man was leaving his home, Reb Shmelke's wife noticed him walking out with the lamp, and so she ran into the room and said to her husband, what have you done? Do you know that lamp is worth hundreds of rubles! When Reb Shmelke heard this, he got up and ran outside, chased down the poor man, and yelled, "It is worth at least 300 rubles, make sure you are not cheated!"

Hashem is telling Moshe, 'Let the people know the true value and worth of Shabbos!' Sure, you can use Shabbos as a day of simply resting from hard labor, to catch up on your sleep, or to relax the body. But this is not its full worth or ultimate value. You can sell it cheap, as it were, but you can also cash in, so to speak.

Let us not waste our Shabbos on *just* eating finer foods and drinking better wines, having a little extra sleep, or sitting around chatting with friends and family — as good and nourishing as all of these activities may be. Certainly, these can all be included within the general sense of Divine pleasure, as we have the ability to extend our 'Divine pleasure' into all areas of life, including eating, drinking, intimacy, sleep, and conversation. If we are not doing these things from a place of *Cheser* / lack and neediness, rather, from a place of *Sheleimus* / wholeness and satisfaction, they too can be *Shabbosdik*. Yet, we ought to always keep in mind what the true gift of Shabbos really is; a time to experience something deeper, something more real, holy and transcendent than the constant drudgery of the proverbial six days will allow, something that we can eventually assimilate into our mundane life as well.

Remember:

Not only is Shabbos holy; through Shabbos we become holy.

Not only do we observe the sanctity of Shabbos; Shabbos sanctifies us.

Not only do we rest on Shabbos; Shabbos brings us rest.

Not only do we keep the Shabbos; Shabbos keeps us.

02

LIVING YOUR PURPOSE WITH BIG PICTURE VISION

S HABBOS IS *SHELEIMUS* / WHOLENESS, AS EXPLAINED; IT is the 'whole,' the big picture vision of our lives, providing focus, purpose and direction to every moment. Shabbos can either be a once a week occurrence, or, as mentioned, it can become the sustaining roots of our very identity, as in, "A wise person is called *Shabbos*." We can be *Shabbosdik*, or live from a Shabbos paradigm and a place of wholeness, every day of our lives.

In general, there are two approaches to life: one is *Rav* / a lot and one is *Kol* / everything.

In the lifestyle of *Rav* / a lot, we feel like there is always 'a lot' of individual, conflicting things going on in our lives — a job, family, social responsibilities, physical and mental well-being and spiritual development. In a paradigm of *Kol* / everything, we perceive that there is an overarching theme to our lives and acknowledge that everything is rooted within that unifying context.

Our lives are either experienced as a collection of many disjointed ideas, feelings, sensations and things, or it is experienced as a unified whole that *includes* many ideas, feelings, sensations and things. In the former, we may feel scattered, pulled in different directions, and perhaps overly busy or stressed. In the latter we feel more at ease, unified, focussed and restful.

After many years of being estranged, Yaakov encounters his brother Esav, the archetype of the unrighteous one, and they both begin talking about their lives, their wealth and blessings. Esav says, *Yesh Li Rav* / "I have so much," whereas his brother Yaakov says, *Yesh Li Kol* / "I have everything." On the surface these two statements seem quite similar, although they are radically different.

There is a profound difference between thinking in terms of 'a lot' or 'much' versus thinking in terms of 'everything.' A person can have 'a lot' and not have everything they need; while on the other hand, a person can have very little and yet feel like they have everything they need. There is a deep distinction between relating to life from a perspective of 'having a lot' and one of 'having everything.'

'A lot' is not merely a quantification, but a statement of quality as well; what you have feels like a multitude of disjointed possessions and responsibilities that are all competing for your time. Nothing receives quality attention. The unified perspective of 'having everything' (see *Medrash Rabbah*, Vayikra, 4:6) is a 'whole picture' vision in which everything is valued and connected. From this vantage point, everything in your life fills in the frame and all the details are harmonized within the context of the whole. Shabbos is that frame.

We live in a culture that thinks in terms of 'having a lot.' People say, 'I have a good relationship with my parents, spouse or children, I also have a home, apartment, car, I have a computer, iPad, iPhone, and also have a certain amount of money in my accounts...' There is nothing really connecting the dots; there is no harmony. In other words, there is a *Cheser* / lack of focus or purpose. Even though they have a lot in life, they are always missing an abiding sense of satisfaction. There will always be a newer phone to acquire, a faster system, a higher rung to achieve, another million dollars to make. Today you may have a lot, but tomorrow you will want more. This is a life lived only from a six-days perspective.

A person, for example, buys a new gadget or a new pair of shoes, feels elated and then calls a friend to share the euphoria. But in a very short period of time, maybe even as soon as he gets off the phone, the nagging, restless emptiness resurfaces. Once again he finds himself on the lookout for the next exciting thing.

This is a fragmentation of one's reality; there is one gadget, a second one and third. There is a sense of needing to catch up, to rush into the future, because there is no ground of wholeness or presence to stand on. From an 'everything' perspective there is an understanding of the whole picture, the entire Gestalt of life; all the things in our lives together form a unity that is greater than the sum of its parts. That unity is Shabbos.

To create a template of wholeness, of unity and harmony, to enter a *Kol* / everything paradigm (without — or with a less intense — *Yetzer* / inclination towards negativity and disharmony. See *Baba Basra*, 17a), we need to glimpse the big picture of our lives and ourselves. The way to do this is by uncovering our deepest purpose. Why are we here? What is our Divine mandate? Why were we born at this period of time, to this set of parents, with these siblings, these genetics, in this culture and upbringing? Why were we born in this particular environment with its inherent challenges and gifts?

We need to think deeply about our uniqueness, and how we can offer our uniqueness to help make this world a better, more refined and holy place. Think about your talents, proclivities, tendencies, natural strengths, and the things you do that make you feel most alive and connected. Channel these into being the best person you can be. Direct them into articulating your highest spiritual, mental, emotional and physical potential; for the betterment of yourself and the betterment of the world around you.

When we uncover and rediscover our mission and pursue it, this becomes the 'everything' in life, the unifying underlying principle that guides us and includes all the details of life. Then, all things are included in this 'everything.'

Chazal debate whether the word *Kol*, when it appears in the Torah, only means 'everything,' or if it can also suggest "a little of the everything" (*Bechoros*, 3a. *Chulin*, 88a). Perhaps all sages agree that the simple meaning of the word *Kol* is 'everything,' yet since everything within the 'unit' of a Kol is an integral, interconnected part of the Kol, every little detail of the Kol can also be called 'the Kol.' Similarly, the Baal Shem Tov says, "When you grasp a little bit of the essence, you are grasping the whole" / כשאתה תופס במקצת מן העצם אתה תופס בכולו (*Keser Shem Tov*, Hosafos, 16. Rebbe Rashab, *Hemshech Samach Vav*, p. 522).

'Kol,' the big picture vision of our life, is the essence of Shabbos; Shabbos is "a taste of the World-to-Come" (*Mechilta*, Shemos 31:13. See also *Berachos*, 57b) and Kol too is "like a state of the World-to-Come" (*Baba Basra*, 17a). Shabbos gifts us the opportunity to stop thinking in terms of 'a lot,' if and when we are inclined to do so, and to begin thinking in terms of Kol, the 'everything-ness' of life.

On all the days of Creation, the Torah says, "and He saw that it was good." However at the conclusion of the Six Days, as Shabbos is about to begin, the Torah says, "And He saw *Kol* / everything that He had made..." (Bereishis, 1:31). Shabbos is the ingathering of all the goodness of the week and of all phenomena into a unified Kol reality.

Shabbos is the Kol of the Rav of the week; it removes us from the inherent limitations of the Rav perspective and allows us to "see *Kol* / the *everything* that He has made," and start living from there.

There is a marked distinction between the liturgies of Shabbos and those of the week. During the workweek we open the blessing of the Shema with the words *HaMe'ir la'Aretz* / "Who illuminates the earth..." and on Shabbos we exchange this opening, for *Ha-Kol Yoducha veHa-Kol Yishab'chucha* / "All acknowledge You and all praise You..." In the Ashkenaz (as distinct from the Sefard and

Arizal's version) *Nusach* / version of the *Siddur* / prayer-book, one recites during the week the phrase *Ma Rabu Ma'asecha* / "How great (*Rav* / many) are Your works." However, this phrase is glaringly omitted on Shabbos. This seems puzzling; what about that phrase is not *Shabbosdik*? The answer is that Shabbos is all about the Kol, the all, the everything, and not about *Rav* or *Rabu* / the many. Thus, on Shabbos, we focus deeply on the perspective that "All praise You" — You, the Creator who is the *Yotzer haKol* / Creator of All.

As Shabbos enters the Torah tells us (Bereishis, 2:1-2), "Now the Heavens and the earth were completed…" / ויכלו השמים והארץ The root word of ויכלו / *VaYechulu* / completed, is *Kol* / completeness, allness. Here the Torah is telling us that it is specifically on Shabbos that the disparate aspects of creation, represented here by the "heavens" and the "earth," are woven together into a unified state of higher integration and completeness, one of "all-ness." The narrative continues, "And Elokim completed on the Seventh Day…" / ויכל אלהים ביום השביעי The Divine Name Elokim, which signifies *Rav* / multiplicity, also shifts into a state of Kol in the context of the seventh day. The verse then ends, "…and He rested on the Seventh Day *from all* His work." / וישבת ביום השביעי מכל־מלאכתו אשר עשה It appears that Elokim shifts into a state of Divine rest "from," or as a result of, the fact that all of the "work" (all of the *Ma'aseh Bereishis* / Acts of Creation) are now seen as *Kol* / an integral and cohesive wholeness. This shift in consciousness is precisely what brings about the state of Divine 'rest.'

Kol (Chaf/20, Lamed/30) is numerically 50 (*Medrash Tehilim*, also known as *Medrash Shochar Tov*, 13:3). The number 50 alludes to the *Yovel*

/ Jubilee Year, the year of complete freedom, when land and indentured servants return back to their original status and perfected state. On the Seventh Day the objective and purpose of the entire Creation in all its individual details and 'many-ness' was realized as Earth and Heaven returned to their original wholeness, freedom and perfection.

Another way of saying this: on Shabbos the Creator rested from *creating* everything and infused the Seventh Day with the ability to make us aware that every little detail of Creation is an aspect of 'everythingness.' Each part contains the whole.

Humanity was originally born in a state of perfection, in *Gan Eden* / Paradise, the paradigm of the Tree of Life, the reality of oneness and wholeness. We too are born into this state prior to any brokenness and duality. The meta-narrative of our collective history is recapitulated in the microcosm of our own individual lives. Just as Adam and Chava were born into a state of wholeness or *Kol*, so are we. When we eat from the 'Tree' or paradigm of Knowledge, of Good and Evil, we enter into a world of fragmentation, brokenness and disjointed many-ness. Shabbos allows us to undo this splintered consciousness and re-enter Gan Eden, to live at least temporarily from a place of wholeness and completion, from a place of Kol without *Cheser* / deficiency. Shabbos reminds us and refreshes us with an experience of our primordial and perfect origins, as well as our Messianic potential in the future.

Just as Adam and Chava (before their expulsion) on Shabbos, we return to the 'Paradise' of Gan Eden, our original state of effortless wellbeing. In an image of our sages, when Adam "would dine in the Garden of Eden, the ministering angels would roast meat for him and strain wine for him" (*Sanhedrin*, 59b). This points out the fact that there is no Melachah in Gan Eden; everything is served to Adam and Chava without exertion or toil. Adam and Chava were perfectly performing the will of Hashem, and thus, "their work was performed by others, as it is stated (Yeshayahu, 61:5), 'And strangers will stand and feed your flocks'" (*Berachos*, 35b). On a deeper level, when one works with a Shabbosdik perspective of the *all*, they are aware that their efforts, their creations, their successes are not attributable to themselves alone, but truly that angels and emissaries, and even Hashem Himself, is invested and involved in all of their pursuits. This very consciousness of Hashem's presence in all that we do introduces the quality of Kol to each individual task or goal we accomplish.

On Shabbos itself, as we enter the Gan Eden of Shabbos, we realize that everything can be fixed, that all our mistakes can be repaired, even our "eating" or internalizing the paradigm of fragmentation. On a more profound level of Shabbos consciousness, we realize that there are no mistakes at all, and what we previously thought of as purposeless or a wrong move was Divinely orchestrated and meant to be, and in fact, it is the reason why you are who you are at this present moment.

On Shabbos we are invited and encouraged to enter into the world of *Yichud* / unity by means of refraining from the 39 *Melachos* / prohibited actions of Shabbos. *Melachah*, as mentioned, comes from the word *Hiluch* / walking, moving — suggesting a separation between 'here' and 'there.' We *need* to do Melachah and hard work during the week because of the curses of Adam and Chava, interestingly both focused on their negative experiences of 'labor,' including childbirth and agriculture, which followed as a result of their eating from the Tree of dualistic Knowledge. Because we now function in a world of *Pirud* / separation we need to perform Melachah, not only during the six days, in which we physically 'produce' and proliferate, but also spiritually, to help us 'move into' the place of unity and blessing of Shabbos.

Following their eating from the Tree of Knowledge, Hashem tells Adam and Chava, "Cursed be the ground for your sake; with toil shall you eat of it, all the days of your life. And it will cause thorns and thistles to grow for you...With the sweat of your brow you shall eat bread..." (*Bereishis*, 3:17-19). Overall, there are 39 curses: ten on Adam, ten on Chava, ten on the snake, and nine on the earth. These correspond to the 39 Melachos, the primary labors that we (and certainly those living an agricultural lifestyle) perform during the workweek (*Tikkunei Zohar*, Tikun 48. Perhaps this also corresponds to the 39 times the word *Melachah* / work appears in the Torah. *Shabbos*, 49b. Yerushalmi, *Shabbos*, 7:2. See Rabbeinu Chananel, *Shabbos* 49b. *Tosefos Yom Tov*, *Shabbos*, 7:2, regarding which (appearances of the word) *Melachah* are counted and which are not). Ultimately, the effect of Adam and Chava entering the world of separation, as a result of eating from the Tree of Knowledge, is that now there is a 'separation' in the process of producing food; "When you sow the earth with various species of seeds it will sprout thorns and thistles" (Rashi, ad loc, *Medrash Rabbah*, Bereishis, 20:10). There is a disconnect between what you sow and what may grow. And even when you sow grain and grain does grow, it comes about only with "toil" or hardship, with the "sweat" of effort, as there is a disconnect between the farmer, the seed and the soil.

Such is the reality of the workweek, we toil, we sweat and we do *Avodas Perach* / hard labor (the word *Perach* in At-Bash (Aleph and Tav interchangeable, Beis and Shin interchangeable, etc.) is Vav/6, Gimel/3, Lamed/30 = 39, alluding to the 39 Melachos (*Tosefos, Pesachim* 117b). לפי שבמצרים עבדו בהם בישראל בפרך ופר"ך בא"ת ב"ש וג"ל שהם מלאכות ארבעים חסר אחת וכשנגאלו ממצרים הזהירם על השבת לשבות מאות' ל"ט מלאכות. Interestingly enough, the idea of exchanging letters to reach the number 39 is also found in the *Yerushalmi*. The Yerushalmi says that we exchange the Hei in אלה to a Ches as in אלח and thus arrive at the numerical value of 39 (*Shabbos*, 7:2. See also Rashba, *Shabbos*, 105a). דאנו דורשין ה"א בחי"ת. Perhaps the weekday reality of toil is an At Bash-like "exchange" or inversion of the true reality, the world of perfection, Shabbos). On Shabbos, we use the various Melachos in our striving and laboring to undo the effects of the Tree of Knowledge and return to the Tree of Life reality, Gan Eden. How so?

The number 39 is the numerical value of the words, *Hashem* (26) *Echad* (13) / "Hashem is One" (*Shulchan Aruch*, Orach Chayim, 11:14, regarding the tying of Tzitzis). During the week, we employ the 39 Melachos in our life's work, accomplishing our goals and manifesting our view of what the world should look or be like. Shabbos, on the other hand, is "a day to Hashem."* On Shabbos, by refraining from all the 39 Melachos and their derivatives, we reveal the *Reshus ha-Yachid* / the 'private' or unified domain; we reveal *Hashem Echad* /

---

* There are four possible ways to spell out the four letters of the Name Hashem, Yud-Hei-Vav-Hei. For example, Hei can be spelled Hei-Hei or Hei-Aleph. These four ways are also known as the Four Names of Hashem, based on their numerical values: *Av* (72), *Sag* (63), *Mah* (45), and *Ban* (52). When all of these four spellings of the Name are spelled out, there are 39 letters in total. Shabbos is the fullness, the Kol / all-ness of the Name of Hashem, and thus we refrain from the 39 (Lamed-Tes) Melachos and enter the world of the *Tal* / Dew (Tes-Lamed) of Resurrection and Unity.

the Oneness of Hashem.*

* The main idea of Shabbos is to refrain from moving out of the *Reshus haYachid* / private domain (the place of non-movement where Hashem's unity rests, the place of Echad) into the *Reshus haRabim* / public domain, the place of apparent duality and movement (and kindling fire). In the words of the Medrash, מה היא שימור של שבת מלהבעיר בה אש ומלעשות בו מלאכה ומלצאת ומלבא חוץ לתחום אפי' רגל אחד ומלהביא דבר בידו ולהעבירו ארבע אמות ברשות הרבים ולהוציא מרשות לרשות, חו היא שמירתה של שבת (*Pirkei d'Rebbe Eliezer*, 18:8). For this reason, the main Melachah of Shabbos is *Hotza'ah* / moving an object from a Reshus haYachid, literally 'domain of the unified,' into a Reshus haRabim, literally 'domain of the multiple,' or the opposite, moving an object from a public domain to a private domain. The latter is called *Hachnasah* / bringing something inside, but is also referred to with the general term *Hotza'ah* (*Shabbos*, 2b. *Shavuos*, 5a-b), as every Melachah of carrying is a form of *Hotza'ah* / moving it from its space. It is perhaps for this reason that it would have even been possible for the *Beis Din* / high court to make the mistake of ruling that while we are not allowed to carry from inside to outside, we may carry from the outside to inside (*Horayos*, 4a), as it would appear as an act of bringing multiplicity into the Domain of Unity.

The entire tractate of Mishnah and Gemara of Shabbos begin with, "the carrying out of Shabbos" / *Yetziyos haShabbos* (even though carrying may seem like a 'weak Melachah' (Tosefos, *Shabbos* 2a), as transferring from the 'private' domain to the 'public' domain is the essential Issur of Shabbos. Carrying, in fact, may be the *only* Melachah that the Torah singles out — "A person may not leave his home (carrying an object)" to a public space (*Divrei Eliyahu*, *Shabbos*, 1a). Lighting a fire may be singled out only to teach us about the other 38 Melachos. *Shabbos*, 70a. See also *Shemos*, 34:21). The ultimate Reshus haYachid is Atzilus, the World of Unity and Stillness, whereas the lower worlds are a part of the Reshus haRabim, the worlds of multiplicity and movement (*Tikkunei Zohar*, Tikun 24. Radbaz, *Metzudas David*, Mitzvah 91. *Likutei Torah* [Arizal], Beshalach. *Toras Menachem*, 9. p. 121). The Reshus haYachid is Hashem's Unity and Domain. The minimum area of a Reshus haYachid is ten *Tefachim* / hand-breadths by four Tefachim. There are four letters in the Name Hashem, and there are Ten letters in the Name when it is filled with an Alef. In the words of the *Tikkunei Zohar*, (12a) ושכינתא שבת יחידה, איהי רשות דיחודא דעלמא דאיהו גבהו עשר אתוון דשמא מפרש יו"ד ה"א וא"ו ה"א, ורחבו ד' יהו"ה The above helps explain a puzzling Medrash (*Likutei Sichos*, 14. p. 68), Turnus Rufus once asked Rabbi Akiva, "If Hashem honors the Shabbos, then He should not blow winds on it, He should not cause rains to fall on it and He should not cause the grass to grow on it!" Rabbi Akiva answered him, "If two people live in one courtyard, unless they both contribute to an Eruv (a device rendering the shared courtyard their private unified domain), they are not permitted to carry in the courtyard. Yet, if one person lives there, his courtyard is his private domain and he can carry there at will. Hashem is the Creator of life and the entire world is like His private

The word *Tal* / dew equals, 39, the number of prohibited Melachos on Shabbos. Tal is also connected with the concept of *Techiyah* / Resurrection. In this sense, Tal is a mystical, otherworldly

domain (*Medrash Rabbah*, Bereishis, 11:6). This merely answers how Hashem can let rain fall in His private domain — but isn't growing and plowing also prohibited on Shabbos? The answer is that all Melachah prohibited on Shabbos is an act of 'taking out' from the private domain of the Creator (where the world is perfect) and bringing it into the world of the public, the world of movement and imperfection. Cooking and sowing, for example, are acts of taking something from its Reshus haYachid status, where everything is perfect as Hashem created it, and changing the status, moving it into the world of *Rabim*, of movement, growth and change. From Hashem's perspective, as it were, nothing ever changes or is transferred; all existence is always-already absorbed within the Unity of Hashem.

The *Rabim* / multiplicity of Melachah and the *Yachid* / singularity of *Menuchah* / resting from Melachah is illustrated by the following Halachic reasoning. Someone who knows that today is Shabbos, yet forgets that certain Melachos are prohibited on Shabbos, is liable for each separate Melachah and must bring a separate offering for each prohibited act that he has performed (*Shabbos*, 67b). In other words, even though he has only transgressed one general prohibition, namely *not to do Melachah on Shabbos*, still, he is liable for each specific Melachah. Why is this? When someone eats two measurements of forbidden fats, and then becomes aware of his transgression, he brings only *one* offering (*Krisus*, 11b). Why don't we bring only one offering for the general transgression of performing Melachah on Shabbos? Our sages bring three reasons:

1) Since the Torah singles out one of the prohibited Melachos — fire — we learn that each Melachah is, in the same way, an individual *Lav* / prohibition, and thus, each Lav performed incurs another offering (*Tosefos Rid,* Shabbos, 138a). In this way, the Melachos can be called שמות מחולקין / separate names.

2) All of the Melachos are like גופין מחולקין / separate bodies. This is comparable to a case, where a man was intimate with five different women who were all Nidos, but he did not know, in which case, he is liable for every separate action.

3) It is simply a גזירת הכתוב / *Gezeras haKasuv* (See *Totza'os Chayim*, Siman 5. *Marcheshes* 1, Siman 13).

In any case, when we observe, *"Lo Taaseh Kol Melachah* / you shall not do any work," we are tapping into the inclusive unity of Menuchah, whereas if we transgress a specific prohibition, Chas veShalom, we are entering the realm of multiplicity, so to speak.

moisture that can give life to the lifeless and resurrect what is dead. It was this dew that returned our souls to our bodies after they departed in ecstasy at Mount Sinai (*Shabbos*, 88b), and with this dew, all of life will be resurrected in the times of Moshiach when the entire world will reveal the Oneness of Hashem. Death defines the world of separation, while Tal revitalizes life by imbuing it with a sense of ultimate Unity. Additionally, when we study Torah (*Kesuvos*, 111b. Yerushalmi, *Berachos*, 5:2. *Ohr Torah* (Rav Yitzchak Chaver) Os 68), which is also likened to water and described as being *Sam Chayim* / an elixir of life and refrain from the 39 Melachos on Shabbos, we enter into the world of Yichud and Unity (Tal is the *Mon* / Manna; מטל השמים, זה המן. *Medrash Rabbah*, Bereishis, 66:3. See also *Idra Zuta*, 292b).

On Shabbos we stop working, manipulating and trying to change reality; we let go of our need to control and allow for a revealing of the Kol, the Whole, the Unified world of perfection, where everything has reached its potential, everything is complete, and everything effortlessly reveals its inner purpose for being created.

Ultimately, we need to marry the *Kol* / Unity of Shabbos with the *Rav* / *multiple* labors of the week. When we bridge these two paradigms, even our workweek will express and be an expression of the wholeness of Kol.

03

SHABBOS AS REMINDER: CREATION *VS* REDEMPTION

I F A PERSON HAS BECOME LOST IN THE WILDERNESS AND DOES NOT know which day is Shabbos, and they do not have any devices with which to determine it, which is the most proper and appropriate day to stop, start, and keep Shabbos? One opinion is that he should count six days and then keep the seventh day as Shabbos. This is similar to the Creation story of the world, in which Shabbos was the Seventh Day of Creation. The other opinion is that he should immediately observe Shabbos, and after that day of rest count six days and establish the subsequent Shabbos. This is similar to the creation of Adam and Chava (i.e. humanity), who were created on the Sixth Day of Creation; with sunset they encountered Shabbos, and afterward they counted six weekdays (*Shabbos*, 69b) before the next Shabbos. These are the ways in which this question is discussed in *Gemara*.

On a deeper level the question is whether Shabbos is a final destination or an origin point. Does Shabbos complete the previous week or give birth to the next week?

REMEMBERING CREATION & REMEMBERING THE EXODUS FROM EGYPT

When the Torah introduces us to Shabbos, in the Ten Commandments engraved in the First *Luchos* / Tablets, it says, "*Zachor* / remember the Shabbos day to sanctify it. Six days may you work and perform all your labor; but the Seventh Day is a Shabbos to Hashem your G-d; you shall do no work... six days G-d made the heavens and the earth, the sea and all that is in them, and rested on the Seventh Day. Therefore, G-d blessed the Shabbos day and sanctified it" (*Shemos*, 20: 8-11). Shabbos is, in this way, "a remembrance of Creation." By means of practicing Shabbos we remember the Creation of the world and, what's more, appreciate the fact that there is an intention to it — personal and collective life is not mere random coincidence. In other words: we remember that there is a Creator of all life.

When we remember that "six days Hashem created... and rested on the Seventh," it is not merely a remembrance of *things past*, that Creation arose long ago with intention and purpose. A "remembrance of Creation" is becoming viscerally aware that the Divine Light is right now creating and sustaining the world, and it is That which gives life to all of Creation from moment to moment. Every day and every moment Creation is renewed through the cosmic process and structure of the 'six days' (or six Sefiros) of creativity and the seventh of *Menuchah* / rest (Malchus). This circuit repeats and imprints itself in every instant, in every point in space, and in the life-force of every living being. This is one aspect of Shabbos.

At the beginning of the Ten Commandments the Torah says, "I am Hashem your G-d who has taken you out of Egypt." This seems to suggest that all of the Commandments which follow are connected with our experience of going out of Egypt. Indeed, in the book of Devarim, we find that on the Second *Luchos* / Tablets it says, "*Shamor* / Observe the Shabbos day and sanctify it... the Seventh Day is a Shabbos to Hashem, your G-d; you shall perform no labor, neither you, your son, your daughter, your manservant, your maidservant, your ox, your donkey, any of your livestock, nor the stranger who is within your cities, in order that your manservant and your maidservant may rest like you. And you shall remember that you were a slave in the land of Egypt, and that Hashem your G-d took you out from there with a strong hand and with an outstretched arm; therefore, Hashem, your G-d, commanded you to observe the Shabbos" (Devarim, 5:12-15).

Here, Shabbos is depicted as "a remembrance of the going out of Egypt". The Torah thus offers two reasons for Shabbos: we are to 'remember Creation' and also to 'remember going out of Egypt' (*Ramban*, Devarim, 5:15. Although see, Tur, *Orach Chayim*, 271, who learns that the remembering of going out of Egypt is actually connected to the *Moadim* /

holidays). These two purposes are expressed in the Nusach (liturgy) of the Friday Night Kiddush in which we first declare that Shabbos is *Zikaron l'Ma'aseh Bereishis / a remembrance of the act of Creation*, and then that Shabbos is *Zeicher l'Yetzias Mitzrayim / a remembrance of the going out of Egypt.* Shabbos connects us to Creation and Redemption — and by extension, it also connects to the teleological purpose of the Redemption from Egypt: the Revelation of the Torah at Mount Sinai.

Shabbos 'reminds' us, makes real to us, that not only is Hashem the purposeful Creator of all life, but that the Creator is lovingly involved with Creation. Hashem took us collectively out of Egypt and also takes each of us out of our own personal 'Egypts,' our places of limitation, constriction and *Avodas Perach /* incapacitating 'slave-labor.'

Additionally, not only is the Creator intimately involved with Creation and with bringing living beings out of exile, there is also 'Revelation,' Divine self-disclosure bridging the apparent chasm between an Infinite Transcendent Creator and a finite, immanent Creation. After being taken out of Egypt, the People of Israel were collectively touched by Infinity. The Torah, the moral and spiritual/ (physical) manual for living received at Mount Sinai, was also a conduit of the Divine Presence on earth, a revelation of the Oneness of all reality, whose reverberation is heard until this present moment. In this way, we can see how Shabbos connects us equally to the creation of the world, the liberation from Egypt, and our experience in the present moment.

Shabbos can thus be called *Yoma d'Zechira /* a day of remembrance (*Sefas Emes,* Yisro, Tof/Reish/Samach/Beis), a day when we remember the Divine source of all Creation, the Divine power to redeem the oppressed and enslaved among us, and the very purpose of our existence; to be a locus of Divine Self-revelation. On Shabbos, we remember with clarity that we are intentionally created, not merely a random coincidence; and that we have a blueprint, a guide, the Torah that shows us how we can achieve our distinct purpose and mission in the world, both collectively and individually.

'Remembering Bereishis' and 'remembering Yetzias Mitzrayim' are related to the two basic paradigms of Shabbos: 1) a culmination of the six days of creative work, a destination to get *to*, and 2) a 'parent' that gives birth and quality/direction to the coming six days, an origin to come *from*.

In the paradigm of 'remembering Bereishis,' Shabbos (which comes after the Six Days of Creation), our rest, is the culmination of all our hard work during the week. Our rest, in fact, corresponds to how hard we worked. The week is like a line, with Sunday as the beginning of the line and Friday afternoon as the end of the line. In this sense, there is a linear progression from 'doing' to 'being,' from Day One to Day Seven.

In this paradigm, the days of the week impregnate Shabbos. The more tired we are, the more physically or emotionally drained we are, the more we desire rest and appreciate it when it comes. Shabbos allows us to recover from the week, as the Torah suggests, "Six days you may work, and on the Seventh Day you shall rest; (even) at plowing (time) and at harvest (time) you shall rest" (Shemos, 34:21). Although the following is absolutely not the intended Torah law, this verse can be mistakenly viewed as suggesting that in a year of total rest from the work of plowing and harvesting, as in the year of Shemitah (when the entire land must lay fallow), there is no reason for an actual seventh day Shabbos (*Horiyos*, 4b. מהו במאי טעו בהדין קרא בחריש ובקציר תשבות בזמן דאיכא חרישה איכא שבת ובזמן דליכא חרישה ליכא שבת), since Shabbos is defined as rest from work.

In the paradigm of 'remembering Yetziyas Mitzrayim,' first comes the holy day of Shabbos and then the six days of the week follow. This corresponds to the Shabbos of Adam and Chava, as they were created right before Shabbos and did not experience a week leading up to it. In this perspective, Shabbos gives *birth* to the weekday; the introspective rest and focus of Shabbos lends context and meaning to the workweek that follows. It is not, of course, that we plan or even think about the coming week on Shabbos which would contradict its spirit. Rather, we are completely immersed in the holiness of Shabbos rest, and the inward 'present moment' of Shabbos, and this consciousness itself secures a mentally healthy and spiritually vibrant week to come.

From this perspective, Shabbos is the 'being' state, from which our workweek of 'doing' flows. *Sheva* / (day) seven is related to the word *Savuah* / satiated, full. On Shabbos we fill ourselves up, become satiated with holiness and clarity, which elevates the week that follows. On Shabbos itself we are simply *being*, with no movement or change, and from that space our subsequent *doing* streams forth. Here, we are not essentially moving *towards* Shabbos, we are coming *from* a Shabbos state as we enter and make our way through the subsequent six days of the week.

Everything pertaining to Shabbos is "double" (*Yalkut Shimoni*, Tehilim, 247, 843. Medrash, *Shocher Tov*, Tehilim, 92. *Rabbeinu Bachya*, Bamidbar, 28:9. *Kol Bo*, 24. *Beis Yoseph*, Orach Chayim, 263). 'Double' can mean a symbolic increase, suggesting that on Shabbos our blessings and holiness is increased, but it can also mean literally double, two. There are two categories of Mitzvos of Shabbos: *Zachor* / 'remember the Shabbos,' the positive commands, and *Shamor* / 'safeguard the Shabbos,' the negative commands for us to refrain from certain actions on Shabbos.

In the first set of Luchos the command of *Zachor* is featured, and in the second set, the command of *Shamor* is featured. Say our sages, when the commandment of Shabbos was actually given, Hashem spoke only one utterance, yet we heard two: *Zachor* (the positive Mitzvah) and *Shamor* (the negative Mitzvah) (*Shavuos*, 20b). This 'hearing two' is rooted in the idea that Shabbos contains both basic dimensions as one. Shabbos is one reality which refracts into two, the double paradigms of Shabbos; completing the previous week, corresponding to the idea of *Shamor*, and inspiring the coming week, corresponding to the idea of *Zachor*.

Shabbos is thus *double*, as it is both a place to go to and a place to come from. Shabbos is both the end and the beginning, the fruit and the root, the receiver and the giver.

Shabbos is *Menuchah* / rest in relation to the hard work of the week, and a culmination of the 'Work of Creation.' Shabbos is also *Cheirus* / freedom beyond the issue of work, a 'going out of Mitzrayim.' This *Cheirus* is not only freedom 'from' oppression and hard labor, it is a freedom 'to' pursue matters of the spirit. Rest from past slavery and exile is a vital elimination of negativity, from there, we can also be free to soar beyond the very world of slavery and exile altogether. On Shabbos, we can experience the double blessings together of both Menuchah and Cheirus.

This 'double' quality of Shabbos is the reason that our sages say, "If we kept *two* Shabbosim appropriately we would be redeemed immediately" (*Shabbos*, 118b). Yet, there is also a teaching that says, "If we kept *one* Shabbos correctly, the son of David (Moshiach) would immediately come" (Yerushalmi, *Ta'anis*, 1:1). These two sayings do not necessarily contradict each other. "One Shabbos" can indicate our full connection to the two paradigms of Shamor and Zachor, the "higher and lower Shabbos" (*Zohar* 1. 5b. *Likutei Torah*, Behar, p. 41), in the course of a single day. When we celebrate Shabbos as both the goal and the source of our lives, celebrating one day of Shabbos encapsulates and unifies each of these 'doubled' dichotomies as one.

RUNNING AND RETURNING

Another way of phrasing these two models or dimensions related to Shabbos is: רצוא ושוב / *Ratzo v'Shov* / running and returning. The weekday is our *Ratzo*, our outward movement of 'running' with ambition, chasing opportunities and trying to manipulate the world. Shabbos is our *Shov*, which shares the same root as *Shav* / rest; it is our return to center. Within the category of Shabbos rest there are two levels: the lower level is rest from the past week's work, and the higher level is rest that is beyond work as the foundation of the coming week.

As mentioned, Shabbos is called a *Yom laHashem* / a day to the Infinite Transcendent One (Devarim, 5:13), as we recite in the liturgy of the Amidah on Friday night, "You have sanctified the Seventh Day, to Your Name." Both the higher and lower levels of Shabbos rest are "to/for" Hashem's Name, however, currently, the Name of Hashem is written-out one way (Yud-Hei-Vav-Hei) and pronounced another way, as *Ado-noi* (Although the Name Hashem, the way the Name is actually written, Yud-Hei-Vav-Hei, is not the Name Ado-noi (Rambam, *Hilchos Yesodei haTorah*, 6:2), with regards to pronunciation, the Name Ado-noi is like the Name Hashem (Rambam, *Hilchos Avoda Zarah*, 2:7). This is because, today, Hashem is *pronounced* as Ado-noi (*Pesachim*, 50a), and thus, with regards to pronunciation, Ado-noi has the same laws of the Name Hashem, as the Brisker Rav (Griz) on the Rambam, ibid, explains). The Name as it is written is the unspeakable 'higher Name' of Hashem, corresponding to the aspect of Shabbos that transcends any relationship to work. The lower, revealed Name, Ado-noi, meaning Master, is connected to the world of *Din* / judgement and physicality, and it corresponds to the lower aspect of Shabbos that is a rest and respite from work.

WORKWEEK	SHABBOS IN GENERAL	SHABBOS LOWER LEVEL	SHABBOS HIGHER LEVEL
RATZO	**SHOV**	**ADO-NOI**	**HASHEM**

These four qualities, Ratzo, Shov, Ado-noi and Hashem, are reflected in the numerical value of the word *Shabbos* which is 702 (*Bris Kehunas Olam*, Ma'amar Shabbos).

The words רצוא ושוב / *Ratzo v'Shov* are numerically 611*. This is, incidentally, also the numerical value of the word *Torah*. The Name Hashem is 26** and the Name Ado-noi is 65***. Thus the combination of *Ratzo v'Shov* (611), Hashem (26), and Ado-noi (65) = *Shabbos* (702).

---

* *Ratzo:* Reish/200, Tzadik/90, Vav/6, Aleph/1. *V'Shov:* Vav/6, Shin/300, Vav/6, Beis/2 = 611.

** *Hashem:* Yud/10, Hei/5, Vav/6, Hei/5 = 26.

*** *Ado-noi:* Aleph/1, Dalet/4, Nun/50, Yud/10 = 65.

Shabbos is the ultimate *Yichud* / unity between Ratzo and Shov and also between the name of Hashem and Ado-noi.* On Shabbos, when we rest (*Shov/Shav*) from toil and aspiration (*Ratzo*), we are resonating with the Name Ado-noi. When we enter a 'higher' place of internal rest that is beyond all work, we are resonating with the Name of Hashem, the world of perfection and unity. Shabbos is related to our world of work and part of the seven day cycle of natural time; it is also part of the timeless future world, the *Olam haS'char* / world of reward, where we bask in the Light of Hashem's unity, beyond any need for work, as the world in this state is always-already perfect and completed.

---

* Shabbos is "a day to Hashem" and the Name Hashem is 26. The vessels that transmit the Light of Hashem into this world are the Aleph Beis. There are 27 letters in total: 22 plus the 5 end letters. 27 x 26 = 702, yielding the same value as the word *Shabbos*. Shabbos is the fullness of Hashem's revelation into and through the world. Shabbos is a manifestation of the highest levels of Keser, which numerically is 620; Chochmah has 32 Paths, and Binah has 50 Gates. Combining these three levels of higher consciousness reveals the same numerical value as *Shabbos* (620, 32, 50 = 702).

04

A GLIMMER OF PERFECTION & PERFECTION ITSELF

T ORAH SHE-B'KSAV / THE WRITTEN TORAH REVEALS THAT SHABBOS is both a "remembrance of Creation" and a "remembrance of the going out of Egypt"; which pertain respectively to the past and present. Additionally, our sages intuit that Shabbos is also connected with the redeemed world of the future. Shabbos, they tell us, is "a taste of the World-to-Come" (*Mechilta*, Shemos, 31:13), a "sixtieth of the World-to-Come" (*Berachos*, 57b), and "a drop of the World-to-Come" (*Medrash Rabba*, Bereishis, 17:7).

The phrase, *Os Hi l'Olam* / "(Shabbos) is an eternal sign" (Shemos, 31:17), also implies that Shabbos is a 'hint' or 'semblance' of eternity, of the eternal *Olam* / World-to-Come that is accessible to us on Shabbos in this world. Shabbos is other-worldy, a manifestation of a dimension beyond this world. As our sages tell us, Shabbos was created before the Creation of the World (*Pirkei d'Rebbe Eliezer*, 3). It comes from a 'place' outside of place and time.

This 'taste' or 'drop' of a redeemed future is a third dimension of Shabbos — a micro-image or dose of the eternal Shabbos of perfection. However, a *taste*, a *drop*, or even *one-sixtieth* of something is by definition not its full manifestation or potential. As such, there must be a higher or deeper level of Shabbos; a timeless time in which every day is Shabbos, *Yom sheKulo Shabbos* / a day when all is Shabbos. This is the fourth dimension of Shabbos, when the ultimate unity of Shabbos permeates all of creation all the time.

Every day, in the Beis haMikdash, the Levites sang a particular song related to each individual day of the week. On Shabbos, they sang *Mizmor Shir l'Yom haShabbos* / a song for the day of Shabbos... (Tehilim, 92). This song is called, "a song for the future, for a day that is eternally Shabbos" (*Tamid*, 33b. *Rosh Hashanah*, 31a).

Just as the six days of the week culminate in the seventh day of Shabbos, the six millennia, which began with the birth of Adam and Chava, will culminate in a seventh millennium which is a Messianic era, a 'day' that is eternally Shabbos. In this way, the days of our week correspond to the six millennia, and our day of Shabbos corresponds to *Yemos haMoshiach* / the Times of Moshiach, a future time when every day will be Shabbos (*Sanhedrin*, 97a. *Avodah Zarah*, 9a. Ramban, *Bereishis*, 2:3. Rabbeinu Bachya, ibid. Ramban, *Sha'ar haGemul*, 58. *Pirush* haGra, *Safra d'Tziniusa*, 5).

In this *Yom sheKulo Shabbos*, every moment and experience will be infused with Shabbos. Today, our experience of Shabbos is, for the most part, just a glimpse of the World-to-Come, we only get a whiff or a trace of eternity in time. Yet, deep within every moment of Shabbos — in the now — is the *Nekudah* / point of the future, and if we go deep enough into this Nekudah we can behold eternity, immortality within this very moment. (As Shabbos is unity and immortality, there is no decomposing on [the level of] Shabbos. אין הרמה שולטת במתים בשבת. Baal HaTurim, *Shemos*, 16:24).

"There is a bird (a phoenix) in the world called 'Chol' that lives eternally because it did not taste of the Tree of Knowledge to come under the spell of death" (Rashi, *Iyov*, 29:18. See *Medrash Rabbah*, Bereishis, 19:5). In our context this means that within the world of mortality and finitude, which is the idea of *Chol* / weekday, there is a Nekudah that is immortal and always connected to the Tree of Life. Therefore, not only is there a glimpse of the eternal Shabbos within the world of limitation and Chol, but there is actually something called "Chol"; which itself is Shabbos-like and connected to the Tree of Life and immortality.

This dimension of Shabbos is not a mere glimpse of a future World-to-Come or a glimmer of *Gan Eden* / Paradise, rather it is the full presence of the World-to-Come, Gan Eden, in this world, right here, right now.

Hashem tells Moshe, "I have a precious gift in My Treasure House, and its name is Shabbos. I want to give it to Israel. Go and tell them this" (*Beitza*, 16a). Say the Chassidic Rebbes, not only did Hashem give us a gift from his Treasures Above, as it were, rather, on Shabbos, HaKadosh Baruch Hu puts us *in* the Treasure House. We are not given a mere glimpse of eternal Heaven, we are there; we are aligned with, and integrated into the Heaven and Eternity of Olam haBa in *Olam haZeh* / this world. Shabbos is not just a glimmer of some future Gan Eden, it is a timeless reality that can manifest equally and fully in the past, present and/or future.

05

FOUR LEVELS OF SHABBOS IN TIME

A S WE HAVE SEEN, THERE ARE FOUR DIMENSIONS OR PARADIGMS of Shabbos: 1) remembering Creation, 2) remembering the Exodus from Egypt, 3) a taste of the World-to-Come, and 4) an immersion in the World-to-Come.

These four aspects of Shabbos are related to the four dimensions of time: 1) past, 2) present, 3) future, 4) and inclusive-eternity, an eternal moment that includes past, present and future.

In greater detail:

1) זכר למעשה בראשית / *Zeicher l'Maaseh Bereishis*: Shabbos allows us to remember and keep in mind that Hashem created the world (although the creation of the world is actually continuous, not only

in the 'past'). As we 'remember' this 'primordial' dimension of Shabbos we become intimately aware that Creation was founded in, and is based in, Divine intentionality and purpose.

2) זכר ליציאת מצרים / *Zeicher l'Yetziyas Mitzrayim*: Shabbos allows us to "remember" the going out of Egypt, and the eventual giving of the Torah, which is connected to the present; "In every generation, each person must regard himself as if he had come out of Egypt" (*Mishnah Pesachim*, 10:5). Not only each generation, but each day a person must regard himself as if he had come out of Egypt (*Tanya*, 47); each day should be as if you had personally left Egypt today (Rashi, *Shemos*, 13:4, as explained by the Chasam Sofer, *Derashos l'Pesach*, p, 521). In a deeper way, Hashem is taking us out of our inner Egypt at every moment (as the Rebbe would often add; see for example *Sefer haSichos*, 5751, Shemos). On Shabbos we experience the fullness of our personal redemption from our personal 'Egypts,' our places of constriction and limitation. Although this Shabbos remembrance is of the 'past,' it fully impacts our lived experience in the present.

3) The experience of Shabbos, as מעין עולם הבא / *Mei'ein Olam haBa* / a taste of the World-to-Come — connected to a future world, as described in the previous chapter.

4) יום שכולו שבת / *Yom sheKulo Shabbos* / a day when all is Shabbos — the word 'all' suggests eternity, a construct of time that includes *all* of time, past, present and future. Shabbos is an eternal sign (Shemos, 31:17) of the eternity of the moment that embraces all dimensions of time.

With regards to the Six Days of Creation, the Torah says at the end of each day, "There was evening and there was morning, Day One." "...Day Two," etc. At the conclusion of Shabbos, however, there is no such statement; it does not say, "There was evening and there was morning, Day Seven." This glaring omission suggests that Shabbos does not conclude, rather it continues throughout all time. Shabbos is the depth of eternity that exists within every moment, forever and always. This is the *Yom sheKulo Shabbos* that manifests in the present.

REMEMBRANCE OF CREATION	REMEMBRANCE OF LEAVING MITZRAYIM	A TASTE OF THE WORLD-TO-COME	A DAY THAT IS ALL SHABBOS
PAST: Shabbos experienced as the completion of our six-day week of creative work	PRESENT: Shabbos experienced as an ongoing liberation leading to revelation (as at Mount Sinai)	FUTURE: Shabbos experienced as a glimpse of the coming Complete Redemption and the revelation of Moshiach	ETERNITY: Shabbos experienced as a perfection that is inclusive of past, present and future; the future that is always-already fully present.

FOUR MEALS — FOUR TIME PERIODS

These four aspects of Shabbos, and the four dimensions of time, are related to the four *Seudos* / meals of Shabbos. There are three meals eaten on Shabbos itself and the fourth meal is the *Melaveh Malkah* / the Escorting of the Queen after nightfall on Saturday night. We learn that we eat three meals on Shabbos from the *Pe-*

sukim / verses speaking of the *Mon* / Manna (Shemos, 16), in which the word *haYom* / *today* is mentioned three times (*Shabbos*, 117b).

On Shabbos we receive a *Neshamah Yeserah* / extra soul. This extra measure of soulfulness and spirit enlarges our 'vessels'; including our spiritual appetite and desire. As our spiritual appetite increases, so does our appetite for everything in life. Thus, our desire to *receive* expands on Shabbos. In its most dense manifestation, of this pure desire, our extra soul is expressed in our augmented desire for physical things such as eating more food (Rashi, *Beitzah*, 16a. רוחב לב למנוחה ולשמחה ולהיות פתוח לרוחה ויאכל וישתה ואין נפשו קצה עליו). On Shabbos we therefore eat three meals, one on Friday evening and two during Shabbos day; early afternoon and late afternoon.

The three meals and the three time periods of Shabbos; night, early and late afternoon correspond to the three dimensions of Shabbos; the Shabbos of Creation, the Shabbos of Leaving Egypt and Receiving Revelation, and the Shabbos of the Future and Redemption (*Tur*, Orach Chayim, 292, see, *Bach* ad loc). The fourth meal after Shabbos, the *Melaveh Malkah*, corresponds to a Day when All is Shabbos.

REMEMBRANCE OF CREATION	REMEMBRANCE OF LEAVING EGYPT, REVELATION OF TORAH	A TASTE OF THE WORLD-TO-COME / COMPLETE REDEMPTION	A DAY THAT IS ALL SHABBOS
Celebration of Past	Celebration of Present	Celebration of Future	Celebration of Eternity in the Present
Friday Night	Shabbos Day	Late Afternoon / Third Meal	After Nightfall / Melavah Malkah

1) *Zeicher l'Maaseh Bereishis* / remembrance of the work of Creation along with celebrating/recognizing the 'past' correspond to the Friday evening meal, as Shabbos is the culmination of the past workweek; first come six days of the week and then Shabbos.

On Friday evening, there is an acute and visceral sense of having just disentangled from, and transitioned out of, the previous days. We are no longer enslaved to our work as we step back and simply let it go. The rest of Friday evening is thus a rest from the week. As such, there is still a strong sense of dichotomy; having left behind the workweek, having broken free from labor and productivity, having released our engagement with the created world, and now having settled down to celebrate Shabbos, we are challenged and able to remember that Hashem created the world and is the Master of the Universe.

2) *Zeicher l'Yetziyas Mitzrayim* / remembrance of the going out of Egypt and celebrating/recognizing the 'present' correspond to the first daytime meal. Klal Yisrael left Egypt on a Thursday, in the pre-glow of Shabbos. The climax of the Exodus — the Giving of the Torah on Mount Sinai — was on Shabbos (*Shabbos*, 86b), and the first daytime meal occurs soon after the reading of the Torah, which is a manifestation of the revelation at Mount Sinai. The focus of this meal is Shabbos providing blessing and focus to/for the coming week.

Enjoying a meal on Shabbos midday or afternoon, after a good night's sleep and an uplifting Davenning, you are no longer affected by the exhaustion or stress of the past week. You can sense that, now, Shabbos is taking you out of all your deeper *Meitzarim* / constrictions and inner exiles, and 'opening you up' to the revelation of Divine wisdom. This allows you the space, time, and freedom to dream and contemplate what you 'want' to do, rather than only what you 'have' to do. Divine purpose and deeper meaning transform the nature of our work, from exhausting to exhilarating, from restricting to rewarding, from mundane to Messianic. This shift in our consciousness takes us *beyond* work, as work is normally thought of.

We feel this type of rest 'beyond work' more on Shabbos day, as work is already a distant past, and we feel more the inner-modality of Shabbos. Now we can also feel how Shabbos and rest is impregnating the upcoming week and imbuing it with soulfulness.

Zeicher l'Maaseh Bereishis and *Zeicher l'Yetziyas Mitzrayim* are the two main aspects and purposes of Shabbos, as stated clearly in the Torah. As such, the two corresponding meals are the most essential meals of Shabbos, and this is why our sages say that on Shabbos we eat "two (major) meals" (Rabbeinu Bachya, *Bamidbar* 28:9, in the name of the Medrash).

3) *Mei'ein haOlam haBa* / a taste of the World-to-Come together with celebrating/recognizing the future Redemption correspond to the Third Meal. Now, not only are we not resting from the previous week of creativity — we are also no longer focusing on the leaving behind of our deeper inner Egypt. At this stage we enter into a quieter, more expansive, inner space that is a glimmer of the Shabbos of the future. The eating of the Third Meal is learned from the third time the Pasuk says, *Hayom* / "today" when referring to the Mon / Manna. However, there it says *Hayom Lo* / "today [you shall] *not*..." The full verse is as follows: "And Moshe said, eat it *today*, for *today* is a Shabbos unto Hashem; *today* you shall *not* find it in the field" (Shemos, 16:25).

The first two mentions of "today" ("Eat it today, for today is a Shabbos...") are direct instructions to eat *today*. These two references/meals correspond to the past and present, which are both very much alive and able to be sensed *today*. Today is a reality that was created by the past, but it is also a free moment in the present. These are the first two meals and first two constructs of Shabbos, and thus, we eat a full meal for each one. However, the phrase "today... not" suggests a type of reality that is 'today,' but not yet fully present. It is a hint at what is possible, the future. The message of this third meal is: to Stay engaged in "today," eat a third meal; yet, also recall the theme of "not." This is a meal that is 'not yet,' the present as a precursor to the future, and as such, we eat a light (rather than a full) meal. (Note, many sources teach that Moshe passed away late Shabbos afternoon, "ומזה הטעם נמי הנהיג ר"ת שלא לקבוע אז סעודה / and for this reason, the custom of Rabbeinu Tam was not to sit down to a full meal during this time period" Tur, *Orach Chayim*, 292.)

In a way, the 'not' also represents a reality of *Lo Ta'aseh* / do not do; in other words, we are asked to experience something that is higher than a 'doing' or a proactive effort. While it is true that we may no longer want to eat after a large day meal, the point is that the Third Meal is higher than the act of eating; it is primarily a time to glimpse the world of the future (see, Rabbeinu Bachya, *Shemos*, 16:25). The experience of the Third Meal is therefore "not found in the field" of the conventional 'present.'

Every week is a new Creation. Speaking of the observance of Shabbos, the Pasuk says *Ki Sheishes...* / "Six days did Hashem create heaven and earth and on the Seventh Day..." (Shemos, 20:11). Grammatically speaking, it should have said, *B'Sheishes* / "*In* six days" not just *Sheishes* / "Six days" — it would make more sense for the Pasuk to say, "*In* six days Hashem created heaven and earth…" (The *Zohar*, Yisro, 89b, asks this question, as does the Rashba, *Teshuvas HaRashba* 1, Siman 423). Regarding this, the Ohr haChayim explains that the Creator created the world to last for only six days (and every six days; the potential and power of the world to exist expires) followed by the Seventh Day of rest and renewal (Ohr haChayim, *Shemos*, 20:1. Ohr haChayim, *Bereishis*, 2:3).*

Some time, on late Shabbos afternoon, there must arise a new Divine desire to create a new week so that another six days of Creation shall ensue. The Third Meal is a time when this cosmic desire to create was and is initiated (*Zerah Kodesh*, Chukas, in the name of Rebbe Mendel of Rimanov). Indeed, the third meal is called *Ra'ava d'Ravin* / the Divine 'Desire of Desires' (*Zohar* 2, 88b).

This is the special energy and enchantment that occurs on every Shabbos, during late afternoon; the Divine desire to create a new week is aroused. And, as we explored regarding the original Creation, the initial desire and dream of creation is perfect and whole.

---

* Perhaps an allusion to this idea, and that "seven days" is the essence of time, is found in the *Yerushalmi* that says, Rebbe Chiya told Rav that a person should aspire to eat his food in ritual purity, and if not possible the entire year, do so for "seven days of the year" (*Shabbos*, 1:3). Many interpret these seven days to be the seven days between Rosh Hashanah and Yom Kippur (Rabbeinu Nisan. Rosh, *Rosh Hashanah*, 4:14. Ran, *Rosh Hashanah*, 12b. Tur and Mechaber, *Orach Chayim*, 603:1). Yet, as the Ohr Zaruah writes, its possible דלא צוהו ר"ח לרב / אלא על שבעה ימים בשנה איזו שיהיו / "that Rebbe Chiya told Rav regarding *any* seven days of the year." In other words, perhaps "seven days" within the year is the embodiment of the entire year. Note, *Yerushalmi*, אחת לשבע שנים הקב"ה מחלף את עולמו / "Once every seven years HaKadosh Baruch Hu changes the world." *Shabbos*, 1:3.

In other words, it is at this primordial moment before Creation that the vision and potential of the redeemed World-to-Come is conceptually created.*

In this way, the time of the Third Meal is not just a culmination of Shabbos or a 'third' meal following two other meals, rather, it is also the foundation of a new creation. It is the beginning both of the new week and of the World-to-Come. The Third Meal, in the language of the Rishonim (early post-Talmudic commentaries), is the "Beginning of the Beginning" (*Rabbeinu Bachya*, Shemos, 16:25).

---

* Although the Third Meal is not a full meal, unlike the first two meals in which מרבין לכבוד השבת ובסעודה / "We increase the joy and the meal in honor of the Shabbos" (Tosefos, *Kesuvos*, 7b), and thus, דשבת וי"ט ראשון ושני הוי כפנים חדשים בסעודת הלילה ושחרית אבל לא בסעודה שלישית / "...Shabbos and Yom Tov are "new faces" at the meals of the night and morning, but not the Third Meal" (*Shulchan Aruch*, Even Ezra, 62:8), as the Third Meal is not qualified Halachically as a full festive meal. Still, it is precisely during the Third Meal that Torah is recited, causing a great spiritual joy (*Ramah*, ibid ה"א ...'ג בסעודה ברכות ז' לברך אלו במדינות נהגו ועכשיו חדשות כפנים הוי והדרשה לדרוש דרגילין מטעם). The time of Minchah on Shabbos is a time of Divine desire and spiritual delight. During the week, the time of Minchah is a time of Din (and Yitzchak) yet, on Shabbos, the time of Minchah is literally the opposite, a time of desire. These are the words of the Zohar: דינא, תא חזי, בכל שיתא יומי דשבתא, כד מטא שעתא דצלותא דמנחתא, דינין וכל דינין מתערין. אבל ביומא דשבתא, כד מטא עדן דצלותא דמנחתא, תקיפא שלטא / רעוא דרעוין אשתכח "Come and see, all the six days of the week, when the time comes to pray Minchah it is a time of harsh *Din* / judgment, and all Dinim are awakened. Yet, on Shabbos, when the time of Minchah comes, it is a time of 'desire of desires'" (*Zohar* 2, 88b). What is the difference? Simply, at Minchah time during the week, it is towards the end of the day, end of sunlight, and it is a period moving into the night, into darkness, and thus a time of Din and concealment. (The Din continues until midnight, because once midnight occurs, the night is inclining towards the day, the rising sun, a time of revealing, of Chesed.) Whereas the Minchah of Shabbos is the cosmic time of the desire to create, to begin the creation of a new week, new *Chayus* / life, vitality; thus, it is a time of tremendous *Ratzon* / will and desire. Parenthetically, perhaps this is the reason why the Sefardic *Nusach* / liturgy for Minchah of Shabbos is to say the three verses of *Tziduk haDin* in a sequence from the earlier chapters in Tehilim to the later chapters — a verse from Chapter 36, then from Chapter 71 and then from 119 (whereas in Nusach Ashkenaz the order is reversed). This movement from earlier to later symbolizes a flow from Above to below, indicating a flow of Chesed and Ratzon from the Divine Above to the world below.

It is both an end of Shabbos and, maybe most importantly, a new beginning of beginnings.

This distinction of the three dimensions of Shabbos reflected in the three time periods of Shabbos also shows up in the *Nusach* / wording of the liturgical prayers. During the Friday evening Amidah, which is the essence of the service, we declare, "And Hashem completed the Heavens and earth... and Hashem rested on the Seventh Day." We also recite, "You sanctified to Your Name the Seventh Day, (which is) the *Tachlis* / ultimate culmination of the Creation of Heaven and earth." These verses describe the culmination of the past, and define Shabbos as the peak of Creation, inspiring us to *Zeicher l'Maaseh Bereishis*.

During the morning Amidah we declare, "Moshe rejoiced with the gift bestowed upon him... as he stood before You on Mount Sinai..." Here we speak about the Revelation of the Torah. This, again, is the idea of Shabbos as a dimension of *Yetziyas Mitzrayim*, which culminates in the Giving of the Torah.

During the afternoon Amidah we exclaim, "You are One, and Your Name is One... a day of rest... you gave to Your People... a rest of peace, serenity and tranquility..." This peace and serenity of Shabbos is part of the glimpse of the World-to-Come, when there will finally be true and lasting peace and tranquility in the world.

FEMININE, MASCULINE & UNITY

These three aspects, three meals and three time periods of Shabbos, are also connected with the 'feminine,' the 'masculine,' and the 'unified' dimensions within Shabbos.

On Shabbos evening (Friday night) Shabbos is called *haMalkah* / the Queen, revealing a feminine quality present during this time. Experientially, the amount of effort and toil we put into the prior six days of the week dictates the amount of our sense of relief and rest that we experience when Shabbos arrives. "One who toils before Shabbos eats on Shabbos" (*Avodah Zarah*, 3a). In this way, Shabbos 'receives' from the week, a feminine quality in relation to the week. This is the Shabbos of Creation.

In the morning, Shabbos begins to take on a quality of the masculine. After a night's rest, our Shabbos experientially assumes a more active posture, in that Shabbos is no longer a destination but an origin. We are fully *being*, and Shabbos becomes the *Mekor haBerachah* / source of blessings and revelatory wellspring of the future week. This is a masculine, 'giving' mode, offering guidance and wisdom to the coming week, as in *Matan Torah* / *Giving* of Torah. This is the revelatory phase of Shabbos, in which we may spend more time giving over our understanding of the *Parshah* / weekly Torah portion to others. This is the Shabbos of revelation.

During the late afternoon on Shabbos, our experience of Shabbos is a glimmer of the future. The feminine and masculine attributes of Shabbos collapse into a perfect unity and begin to give birth to a new reality. It is thus not only 'receiving' from the past week or 'giving' to the following week, rather, it is 'creating' a new week, a new world, and potentially the perfect World-to-Come.

The Mitzvah of Shabbos was given to us in both the first and second sets of Luchos. In the first set of Luchos the phrase that informs our relationship to Shabbos is *Zachor* / remember, in the second set it is *Shamor* / safeguard, protect. Say our sages (*Shavuos,* 20b), when the commandment of Shabbos was actually revealed at Mount Sinai, Hashem spoke it in one utterance, but we heard it as two utterances; *Zachor* / the positive, 'to remember,' and *Shamor* / the negative, 'not to forget.' Indeed, in the order of the Luchos, first comes *Zachor* and then *Shamor*. Yet, in the opening paragraph of *Lecha Dodi* (the mystical poem written in the 16th Century by Rav Shlomo Alkabetz to usher in the Shabbos Queen), the verse begins with, *Shamor v'Zachor b'Dibur Echad* / "Safeguard and Remember (what was said) in One Utterance." Why are they in the reverse order in this *Piyut* / poem?

This is because *Shamor* represents the evening of Shabbos, the feminine, while *Zachor*, as in the word *Zachar* / male (*Zohar* 2, Raya M'hemnah, Yisro. Note the Gemara (*Baba Basra,* 21b), where *Zachor* and *Zachar* are possibly interchangeable. Shamor with a Vav (Devarim, 5:12), a masculine letter, represents the elevation of Malchus to the world of masculinity. *Heichal HaBeracha,* Bamidbar, 8:26), corresponds to the day of Shabbos, the masculine element of Shabbos (*Shamor* and *Zachor* are the feminine and masculine aspects of Shabbos. Ramban, *Emunah u'Bitachon,* 19. Radbaz, *Metzudas David,* Mitzvah 91. *Tola'as Yaakov,* Sisrei Tefilos Shabbos uMoadim). The Zohar says that, in general, Shamor is connected to the night, the feminine, and Zachor to the day, the masculine (*Zohar* 3, 115b. See *Ohr haChayim,* Vayikra, 19:3). *Shamor* is to protect what already is, alluding to the past. *Zachor* is to remember the past in the present, in order to inform and impregnate the future.

"And the people of Israel should *Shamor* / observe the Shabbos" (Shemos, 31:16), means to 'safeguard' it so that they can 'observe' it (*Megaleh Amukos,* Ki Tisa, 2:2). 'To observe' is a proactive, positive posture corresponding to Shabbos day. We must first safeguard Shabbos by avoiding and refraining from 'doing,' and this feminine non-doing, a more passive or 'negative' quality, ensures that there is a proper context for doing positive actions. We first need to let go of the past workweek in the mode of Shamor, the consciousness of Shabbos night; only then can we be fully present in the now of Shabbos day, in order to properly affect the future.

On late Shabbos afternoon, however, a unity between the two opposites begins to emerge. Shamor and Zachor, past and present, feminine and masculine, night and day, refraining and reframing, begin to morph into one seamless construct. Shamor and Zachor were "uttered as one," but received by the people as two; now, during the third meal, they return to "one." Hashem is the Ultimate in unity, while Creation, by definition is based in duality, two-ness. This is why the Torah's account of creation begins with the letter Beis, the second letter of the Aleph-Beis. On Shabbos, late afternoon, following twenty-two hours or so of being bathed in the holiness of Shabbos, we begin to slip into a consciousness of unity, in which all dualistic dynamics begin to fade. As we begin to enter into a world of Unity, we can perceive and experience a glimpse or ray of the World-to-Come.*

---

* The Name Adam, referring to the archetypal human being, is an acronym of three names: Adam, David and Moshe. Adam, the first human being, is connected to Shabbos of Creation. Moshe, the redeemer from Egypt and receiver of Torah, is connected to Shabbos of Going out of Egypt and Revelation. King David is connected to the Third Meal and the time of Redemption, which will be birthed by Moshiach ben David.

LITURGY

This unfolding of Shabbos, from the feminine to the masculine to the unity between them, is also reflected in the subtle change of one particular word within the liturgy of Shabbos.*

In the Evening Amidah we say *V'Yanuchu Vah* / we rest in *her*.
In the Morning Amidah we say *V'Yanuchu Bo* / we rest in *him*
In the Afternoon Amidah we say *V'Yanuchu Bam* / we rest in *them*.

Shabbos as *Bah* / "in her" is associated with the entire complex of feminine images poetically employed during Friday evening; whereas the weekdays project a masculine, outwardly active and sometimes even aggressive image. On Friday evening we first welcome the Shabbos Queen with the invitation, *Bo'ee Kolah* / "Enter, O Bride" (*Baba Kama*, 32a. *Shabbos*, 119a, Rambam writes that we welcome the King. *Hilchos Shabbos*, 30:2). The idea of Shabbos at this time is represented by the image of a *Kolah* / Bride (*Rabbeinu Bachya*, Shemos, 16:25). There is also a prevailing custom to recite or sing *Aishes Chayil* / "A Woman of Valor," addressed to the woman of the home — and in a sense to the Divine Feminine aspect, as well as the collective feminine soul of Klal Yisrael. On Friday night, we are all embodying *Shamor*, the feminine state of non-doing and receptive passivity.

---

* This change of liturgy is found in many Sidurim that are based on the teachings of the Arizal and Kabbalah (See *Haga'as haRamaz. Mishnas Chassidim. Siddur Baal haTanya.* And see *Magen Avraham*, 268:3. *Shiyureh Keneses haGedola*, Siman 265. Note: *Ohr haChayim*, Vayikra, 19:3). Although this is not found clearly in the writings of the Arizal (see *Kaf haChayim, Orach Chayim*, 248:2), and thus many, such as the Rashash, who in fact follow the Arizal, do not have these liturgical changes, and by Minchah they say Ba (See *Ben Ish Chai*, Vayera).

Shabbos as *Bo* / "in him" is associated with all the masculine phenomena of Shabbos day. This stage of rest and rejuvenation actively injects focus and blessing into the coming week, as at Mount Sinai when we were charged with a mission to transform the world. Here/now, Shabbos impregnates the weekdays with holiness and higher meaning.

Shabbos as *Bam* / "them" is associated with the unification of the masculine *Bo* and the feminine *Bah*. It is also the merging of the weekday and Shabbos paradigms in perfect unity, an infinite 'circle' of oneness. Shabbos is the center that both receives from and infuses the preceding and following weeks.*

---

* The progression and movement towards unity is also expressed in another change of liturgy. The Arizal teaches that in the Shabbos evening Amidah, when we say, "You have Sanctified," this represents *Kidushin* / betrothal. In the Shabbos morning Amidah, when we say, "Moshe is joyous with the gifts," this refers to the gifts that are sent to the Bride. During the Shabbos Musaf Amidah, when we say "You have prepared," this refers to the wedding meal. During the Shabbos Minchah Amidah, when we say "You are One," this refers to the actual Unity between the Bride and Groom. The Avudraham writes something very similar. From the Arizal it seems clear that the peak of Shabbos is Shabbos afternoon, as Shabbos gets deeper and deeper, and the time of Minchah is the time of Yichud (*Pri Etiz Chay*im, Sha'ar haShabbos 6. *Shaloh*, Shabbos, Torah Ohr, 35. *Likutei Torah*, Emor, 36b). Yet, other sources teach that Shabbos evening is the peak of the Kedushah of Shabbos (*Zohar* 2, 88a. *Zohar* 3, 288b. See also *Siddur Im Dach*, p. 173a). How can we reconcile these two opinions? There are two principles regarding matters of Kedushah. On the one hand, כל המקודש מחבירו קודם את חבירו / "Whatever is more Kadosh than the other comes first" (*Zevachim*, Mishnah, 10:12). In a case where two offerings need to be offered, whichever one is holier, more Kadosh, is offered first. And yet, on the other hand, there is the principle of מעלין בקדש / "We increase in matters of Kedushah" (*Shabbos*, 21b). This principle seems to contradict the previous principle that, "whichever is more Kadosh is first," as it implies that the less Kadosh item should come first. The answer is that it depends on the situation. Normally, whatever is more Kadosh is first. Yet, in situations where there is a *Tahalich* / process or gradual unfolding, then we need to increase in Kedushah. The Kedushah of Friday Night is the higher Kedushah (as, for example, the Kiddush of Friday Night is *d'Oraisa* / a Biblical command). Thus, we start with the Kedushah of Friday night, as according to the principle of 'the more Kadosh comes first.' Yet, from the process-oriented perspective of Tahalich, although Friday night is the inherently higher Kedushah, the highest Kedushah that we can *attain* is on Shabbos afternoon.

With all this in mind, we can now return to wrap-up our discussion on the inner meanings of the different Shabbos meals and times. The required three meals of Shabbos also correspond to the Three Patriarchs. The Friday night meal corresponds to Yitzchak who embodied the quality of Gevurah, strength, restraint, boundary, receptivity, all considered feminine postures. The day meal corresponds to Avraham, the embodiment of the quality of Chesed / loving kindness and outward flowing abundance, a more masculine (provider) posture. The third meal is linked to Yaakov, who represents an embodiment of the unity between the two (Shaloh, *Maseches Shabbos*, Ner Mitzvah, Chap 40. Other sources align the evening meal with Avraham, the day meal with Yitzchak and the afternoon meal with Yaakov (See *Zohar*, 2, 88b. *Siddur Im Dach*, p. 201d. *Sefer haMa'amarim*, Tav/Reish/Pei, p. 168). Alternatively, the day meal is Yaakov. *Zohar*, Idra Zutah, 288a).

The Third Meal in Hebrew is commonly referred to as *Shalosh Seudos* / three meals, rather than the more grammatically proper term, *Seudas Shelishis* / Third Meal. This, says the Avnei Nezer, is because just as Yaakov included within him both the elements of Avraham and of Yitzchak, the Third Meal includes within it both preceding meals (*Shem Mishmuel*, Korach. Additionally, since it is a meal that is eaten despite not being hungry, it thus retroactively demonstrates that the evening and the morning meals were also both eaten in honor of Shabbos and not simply as dinner and lunch. The Chozeh of Lublin, *Divrei Emes*, Balak).

This Third Meal is thus the unity between the feminine night meal and the masculine day meal, hence it is called [all] 'three meals' in one.

In the strict terminology of the AriZal, the Friday night meal is the *Sefirah* / Divine expression of *Binah* / comprehension, also referred to as the *higher mother*. It is called the meal of *ChaKol Tapuchin Kadishin* / the Sacred Apple Orchard, which represents the Feminine principle (which in this case is Malchus, "the Daughter," but still couched within the primordial feminine image of Binah). The day meal is the Sefirah of *Chochmah* / wisdom, the *father*. This meal is called the meal of *Atika Kadisha* / the Ancient Holy One, a masculine meal.

The afternoon of Shabbos shines with the Sefirah Keser, and represents a crown on, or above, the 'head' of Shabbos. And just like the skull, upon which a crown rests, is a space that includes and contains the opposite parts of the brain — the right hemisphere (Chochmah) and the left hemisphere (Binah) — Keser is the context which includes and unites the various energies and contents of Shabbos. This meal is called the Meal of *Ze'ir Anpin* / the Small Face, as it represents the child that is born when the masculine and feminine are unified.

THE FOURTH MEAL

The fourth meal (which according to Rav Chidka is actually the 'fifth meal.' see *Shabbos*, 117a) is called the Melaveh Malkah, the meal to *Melava* / escort the Shabbos *Malkah* / Queen, and it corresponds to the integration of the 'Future with the Present.' Although, technically, this (ideally hot) meal (see *Shabbos*, 119b) occurs "after" Shabbos, Saturday night, it is still considered a Shabbos-meal, or a meal 'with the Shabbos Queen.'

As such, it is a weekday evening and we are extending the spirit of Shabbos into the weekday and infusing Shabbos throughout the week. This is a subtle manifestation of the Messianic future when "all is Shabbos." This is why the Melva Malkah is called "the Meal of David the King Moshiach," and a meal which 'nourishes the Luz Bone,' the bone from which the resurrection of the body will occur.

As explored earlier, at the end of each week, creation comes to an end, as it were, and in the late afternoon of Shabbos there arises a new Divine desire to initiate a new cycle. As such, over the course of every Shabbos there is the 'death' of the past week and the resurrection of time through the re-creation of a new week. This new cycle of creation, weekly resurrection, culminates on Motzei Shabbos / Saturday night, and appropriately it is connected to the general concept of *Techiys HaMeisim* / resurrection of the dead.

HONOR, PLEASURE, JOY AND UNITY

As explored above, the Torah commands us to both *Zachor* / remember and *Shamor* / safeguard Shabbos. In addition, there are another two Mitzvos that originate in the words of the Prophets.

In the language of the Rambam, "There are four (dimensions) connected to Shabbos; two originating in the Torah and two originating in the words of the Prophets, which are transmitted exposition by the Sages. The two Mitzvos of the Torah are *Zachor* and *Shamor*. The two from the Prophets are *Kavod* / honor and *Oneg* / pleasure, as the Pasuk (Yeshayahu, 58:13) says, "And you shall call the Shabbos *Oneg* / delight, sanctified unto Hashem and *Mechubad* /

honored..." (Rambam, *Hilchos Shabbos* 30:1).*

In other words, there are two Biblical commands of Shabbos: Zachor and Shamor, these are performed in the realm of action. Then, there are two Prophetic experiences we strive to cultivate during Shabbos: Kavod and Oneg.

In terms of actual practice, Kavod is more related to the honor given to Shabbos (even) before Shabbos begins, whereas Oneg is an experience within Shabbos itself. The Gaon of Vilna explains (*Hagahas* haGra, *Orach Chayim*, 529:5) that Kavod Shabbos is to take a bath, dress nicely, light candles for Shabbos; things that are done before Shabbos in honor of its gradual approach. Oneg Shabbos is to eat good foods, to enjoy oneself, and to have pleasure on Shabbos for Shabbos (*Shabbos*, 118b).

SIMCHA ON SHABBOS

In addition to the four "Mitzvos" of Shamor, Zachor, Kavod and Oneg, another vital mode of Shabbos observance is *Simcha* / joy.

---

* The four Mitzvos of Shabbos, Zachor, Shamor, Kavod, and Oneg, can also be correlated with the four purposes and four dimensions of time related to Shabbos. 1) *Shamor* is to protect, suggesting a past (or something that has already come into existence) which needs to be protected and remembered. This is Shabbos as 'past,' as a reminder of Creation. 2) *Zachor* is to remember now, proactively. This is the Shabbos of the present, the Going out of Egypt and the Revelation of Torah; which are still the defining current historical processes and dynamics that inform our experience. 3) *Kavod* / honor is the act of preparing for Shabbos. This is Shabbos of the future for which we are preparing, and is a taste of the World-to-Come. 4) *Oneg* / pleasure is the highest form of Unity ("there is nothing higher than Oneg." *Sefer Yetzirah*) as pleasure is the collapse of one thing or person within another thing or person. Eternity is defined by Oneg, this pleasurable collapse into unity.

The Simcha of Shabbos is alluded to in the Torah, yet it is really only suggested as a Mitzvah by *Chazal* / the sages. In the verse, where the Torah lists the days on which the special trumpets were sounded in the Beis HaMikdash, the Torah says, "On the days of Simcha, on your designated holidays…" (Bamidbar 10:10). Say our sages (Sifri, *Bamidbar*, 10:10), this refers to Shabbos.*

Simcha is thus not actually *commanded*, as the verse does not say 'And you shall be joyous.' Rather, it says, "The days of your joy…" and the sages infer that this refers to Shabbos. The phraseology suggests that Simcha is automatic, an existential inevitability on Shabbos by its own very nature. Certainly, we are "not allowed" to be sad on Shabbos. (*Tosefos* (Moed Katan, 23b) brings down from the Yerushalmi *(Berachos, 2:7)* that the reason there is no mourning on Shabbos is because Shabbos is a place of *Berachah* / blessing, and in the place of Hashem's Berachah there is no mourning.) The Simcha of Shabbos is simply a direct result of truly entering Shabbos, which necessarily yields the experience of Deveikus and the 'transcendent' feelings of Unity.

Joy washes over us when we truly experience Shabbos. Every Mitzvah has a special *Segulah*, an 'omen' or key through which we tap into the Mitzvah. The Segulah of Shabbos is Simcha (*Menachem*

---

* See also *Yearos Devash*, 2, Derush 10. Chasam Sofer, *Orach Chayim*, 168. We do not make the Seuda of Purim on Shabbos (Yerushalmi, *Megilah*,1:4). Not to mix one Simcha with another. *Pri Chadash*, Orach Chayim, 688. However, in a sense, there is no 'obligation' to be joyful on Shabbos (*Magen Avraham*, Orach Chayim, 529:4. *Shu't Rabbi Akiva Eiger*, Hashmatos, 1. See Meiri, *Moed Katan*, 8b. Tosefos, *Moed Katan*, 23b. Ran, ad loc). The above verse does suggest that one of our days of joy is Shabbos, yet we are not literally "commanded" to be joyful, we are just naturally joyful when we feel settled and 'at home.' The Bahag, however, actually rules that there is an "obligation" to be happy on Shabbos. See also Radbaz, *Metzudas David*, Mitzvah 91. *Manhig*, Tefilos Shabbos. *Shibolei haLeket*, 82. *Beis Yoseph*, Orach Chayim, 281.

Tziyon (Rimanov), Yeshayahu). And from a state of joy we eventually slip into a state of Deveikus, unity and internal outflowing bliss.

KAVOD, ONEG, SIMCHA, DEVEIKUS

These four aspects of Shabbos, *Kavod, Oneg, Simcha* and *Deveikus*, are also connected with the four purposes of Shabbos; Creation, Revelation, future Redemption, and Redemption in the present. These, in turn, correspond to the four dimensions of time: past, present, future and eternity.

KAVOD / PAST / CREATION

For the purpose of *Kavod Shabbos* / honoring Shabbos, we prepare our bodies, minds, and homes before Shabbos. While the main time to make preparations for Shabbos may be on Friday morning, each day of the week is a unique phase of preparation for Shabbos. In this way, we develop an acute awareness of Shabbos as the culmination of a weekly cycle, in the image of the Six Days of Creation. Shabbos, then, is a commemoration of the past week and a reminder that Hashem is the one who created our world.

ONEG / PRESENT / REVELATION

Oneg is the pleasure we enjoy on Shabbos itself, as we settle deeply into our state of inner freedom from labor. This is Shabbos of the present moment, and Shabbos as an experiential reminder of the Exodus from Egypt, the place of forced and 'meaningless' labor, pain and hardship. Indeed, the experience of Shabbos is a mini-exodus from 'slavery' every single week.

SIMCHA / FUTURE / REDEMPTION

Simcha is an inevitability on Shabbos, not something we have to manufacture or try to feel, rather, it is simply something that we *will* feel. True Simcha is our destiny; it is a redemptive glimpse of the promised future, *Az Yimalei Sechok Pino* / "Then our mouth will be full of laughter" (Tehilim, 126:2. *Berachos*, 31a). This represents Shabbos as a glimmer of the future, and therefore it is only alluded to within its verse and not explicitly stated as, 'You shall be happy on Shabbos.'

DEVEIKUS / ETERNITY / REDEMPTION IN THE PRESENT

The highest or deepest experience of Shabbos is *Deveikus* / unification, an actual experience of the World-to-Come in *this world*; the world of unity and perfection, in the present. The enraptured experience of Deveikus (which will be further explored later on) is beyond all other emotions, even higher states of joy, pleasure and ecstasy. This is the Shabbos of the future in the eternal present.

REVERENCE & AWE LEAD TO JOY, PLEASURE & DEVEIKUS

At this point it behooves us to explore one more emotional state that is connected to Shabbos. In addition to honor and pleasure, joy and Deveikus, there is also an element of *Yirah* / fear or awe present on Shabbos.

The first and opening word of the Torah, בראשית / *Bereishis*, say the mystics, can be rearranged to spell the words ירא שבת / *Yirah Shabbos* / fear/awe of Shabbos (*Tikkunei Zohar*, 69a. Baal haTurim, *Bereishis* 1:1). Our sages tell us that even an *Am haAretz* / a brute, coarse person, does not lie on Shabbos, because the "fear" of Shabbos is upon him (*Yerushalmi*, Demai, 4:1. Rambam, *Hilchos Ma'aser*, 12:1). In fact, one of the early *Rishonim* / post-Talmudic commentators, Rav Eliezer of Metz (?-1175), writes that it is actually a Mitzvah to experience Yirah Shabbos (*Sefer Yerei'im*, 410. In a similar manner our sages teach, "One does not have fear/awe/reverence of Shabbos itself, but rather, of Him who ordered the observance of the Shabbos. *Yevamos*, 6a-b, although see Rashi, ad loc).

What is Yirah Shabbos? And why is it important to have a sense of Yirah on Shabbos?

In general, the lower form of Yirah, translated as *fear*, is a phenomenon of the self-preserving ego. Fear sets in whenever we sense that our ego or body is in danger, whether real or assumed. We are naturally afraid when we feel threatened. The great root of fear is the fear of death, of no longer existing. All fears share this root, from the fear of being physically hurt or losing a limb, to the fear of being emotionally crushed. The common denominator is a sense of losing the ego.

This 'lower' Yirah is not what Yirah Shabbos is about. Lower Yirah is "for the lowly (unintelligent, spiritually unsophisticated)… but this is not the Yirah of the wise and the mindful" (*Mesilas Yesharim*, 24). Higher Yirah is sensing the numinous, the mystery, the tangible feeling of being in the presence of something unexplainable or beyond us. Yirah Shabbos is thus a cultivated sense of reverence and awe.

On the other hand, the ego is humbled — perhaps even 'threatened' — in the presence of Shabbos, as Higher Yirah is "to make oneself as if he does not exist" (Maharal, *Nesivos Olam*, Nesiv Yiras Hashem, 1). Yet, this loss of ego is, through the frame of Higher Yirah, a deeply positive experience. Similarly, we may feel overawed and overwhelmed by the majesty of a mountain or a beautiful sunset. Such experiences 'eclipse' the ego and render us more transparent to Transcendence, stimulating positive feelings. In developed stages of Yirah Shabbos, just thinking about the holiness, majestic beauty and power of Shabbos, we may feel overawed in the same way, and thereby joyfully take leave of pettiness and negative ego.

Yirah is compared to a key that unlocks the outer gate (*Shabbos*, 31b). Reverence and awe are the 'keys' that open us up to more inner, transcendent emotions and experiences. When a person is in a posture of Yirah Shabbos, not only will they give respect and *Kavod* / honor to Shabbos, they will feel great joy, genuine *Oneg* / pleasure, and even slip into Deveikus, in the presence of Shabbos.

Essentially, awe causes us to take leave of our ego. There is an absence of a sense of 'I,' the self-observing 'me.' Let's say, for example, that you go to a museum and see a beautiful painting. The painting you are viewing is so exquisite that you become completely mesmerized and enchanted by its beauty. You feel yourself 'losing' yourself and becoming subsumed by the great beauty of the painting. Awe manifests in that moment when you are dropping your self-awareness and losing yourself in the painting.

Higher Yirah is the key that opens us up to Oneg, and true Oneg is the experience of unity. The greater the unity, the deeper the pleasure, and the deeper the pleasure, the less we have a sense of being the experiencer of it. The higher and more profound the pleasure, the less the egoic 'me' is present as the presumed separate entity which experiences pleasure. Conversely, the more present the sense of a separate self is in the experience, the less pleasurable it is. Oneg Shabbos, the pleasure *from* (not simply 'on') Shabbos arises from a state of awe. First one experiences an overwhelming awe of Shabbos, losing oneself within the majesty of Shabbos, and then this Yirah organically evolves into a tremendous sense of pleasure, bliss and ecstasy.

Still, pleasure is a sensation, a feeling, and thus there is always some measure of 'I' and duality in it. Ultimate spiritual pleasure dissolves the *Ani* / I into *Ayin* / no-thing-ness. The 'small i' dissolves within the 'Divine I.' This deep Deveikus is available every day, and every moment, but especially on the majestic day of Shabbos.

PERSPECTIVES ON THE FLOW OF THE WEEK

These Four Perspectives of Shabbos, 1) remembering Creation, 2) remembering the Exodus from Egypt, 3) having a taste of the World-to-Come, and 4) experiencing the World-to-Come in the eternal present, are also related to a fundamental understanding of the flow of the week. There are four ways in which to view the six workdays and the Seventh Day of Shabbos, as will now be explored.

06

LINE, CIRCLE & ETERNITY: THE FLOW OF TIME

OW WE MEASURE AND OBSERVE TIME AFFECTS HOW WE experience it. When we observe the natural, cyclical, patterns of the seasons of the year (the movement from spring to summer, and fall to winter, and then back to spring again) we assume that time flows cyclically, in endlessly repetitive circles.

When ancient man observed the cyclical patterns of the seasons with the cyclical nature palpable throughout Creation — sprouting, blossoming, bearing fruit, wilting, lying dormant, and returning again to life — he concluded that not only is time cyclical, but all of nature and all of reality is cyclical and repetitive in design.

FOUR PERCEPTIONS OF TIME

The Torah introduced to humanity a new way of observing and measuring time; in addition to its naturally cyclical repetitions, time also has a linear and progressive, even teleological, element to it. In this new view, time began at Creation, as *time itself is* a creation (Rambam, *Moreh Nevuchim*, 2:13. See also Radak, Seforno, and the Gra on *Bereishis*, 1:1. *Siddur Admur haZaken*, Sha'ar Kriyas Shema). And since time was created and began at a certain point, as it were, it is also moving toward a certain point. Creation is progressively moving forward in a continuous quest for a *Ge'ulah Sheleimah* / Complete Redemption. Time is an unfolding process of Revelation. This way of viewing time allows humankind to envision a better future, and empowers us to develop ourselves and improve circumstances in the world in order to create a better tomorrow for all created beings.

As linear time moves forward from Creation to Redemption, the past impregnates the present and the present impacts the future. The Hebrew word for time is *Z'man*, which is also related to the word *Hazmana* / preparation or invitation (*Sanhedrin*, 47b). As such, the present moment is a preparation for the future, but also an 'invitation' from the future; we are being pulled toward a future of inevitable Redemption. This future thus impacts our activity and consciousness in the present, driving beneficial behavior. Also, when we engage in present benefit, our perception of our past is transformed; our beneficial action in the now changes the valence and import of a seemingly negative past. When you learn from a past mistake and change yourself, it elevates your past; your past thus becomes an essential part of your drive/progression towards

Redemption. Thus, linear time moves not just from the past to the future, but also from the future to the present and even back to the past. The future pulls at the present and ultimately can elevate and transform our past.

This brings us to an understanding of how the Name of Hashem, the Yud-Hei-Vav-Hei, is related to a deeper understanding of the nature of *Z'man* / time. When the letters of the Name are rearranged they spell the words *Hayah* / ה-י-ה / it was (past), *Hoveh* / ה-ו-ה / it is (present), and *Yihiyeh* / י-ה-י [Yud is an elevated Vav] / it will be (future). The Name of Hashem itself represents Eternity, beyond and including all time, past, present and future as one.

There are various ways how these four letters, Yud, Hei, Vav and Hei, can themselves be spelled or 'filled out,' and these fillings produce different numerical values. When the four letters are spelled out as יוד-הא-ואו-הא, they add up to 45, and are therefore called 'the Name *Mah*' (Mem/40, Hei/5). When the four letters are spelled out as יוד-הה-וו-הה, they add up to 52 and are called 'the Name *Ban*' (Beis/2, Nun/50).

Together these two Names, Mah (45) and Ban (52), add up to 97. This is the same numerical value as the word זמן / *Z'man*.* There are multiple levels on which this can be deciphered. What is relevant to our immediate discussion about time is as follows: *Mah* literally means "what" and is also the same numerical value as the word אדם / *Adam* / humankind.** *Ban* (which only has nine letters, one letter less than Mah, indicating a lower stature then Mah) is

---

* *Z'man:* Zayin/7, Mem/40, Nun/50 = 97.

**Adam:* Aleph/1, Dalet/4, Mem/40 = 45.

the numerical value of the word בהמה / *Beheimah* / animal (Beis/2, Hei/5, Mem/40, Hei/5 = 52). Notice that in the word *Beheimah* there is also the word *Mah*. The word *BeHeiMah* can be divided into, *Bah Mah* / בה-מה / "there is in her *Mah*."

To explain: the difference between *Mah* and *Ban* is the contrast that exists between truly being human and being merely a more sophisticated animal. The definition of a human being, an *Adam*, is to be in a constant state of *Mah* / 'what?' — questioning, probing, seeking and yearning for more. To be human is to always be open to learn and grow. An animal, by contrast, or someone living in the paradigm of an animal, is to be a prototype of בה-מה / in her is *what*. In other words, she, the animal, is 'what' the animal is and will be. The 'what' is the animal as it is; there is no perception of a future and no potential for development or shift in her life.

"An ox a day old is called an ox" (*Baba Kama*, 65b). There is no real emotional, mental or spiritual growth for the ox; the *what* is already manifest within the ox from birth. What you see is what you get.

Unfortunately, some people never grow as well, and the exact same struggles they had when they were 20 are what they still have when they are 120. They are what they are, and always remain so. To be a true Adam we need to constantly grow, and live with the mystery of what the future will bring. To be human means to dream, to yearn, to hope and aspire for ever-greater depths and heights.

We need to perceive time progressing from the past into the present, and very presently feel the tug of the future. We need to let the unforeseen and as of yet unrealized future stimulate a movement in the present.

Within a unidirectional time frame, in which time only moves from past to present, there is no 'What?' — no mystery of the future pulling retroactively on the present. This is the worldview of inevitability; what happened yesterday is inevitably imprinted on the present. Born an 'ox,' and an 'ox' will remain so. Genetics, environment, education and infancy/childhood are solid so that they hold an absolute grip on one's life. Life is predictable and inevitable, there is no movement or change possible. However, from an *Adam* or *Mah* worldview, the present is not the inevitable effect of the past. Rather, an infinite, unsoiled and bright future draws the best from the present, which also releases the weight of the past. Every moment is a new moment, with limitless potentials and possibilities, as the timeless Name of Hashem infuses linear time with the light of Mah.

On the other hand, it cannot be disputed that time and nature also flow cyclically, as observed in the cyclical seasons of the year. Indeed, some ancient Kabbalistic texts speak about a grand cyclical rhythm of time, with recurring universes called the Seven *Shemitos* / cosmic eras. The psycho-cyclical nature of time is that it always returns to the moment, to the now.

The dynamic, evolving nature of linear time (the future-in-the-present) is a manifestation of the Name Mah; the now as open to the future. The past-in-the-present is a manifestation of the Name Ban; the inevitability of the past predetermining the nature of the present, defining the present as the necessary effect of the past. There is, however, also a third perspective of Z'man, which is the *Yichud* / unity of Mah and Ban. In Yichud, the present moment is the center of the circle, the point, the axis upon which the past and future meet and revolve. In this way, the infinite future pulls on the present (Mah), even as the present is being pushed by the finite past (Ban).

These three dimensions or perceptions of time are also related to the three letters in the word Z'man / זמן — Zayin, Mem, and Nun.

Zayin is numerically 7, representing the seven days of Creation, which is time as it flows from day one into day seven, from the past into the present and future. This, again, is the idea of natural time, the 'past' as the cause and the present as the effect. This is the dimension of the 'past' within time.

Mem is 40, and represents a construct of transformation, from 'what is' into 'what will be.' There were 40 days of the Great Flood that transformed the earth and a new world was born. There were 40 years in the desert journeying towards the Promised Land. There are 40 days from conception until an embryo is called a fetus. This is time as a *Hazmanah* / preparation for the future, and as the present being impregnated by the future. This is the dimension of 'future' within time.

Nun is 50. Fifty is the time of *Yovel* / jubilee, the fiftieth year following the end of the cycle of seven Shemitos (in this case, a "Shemitah" is a period of seven years) and beginning another cycle of seven Shemitos. In this way, Yovel embodies the cyclical nature of time in which the past, present and future are always the same, forever returning to the beginning. This is the dimension of the 'present' within time.

There is also a fourth element of time: Eternity, the moment that includes all the past and all the future in a timeless embrace. The meta-root of Z'man is the transcendent Name of Hashem; and the Name of Hashem represents Eternity, beyond and including all time, past, present and future (as mentioned, the four letters of the Name spell out *Hayah, Hoveh, Yihyeh* / Was, Is, Will Be). This is the deepest essence of time: the unity of past, present and future — and timeless transcendence — within time. This is the dimension of the 'timelessness' within time, the inclusive transcendence that is beyond, and including, all the dimensions of time.

On Shabbos, we connect with the Eternity of time, the essence that includes the other three dimensions of time. On Shabbos, we experience, if we truly enter it, a total Yichud of time and timelessness. Shabbos is an eternal present, in which we can sense our past as a positive premonition of our future, without nostalgia or fantasy. From moment to moment we feel timelessly perfect and complete, and that 'all our work is done.' And yet, we also know that we have much more to achieve on this planet — not because we 'have to,' but because we want to and we can. This is the coexistence of all perspectives of time while being beyond time.

Our sages tell us (*Medrash*, Bereishis Rabbah 11:8), that each day of the week was created with a counterpart, a match. Sunday, Day One, on which there was the Creation of light, is matched with Wednesday, Day Four, on which there was the formation of the great heavenly luminaries. Day four is the completion of day one. Monday, Day Two, with its division of the waters, is matched with Thursday, Day Five, on which life rose up from the water. Day Five is the completion of Day Two. Tuesday, Day Three, in which there was a revealing of the land mass, is matched with Day Six, the creation of animals and humans which roam the land. Day Six is the completion of Day Three.

Now the question arises, who or what is the match for Day Seven, Shabbos? The answer is, the People of Israel. On Shabbos there is a perfect Shalom and Yichud between the day and who we are. We are 'matched' or unified with the essence of time.

And since Shabbos is the essence of time, the experience and practices of Shabbos include all four dimensions of time. These are revealed in a progressive order as Shabbos unfolds.

SHEIM BAN	SHEIM MAH	YICHUD OF MAH & BAN	SHEIM HAVAYAH
Natural causality of linear time: From past to present to future.	Higher linear time: The future pulling the present and the present retroactively uplifting the past.	Cyclical time: A combination of natural and spiral time.	Eternity of time: Timelessness that includes all time.
-Past	-Future	-Present	-Eternal Present

FOUR MODELS OF TIME / FOUR DIMENSIONS OF SHABBOS

Shabbos is the true essence and purpose of all time and Creation. The four dimensions of time discussed above are also expressed fully in the ways Shabbos is perceived.

1) WEEKDAY — SHABBOS — LINE MOVING TOWARDS SHABBOS

In the first paradigm, the weekdays lead into Shabbos; much like the order of Creation, first the six days then Shabbos. As such, when we are not actually celebrating Shabbos, we are then moving towards the next Shabbos. Rest is the culmination of the work-week. This is the sensation we feel most on Friday evening, as explored earlier.

2) SHABBOS — WEEKDAY —
LINE MOVING FROM SHABBOS

In this paradigm, time begins (so to speak) with the 'end,' the *Tachlis* / ultimate purpose, Shabbos. Since "The beginning is wedged in the end" (*Sefer Yetzirah*, 1:7), Shabbos is the essential moment within time and thus gives birth to the weekdays. In other words, the destination is what necessitates the journey. The rest, focus, and introspection of Shabbos give context to the workweek. To be sure, on Shabbos, we are not thinking about the coming week (which would be the opposite of the spirit of Shabbos), rather, we are completely submerged and immersed in the holiness, rest, and inwardness of Shabbos. This consciousness itself secures a healthy mentality and spiritually productive week to come.

Shabbos is a *being* state; from which our weekday doings stream forth. This stillness and changelessness is the source of all action, movement and change. It is the *being* state that will give birth to our future. This is the sensation that we feel most on Shabbos day, as explored earlier.

3) SHABBOS AT THE CENTER, THE MIDDLE OF THE CIRCLE

The cyclical nature of time is that everything always returns back to this moment, the present. This is related to Shabbos as the center point where all the weekdays surround Shabbos. In terms of geometry, the circle is a type of perfect image. Shabbos is the "midpoint" of the week (Rabbeinu Bachya, *Kad Kemach*, Shabbos), and all the days of the workweek come from *and* lead into Shabbos. Shabbos is both the source *and* the goal. As the middle point, Shabbos is called "the holy *Heichal* / sanctuary" (Maharal, *Derech Chayim*, 5. *Chidushei Agados*, Sanhedrin, 137). Shabbos is the "heart of the week" (Maharal, *Chidushei Agados*, Shabbos, 119a). Many of the body parts are double: two eyes, two nostrils, two ears, two lips, two arms, two legs, etc. But there is one heart that sits in the center of the body that pumps lifeforce, *Chayus* / vitality and vigor to the entire system. Shabbos is the unifying center of time.

Some Mekubalim actually draw diagrams showing Shabbos as the midpoint of the week, and the six days flowing outward from it (*Reishis Chochmah*, Sha'ar haKedushah, 2. *Shaloh*, Maseches Chulin, 32). Shabbos is the middle of the circle and the other six days are the outer circumference. We come from the Shabbos of the past, move always towards the Shabbos of the future, and rest within the Shabbos of the present.

This is the experience and sensation of Shabbos afternoon, Minchah time.

CENTER AND RADIUS

Let us look more closely at this idea that the six days of the week are like the circumference of a circle with Shabbos in its center. Every circle requires a circumference and a diameter, the distance around and across the whole circle respectively. Yet, a circle also has a radius, the distance between the center of the circle and its circumference. Our sages tell us that if something has a circumference of three *Tefachim* / handbreadths then its diameter is about one Tefach (Mishnah, *Eiruvin*, 1:5. See *Melachim* 1, 7:23, regarding the Yam (water) of Shlomo), although it is not exactly a 3 to 1 ratio, as Tosefos explains (Tosefos, *Sukka*, 8a. Tosefos haRosh, *Eiruvin*, 14a). Today this ratio is known as the principle of *Pi*, which is an 'infinite' number, as the digits continue on and on with no repeating pattern: 3.14159265358979323846... *ad infinitum*. The Rambam (*Pirush haMishnayos*, Eiruvin, ibid) writes that, indeed, the exact ratio between the diameter and the circumference is not known and is impossible to know. In any case, approximately six times the length of the radius equals the circumference; if the radius is one inch, the circumference would be a little more than six inches. This mathematical equation, with its roughly 1:6 ratio, illustrates the concept of Shabbos. Perhaps this dynamic of weekdays and Shabbos is the meta-root of the natural phenomena circles show us.

Shabbos, the center point within the circle, is the point from which the radius extends and gives length to the circumference. The six radius-lengths of the circumference correspond to the six days of the week. Despite the fact that the centerpoint takes up no space of its own, without it there is no circle. The ebb and flow of time, past and future, revolves around the axis of Shabbos, the innermost moment from which time extends (as the Rebbe explores, see *Rashimos*, No. 3, p. 46–47).

Time and space are deeply linked as part of the four dimensional space-time continuum. In addition to the above image of Shabbos as the center of a circle, another geometrical image of Shabbos is as the center of a cube and the six days of the week being the six faces of the cube. Each of these six faces also significantly correspond to one of the six *Sefiros* / spiritual attributes and its experiential quality:

DAY	CUBE	COMPASS	ATTRIBUTE	EXPERIENCE
1. Sunday	Right Side	South	Chesed	Giving and Openness
2. Monday	Left Side	North	Gevurah	Restricting and Inwardness
3. Tuesday	Front	East	Tiferes	Harmonizing and Beauty
4. Wednesday	Up	Skyward	Netzach	Victory and Perseverance
5. Thursday	Down	Earthward	Hod	Humility and Gratitude
6. Friday	Back	West	Yesod	Foundation and Relationship
7. Shabbos	Center	Point of Observer	Malchus	Royalty and Receptivity *

* The notion of Shabbos and the seven day weekly cycle is universal. Klal Yisrael who are rooted in Avraham (right), Yitzchak (left), and especially Yisrael (center), acknowledge the cosmic Seventh Day Shabbos, which is Malchus, in the center-line. Shabbos at the center as the seventh day of the week. The children of Yishmael, who are rooted solely in Avraham, and represent an overbalanced side of Chesed, the 'right side' — established their 'Shabbos' to the 'right' of the cosmic Shabbos, on Friday. The children of Eisav, who are rooted principally in Yitzchak, Gevurah, the 'left side' — established their 'Shabbos' to the 'left' of the cosmic Shabbos, on Sunday.

In the diagram of the cube, the reason why the right is south, and the left north, and so forth, is that the proper orientation of the observer is to face east. East is considered the "front" or the "face" (Shemos, 38:13. *Rashi,* ad loc), whereas 'west' alludes to the back or behind. East is also the metaphysical positioning of our collective birth: our sages tell us that the primordial human being, Adam, was created with his head to the east, his feet to the west, his right hand to the south, and his left hand to the north (*Chagigah,* 12a, Rashi (*M'sof*) ad loc. *Sha'ar haMitzvos,* Bereishis 4a).

Each day of the week is intrinsically connected with one of the sides of the cube, including what each direction embodies and represents.

Sunday is to the right (south), the quality of Chesed / *kindness, giving and openness.* On Day One of Creation light was created, which is an expression of kindness, giving and revelatory openness.

On a personal level, on Sunday most people feel infused with optimism and possibility. A new week is beginning and new possibilities are on the horizon. Studies have found that people have less migraines on Sunday than on any other day of the week. It is a day of openness, of 'light' and revealing.

Monday is to the left (north), the quality of Gevurah / *strength, restriction and inwardness.* On Day Two of Creation, dualities and separations were created, most prominently through the separation placed between higher and lower waters.

On a personal level, Mondays can be hard days; many people experience "Monday-morning blues." There is a more pronounced sense of anxiety (inner separation) on Mondays than on any other day of the week. Sadly, studies show that suicides are much more frequent on Mondays.

Tuesday is to the front (east) — connecting and harmonizing the two opposites of right and left; as the quality of Tiferes / *balance, harmony and beauty*. On the Third Day of Creation vegetation was created. Sprouting up from the earth represents a defiance of gravity, reaching up towards the heavens. On the other hand, such upward growth is only made possible to the extent that one's roots are firm and secure, burrowing down into the earth. As such, vegetation is a perfect analogy to the work of connecting and harmonizing the lower and higher realms. When the water of the earth (the lower waters) rises to meet the water that falls from the sky (the higher waters), then vegetation begins to flourish. Barren land begins to produce fruit and teem with life and the landscape is transformed into a beautiful tapestry. This is the harmony and beauty of Tuesday's Creation — elevating that which is below while at the same time channeling and receiving that which is above.

On a personal level, Tuesday manifests the quality of *routine*, as in, for example, 'showing up the next day to work.' To some, 'routine' means boring, tedious and mundane, yet, routine actions are often what bear fruit. To be productively successful in whatever we are doing, we cannot just show up for the 'exciting' first day without also making it for the second day too. We need to *defy gravity*, which is only possible if we are deeply rooted.

Wednesday is connected to the 'above' (heavens), it has an upward posture and is infused with the quality of Netzach / *victory and perseverance*. On the Fourth Day of Creation the two "great lights" above, the sun and the moon, were established. Netzach is perseverance and continuation; Wednesday is the day when the continuous circular motions of the sun, moon, stars and galaxies were initiated.

On a personal level, Wednesday is all about perseverance. On Wednesday, a person is already deep in the routine of the work-week; here, what matters most is the quality of Netzach, perse-vering and pushing through the rest of the week. On Wednesday late afternoon you may feel your perseverance waning and that you could use a break. It is not by coincidence that matinees are held on Wednesdays, and *LeHavdil* / to draw a qualitative distinction, the best time to convene a successful Torah *Shiur* / class is on Wednes-day evening. By the fourth day we are likely to need a recharge to persevere through the end of the week.

Thursday is connected to 'below' (earth), a downward or humble posture and the quality of Hod / *humility and gratefulness.* On the Fifth Day of Creation, animals emerged. Animals have an innate 'humility' before their Creator, as they only do what they were cre-ated to do. There is no inner dichotomy between what they were created to do and how they actually live. Their humble submission to the Creator is much like the angels, some of whom are called *Chayos haKodesh* / holy animals, and were also created on Thursday (or Monday: *Medrash Rabbah,* Bereishis, 1:3). Humility is connected with acknowledging that which is beyond or greater than oneself, giving thanks and offering praise. Every sound emitted from an animal is another revealed sound in the great symphony of the world, as it sings the Creator's praise, like the sweet songs of the angels.

On a personal level, on Thursday we feel as if the workweek is finally ending. There is a certain sense of relief and exhalation; we feel grateful for the passing of the week and we instinctively desire to offer thanks. For better or worse, and without condoning it, the biggest weekday night at bars across the world is Thursday night. *LeHavdil*, on Thursday night many *Yeshivos* / Torah academies and communal leaders convene a *Farbrengen* / spiritual gathering or *Mishmar* / night study session on Thursday night, punctuated with songs of praise.

Friday is associated with facing the back (west), the quality of Yesod / *foundation, connection and relationships*. On the Sixth Day of Creation, the human being was created. Only regarding the human being does the Torah say, "It is not good to be alone." All animals procreate, and some are even monogamous, yet, it is only the human being who seeks intimacy beyond physical procreation, who desires to not be existentially alone. The deepest level of Yesod, of connection and relationship, is intimacy, a human trait.

On a personal level, Friday is the last day of the workweek. It is a time when we begin to reconnect with family, loved ones and friends.

Shabbos is the center, the quality of Malchus* / *receptivity*, the

---

* The seven days of the week are the seven Sefiros from Chesed to Malchus (*Tikkunei Zohar*, Tikun 56). There are *Rishonim* / early commentators who connect Shabbos with the attribute of Yesod (Rabbeinu Bachya, *Bamidbar*, 10:33. *Sha'arei Orah*, Sha'ar 2), being the Seventh Sefirah counting from Binah (Sunday as Binah, and Monday to Chesed, etc.). See also *Ohr haChayim*, Vayikra, 19:3, where he speaks of Shabbos as being connected to Yoseph and the attribute of Yesod, also called *Kol* / everything (as explored in a previous chapter). Yet, most opinions (including the Arizal's) associate Shabbos with Malchus (see Arizal, Sha'ar *Ma'amarei Rashbi*, Vayakhel). The Ramak (*Pardes Rimonim*, Sha'ar 23:21) elaborates on this argument, and writes that Shabbos, according to the count of days, lies between Yesod and

actual 'vessel' that contains all of Creation. On the Shabbos of Creation nothing was created, and 'nothing' was created. On Shabbos, a dimension of *Nefesh* / soul, sometimes referred to as *Ayin* / nothing, was revealed in the world. On a personal level, as we rest and cease from all outward creative expression, we become deeply centered, and receive an experience of our soul.

4) SHABBOS AS ETERNITY: BEYOND TIME & EMBRACING ALL TIME

Shabbos, as just explained, is the center point within the circle of the week, yet, on a deeper level, there is no actual center point within a circle (Rav Yitzchak Chaver, *Afikei Yam*, Moed Katan, 3a). In fact, this is clearly observable. There is no tangible/physical point within the diagram of a circle that you can point at and accurately declare to be the center. Every dot itself has a center, and that center has a center; every point can be divided and subdivided ad infinitum. We can never arrive at a true center within space, as the essence of space and time, is spacelessness, timelessness and Infinite. Imagine you are asked to walk half way from where you are standing to the wall, and then half again, and half of that. Theoretically (if you could make yours steps small enough), you could do this *ad infinitum*, because the essence of space is actually spaceless Infinity.

Malchus, yet the essential attribute of Shabbos is Malchus. There are also higher dimensions of Shabbos that are connected with Keser / Chochmah / Binah / Da'as. The created world is connected to the seven (lower) attributes, from Chesed to Malchus, and the 'lower' Shabbos, the Shabbos of Creation, being Malchus. The higher Shabbos is the Shabbos 'before' the Creation of the world, before the Seven Days of Creation. The first Shabbos 'within' Creation is Shabbos as Malchus.

Despite being an abstraction, the innermost Infinite-Spaceless center point is nonetheless the basis and center from which the 'area' of timespace radiates. The six segments of the circle, and their respective portions of the circumference, are the six days of the week. Without a center there can be no circle. Even though the center point is undefinable, spaceless and infinite, it defines the existence of a circumference and the possibility for a radius. This timeless 'centerpoint' of time is Shabbos. It is timeless, undefinable and ungraspable, and yet, there are no weekdays without Shabbos. The fullness of Creation, the six directions, the six days of the week, the six *Midos* / qualities of consciousness — the entire circle — is founded on Shabbos.

Shabbos is beyond time and space, yet it also embraces and includes all of time and space. In this sense, Shabbos is similar to the *Aron* / Ark of the Covenant (*Zohar*, Hakdamah, 13b). Our sages teach (*Yuma*, 21a) that the "place" of the Aron did not take up any space: מקום ארון אינו מן המדה / "The place of the Aron has no measurement." The Aron itself had a definite measurement; it was 2.5 cubits by 1.5 cubit. Yet, paradoxically, in the Holy of Holies, which in the First Beis haMikdash was 20 cubits by 20 cubits, if one would measure from one edge of the Aron to the curtain wall, it would be 10 cubits, and from the other side of the Aron it would also be 10 cubits. This paradoxical image demonstrates that the place of the Aron did not take up any space. The Aron had a defined measurement, and yet, it was 'beyond' space; it was both within and beyond space. The same is true with Shabbos in the world of time. Shabbos, as the seventh day of the week, has a certain time period, and it affects the preceding and following week, and yet, it is also beyond the world of time. Shabbos is eternal. It is both within and beyond time.

REST AND REDEMPTION OF TIME ITSELF

The Eternity of Shabbos is manifest in the way that Shabbos spreads into the weekdays, especially during the fourth-meal, the feast of Melava Malka, that occurs after Shabbos.

Clearly there is a progressive unfolding of Shabbos, moving deeper and higher, as well as a progressive unfolding of our relationship with time. We move from the 'inevitability' of time, where the past affects the present (experienced on Friday evening), to the present pulled by the unimaginable future (experienced on Shabbos day), to the presence of the present, in which past and future collapse into the present (experienced on Shabbos afternoon), to the eternity and timelessness of Shabbos, which paradoxically flows into and permeates all dimensions of time. This is Shabbos as both Shabbos and *beyond* the day of Shabbos.

The deepest dimension of Shabbos is not only a rest from work and the world of work, but a redemption of time itself.

The eternity of Shabbos allows us to see and experience time beyond its illusory rigidity of past, present or future. Shabbos allows us, through its infinite fractal-like dimensionality, to experience timelessness within time, leading to the realization that the beginning and the end, the purpose and the goal, the past and the future, are all present in this very moment.

These are the four progressive stages of Shabbos, one leading to the next, each one revealing a deeper dimension and way of relating to time — leading to the redemption of time itself. The aspect of infinite timelessness is revealed to be expressed precisely within the finite, defined present moment.

Much like the unity of Infinity and finitude, immeasurability and measurement, which was revealed in the Holy of Holies, Shabbos reveals a paradox within the world of time. On the one hand, Shabbos is a defined seventh day of the week, a finite slice within the rhythm of time and an honoring of time; and yet, Shabbos is also unbounded timelessness and is thus expressed in the *Nekudah* / essential point of 'Shabbos' that shines within all the days of the week, and indeed in every moment, as will be explored.

This is the transcendence and redemption of the entire structure of static time. Infinity and finitude merge, so to speak, on Motzei Shabbos, although it is also the foundational truth of every single moment of time, expressed most potently on the day of Shabbos.

Once we experience the redemption of static time, and reveal its paradoxical nature, we can come to celebrate and understand the innate value of having a 'set' day of Shabbos, allowing us to honor time as we are experiencing it as eternity.

Infinity cannot be grasped, and the only way to tap into and experience something of Infinity, is through a finite interface. Through honoring the specific day of Shabbos, celebrating the 25-26 hours of Shabbos, we come to experience the eternity of Shabbos, the timeless Nekudah of Shabbos that is ultimately accessible within each and every finite moment of time, no matter what day of the week it is.

INFINITY OF SHABBOS
WITH INFINITE RAMIFICATIONS

As Shabbos is infinite, it both permeates and embraces all finitude, therefore everything we finite beings do on Shabbos is magnified and has infinite ramifications. For this reason, the Ramak teaches that the Mitzvos we do on Shabbos reach a higher place than the Mitzvos we do during the week (Note, *Zevachim* 91a, regarding the daily offerings that are offered on Shabbos). Our Shabbos *Tefilah* / prayers are as potent as the prayers we offer during the period between Rosh Hashanah and Yom Kippur (*Rosh Hashanah*, 18a. Pirush HaGra, *Tikkunei Zohar*, Tikun 21. See also *Reishis Chochmah*, Sha'ar haKedushah, 2). As the Ben Ish Chai confirms, one Mitzvah performed on Shabbos, and especially the Mitzvah of learning Torah, is like a thousand ('thousand' being a code word for infinity, note, *Makkos*, 10a) Mitzvos done during the week (Ben Ish Chai, *Hakdamah Shemos*). Conversely, any negative act that we perform on Shabbos has a greater negative effect than acts done during the week (Chidah, *Lev David*, 22. Note, *Nefesh haChayim*, Sha'ar 1:14).

This is the Shabbos of eternity; that which is beyond time and yet is the essential aspect of time, the Nekudah, the Infinite center that nevertheless defines time. As such, the essence of every dimension, every point along the line of time and every slice of the circle of time, is really Shabbos. There is a Nekudah of Shabbos within every moment.

In the first three paradigms of Shabbos, the forward flowing line, the reverse flowing line and the center of a circle or cube, there is still a marked boundary around the sacred day of Shabbos; distinguishing it from the six mundane days of the week. On the level of eternity, however, there are no separations or distinctions; all is Shabbos and every day is a holy day. Yet, paradoxically, due to how our consciousness functions, we need the defined day of Shabbos to reveal to us that every day has an essential undefinable Nekudah of *Shabbos*.

This is Shabbos as the zero-dimensional foundation of spacelessness and timelessness from which all space-time emerges; not merely the end or beginning of a line of time or the center of a circle of time. The eternity of Shabbos can be visualized as the entire circle itself and its area, with no beginning or end. Every point on the circle, every moment, is *Shabbos*; the past and future are united. Shabbos can be conceived of as the infinite ground, upon which such a circle would possibly be constructed; the fertile void from which all dimensionality emerges and expresses itself.

"And there was evening, and there was morning, day one (came to an end)…"

Each of the Six Days of Creation is described by the Torah in this way; every weekday comes to a conclusion. The one day of the week, regarding this description being omitted, is Shabbos. It does not say, 'And it was evening and it was morning, Day Seven.' This suggests that Shabbos is not just 'Day Seven,' not just one day in the weekly cycle. It is something more, something altogether different, beyond mere quantity.

The Baal haTurim (Rav Yaakov son of the Rosh, 1269-1343) writes that the reason for this omission in scripture is that the sanctity of Shabbos can be extended into Friday afternoon and into Saturday night, which is already 'day one' of the next week; the beginning of Sunday in the Hebrew calendar. Extending the 'territory' of Shabbos is called *Tosefos Shabbos* / adding to Shabbos. Technically, portions of the workweek can, in this way, be converted into Shabbos. If someone accepted upon himself Shabbos on late Friday afternoon, then for him it is Shabbos and all the laws of Shabbos apply. One can also extend Shabbos into Saturday evening as long as one wishes.

On a deeper level, the fact that the sanctity of Shabbos can extend and irrigate the workweek, suggests that there is an inner spiritual quality of Shabbos that is also hidden within each weekday. If not, it would be impossible for parts of Friday or Sunday to become Shabbos. There must be some Nekudah of Shabbos within them, already, just waiting to be accessed and activated.

Similar to the expansion of spatial borders, such as with property, there can be an expansion of temporal boundaries as well. Although the *Kedushah* / holiness of *Eretz Yisrael* / the Land of Israel has clearly defined borders, yet, "Whenever Eretz Yisrael is mentioned, the intent is (to include) the lands conquered by the King of Israel or a prophet with the consent of the entire Jewish People." This may include even lands outside the ancient Land of Kena'an (Rambam, *Hilchos Terumos*, 1:2-3). The deeper reason why this transformation is possible, is that there is a Nekudah of Eretz Yisrael within every land and every location throughout the entire world. There will even come a day when the sanctity of "Eretz Yisrael will expand over the entire world" (*Pesikta Rabsi*, 1). The same is true with time. Whereas Shabbos is defined as the seventh day of the week, still, through Tosefos Shabbos we can extend Shabbos; and here also, this is because there is a Nekudah of Shabbos within every day of the week.

Even now, every day of the week has a Shabbos quality within it. For example, just as Shabbos completes the week, Tuesday 'completes' Monday, and Wednesday 'completes' Tuesday (Rikanti, *Beshalach*, 35:1. *Tola'as Yaakov*, Sisrei Tefilos Shabbos uMoadim). Deeply, this is because there is a Nekudah of Shabbos within every day and every moment of the workweek. The weekdays are defined by Melachah, work, *Hiluch* / movement, *Tenuah* / the rhythm of motion, and thus sound. Shabbos, by contrast, is the rest that is beyond the world of Tenuah. Within every movement and sound there is an underlying stillness, an infinite quietness, spacelessness and timelessness; the inner aspect of Shabbos.

In the noisy and dualistic world we live in, this inner Nekudah is not fully revealed. But there will come a time when this Nekudah will be revealed within every moment, when we have attained *Yom sheKulo Shabbos* / a day when all is Shabbos. Even today, in a more concealed manner, the Nekudah of Shabbos glimmers within every day. There is an ever-present aspect of Shabbos within the cycle of the week, within every motion, even now.

THE SIX DAYS OF THE WEEK / SIX DAYS OF YOM TOV & THE SHABBOS WITHIN THEM

In the future, when the Nekudah of Shabbos will expand infinitely, every day will be revealed as Shabbos. Today there are six mundane days of the week with their inner Nekudah being Shabbos. In the Temple era, there were six principal days of *Yom Tov* / holiday, during which Israel would refrain from most mundane activities. These are: two days of Pesach (the first and last day), one day of Shavuos, one day of Rosh Hashanah, and the first and last days of Sukkos. These six Torah-based holidays correspond to the six days of the week.

This alignment of six holidays with six weekdays is not a mere coincidence. Rather, it teaches us that while it may appear that there is one sacred day of the week, Shabbos, and six mundane days, the truth is that every day of the week has latent *Kedushah* / sanctity and spiritual potential within it.

Just as the Kedushah of Yom Tov is rooted in Shabbos, the inner quality of every weekday corresponds to another day of Yom Tov, and as stated, the inner root of every Yom Tov is Shabbos.

Another way of saying this is that every day of the week has four layers of depth:

1) There is the outermost *Hispashtus* / expression, in which every day of the week has a particular quality, a distinct expression; on Sunday one may feel more open and on Mondays more anxious, as explored earlier.

2) This outer sensation is rooted in the six Sefiros; on Sunday there is more Chesed (stimulating a sensation of openness) and on Monday there is more Gevurah (stimulating a sensation of anxiety).

3) The Sefiros and their experiential expressions are each related to one of the six days of the Biblical Yomim Tovim, which are 'internal' expressions of the Divine Will, as will be explained shortly.

4) The deepest core of time, the root and goal of every moment, the *Etzem* / essence of every day, is Shabbos. Shabbos is the undefined, infinite ground of being inside every day, while the particular expression and experience of each day is the *doing*, the manifestation, of that essence.

Everything has an *Etzem* / essence and *Hispashtus* / an expression, and within the Hispashtus itself there are inner and outer manifestations.

Everything is rooted within the Creator. Similarly (*Kaviyachol* / so-to-speak), there is an Essence of Hashem, an Unmanifest Ground of all Being; and there is the way Hashem is *Mispashet* / projected and manifested through the forms of the Sefiros, the Divine screens and filters, revealing finite expressions. The same is true, by extension, with every creation. There is an Etzem of the thing (whether it is a unit of time or a particular point in space), and there is an outer Hispashtus, how it is projected and sensed. This outer Hispashtus is a reflection of its inner Hispashtus or Sefirah.

Shabbos is the Etzem of all time, which is connected to the Etzem of Hashem, the Ultimate Being that is beyond 'expression,' beyond all creating and revealing, and even beyond any of the Divine Names or Sefiros. The external, outer expression of Sunday, for example, its quality of openness and optimism, is manifest because Sunday is a reflection of the Sefirah of Chesed, and the full embodiment of the Sefirah of Chesed is the Yom Tov of Pesach. That is the level of expression, while on an Etzem level, the depths of Sunday, and every day of the week, is Shabbos.

The Etzem of the Creator is beyond definition; It includes timeless-infinity and yet It includes all of time and finitude, "For just as He has the power of Infinity, He includes the power of Finitude."

Similarly, the Etzem of time is timelessness that is paradoxically expressed in all dimensions of time.

When Yom sheKulo Shabbos comes, every moment will be openly linked to the Etzem of time, and in the context of that essence, all expressions and manifestations, all six days of the week, will reveal their internal manifestation, their Divine quality, their fullness as a Yom Tov.

Today, as mentioned, Sunday manifests Chesed, and thus people feel infused with optimism and possibility; Monday is the quality of Gevurah, restricting and inwardness, and therefore people may feel more anxious or irritable. However, there will come a time when the fullness, the 'Yom Tov' of Chesed will be revealed on Sunday and the 'Yom Tov' of Gevurah on Monday. Thus every Sunday will be 'Pesach' and every Monday will be 'Rosh Hashanah' and so forth.

Our sages tell us that in the times of Moshiach there will be no more Yomim Tovim (besides Purim [and Chanukah] (*Medrash*, Mishlei, 9:2. *Yalkut Shimoni*, Mishlei, 944)). The inner reason why the Yomim Tovim will no longer be, is that all days will be infused with the holiness of the Holidays, and there will be no mundane 'weekdays.' Each day of the week will be fully revealed as its inherent Yom Tov quality. In other words: in the future, every day of the week will be revealed as another Yom Tov* (*Leshem Shevo V'Achlama*, De'ah 2. p. 116. *Derushei Olam haTohu*, Cheilek 2, Derush Dalet, Anaf Yud-Beis, Yud).

---

* In the Seventh Millennium, a time of Yom sheKulo Shabbos and the level of 'revealed Etzem,' every day will reveal its Etzem, its Yom Tov, corresponding to its emotive Sefirah. Yet, there are also three higher Sefiros and thus there will also be an Eighth Millennium which will be *Yom sheKulo Yom Kippur*, and a Ninth Millennium which can be called *Yom sheKulo Purim*. After that, there will even be revealed a Tenth Millennium.

Every Sunday, which is the quality of Chesed, will be Pesach. Pesach was a time when HaKadosh Baruch Hu showed us great Divine kindness and lifted us out (despite the fact that perhaps we were not worthy) from "Egypt," meaning from physical / mental / emotional and spiritual bondage. Within the rhythm of time, Pesach is the full expression and embodiment of the Sefirah of Chesed and as such, every Sunday will be Pesach.

Every Monday, Gevurah, will be Rosh Hashanah, the day that embodies all the qualities of *Din* / judgement and severity.

Every Tuesday, Tiferes, will be Shavuos, as Tiferes is the giving of the Torah (*Berachos*, 58a). The Torah embodies the quality of the 'third' (*Shabbos*, 88a), that power which creates harmony between the 'One' and the 'two.'

Every Wednesday is Netzach, and the day in which the sun and moon began to function, thus every Wednesday will be Rosh Chodesh, which is also a *Moed*, a type of Yom Tov (*Erchin*, 10b).

Every Thursday, which is the quality of Hod / thankfulness, will be Sukkos, a time when we say the full Hallel, offering praise and thanks to Hashem every day.

Every Friday, the quality of Yesod / foundation and relationship, will be Shemini Atzeres, the final day of the season of holidays, when HaKadosh Baruch Hu says, "I want to be alone with my children," a time of spiritual intimacy (in general, Sukkos is Yesod. *Tikkunei Zohar*, Chadash, p. 58b).

And Shabbos is Shabbos. Shabbos is not a day of a particular 'expression' or quality, rather it is a time of transparent integration and connection to the Source of all expressions and qualities. There is nothing to do and nowhere to go, just to fully be, like Adam and Chava before the sin, basking in the Light of Hashem, embraced within Gan Eden.

07

IS SHABBOS AT THE END, BEGINNING OR MIDDLE OF THE WEEK?

A S EXPLORED EARLIER, IN DESCRIBING A SEVEN DAY WEEK, usually one begins counting from Sunday, and Shabbos, the Seventh Day, is at the end of the week. However, Shabbos can also be seen as the first day of the week, with Friday as the last day. Furthermore, Shabbos can be viewed as the midpoint of the week, with Sunday, Monday and Tuesday on one side, and Wednesday, Thursday and Friday on the other side.

Let us explore these paradigms a little further.

In the first view, every day of the week is leading up to Shabbos and a 'preparation' for Shabbos. We are always thinking of Shabbos, always building up to it. Our sages report (*Beitza*, 16a), "It has been said of Shammai the Elder that every day he would eat for the honor of Shabbos. How so? If he found a choice animal (to eat), he would say, "This will be for the honor of Shabbos," and he would put it aside for Shabbos. If (subsequently) he discovered another even nicer one, he would put that one aside (for Shabbos) and eat the first one. Hillel the Elder had a different trait, that all his actions (during everyday) were for the sake of Heaven, as it says (*Tehilim*, 68:20), 'Blessed is Hashem, each and every day.'" In other words, if he found a nice piece of food in the market, he would eat it that day and trust that the Creator would allow him to find an even better one on Friday. Additionally, Hillel's actions can be interpreted to demonstrate his belief that Hashem is imminently present and intricately involved with us at every step of our journey on every day of the week. Just as we must "honor Shabbos," we must "honor" the Divine root of each and every day of the week.

SHABBOS AT THE END, THE GOAL

According to Beis Shammai, if you see something nice on Sunday, put it aside for Shabbos; "from Sunday (begin looking forward) to Shabbos." In this view, Shabbos is the culmination of the week and everything is moving towards Shabbos.

This theological/spiritual perspective of Beis Shammai, of the week moving towards Shabbos, is also translated into other areas of Halachah. For example, from three days before Shabbos we are not to board ships, nor schedule certain medical procedures, and so forth, if possible. As the whole week is a movement towards Shabbos, we are highly sensitive to honoring the coming of Shabbos on every day of the week, preparing for Shabbos, and always having Shabbos in mind.

When we are always preparing for Shabbos we marry each weekday to Shabbos. In Hebrew, weekdays are called *Chol*, which is the root of the words *Choleh* / sick and *Chalal* / hollow. In a world without Shabbos, without this all-consuming goal and focus, every day of our lives would be sensed as inherently empty and lacking. We would constantly yearn and desire, causing us to pursue one thing after another, with no satisfaction. We would forever be left feeling 'sick' or deficient, sensing that something is missing. Yet, when Chol is married to Shabbos, we are able to bridge desire and ambition with spiritual satisfaction. Because of this, the sense of unwellness and emptiness of Chol is transformed into desire and yearning for Shabbos. We are able to redirect our physical hunger and psychological longing into spiritual hunger and soulful longing for Shabbos. This transmutation of our innate hungers and longings elevates them in such a way that they in turn may elevate us through their conscious cultivation and creative intention, rather than constantly distracting and sabotaging us along our desired path.

YEARNING FOR SHABBOS

Rabbi Shimon ben Lakish said, "The Holy One, Blessed be He, gives a person an additional soul on Shabbos eve, and at the conclusion of Shabbos removes it from him, as it is stated, 'He ceased from work and was refreshed (וינפש)' (Shemos, 31:17). Since he ceased from work (and now Shabbos has concluded and his additional soul is removed from him), וי / woe for the additional soul (נפש) that is lost" (*Beitzah*, 16a).

In this teaching, it is implied that וינפש is divided into two words: וי / woe and נפש / soul. When the Nefesh departs, then 'woe' is left in place of 'refreshment.' This is the sadness many feel on Motzei Shabbos, the very beginning of the week. Everything has a purpose. What is the inner purpose of this 'woe'? On one level, we realize that we have had the experience of an extra (dose of) soul on Shabbos from the fact that on Motzei Shabbos we feel its departure and its looming absence. On another level, it is precisely this sense of absence that creates the longing and excitement to be connected to the extra soul again, that impels us to actively prepare for Shabbos, to enjoy the *Ohr* / light of Shabbos again; and seek to carry, kindle, and integrate it into the week.

On Shabbos, we receive the extra soul, which manifests as a heightened sense of having arrived, a tangible presence, a feeling of fullness or completion. This sense of deep contentment is a positive experiential proof in and of itself. However, the absence of this extra soul and the corresponding longing and yearning that we experience on Motzei Shabbos, or on the first days of the week, is arguably more precious and productive, as it is a prerequisite for such a positive experience. And it is Reish Lakish, the Baal Teshuvah, who gives us this teaching, as he knows the benefit and purpose of yearning, separation, and discontent. These restless feelings are fuel for the fires of the soul. From a place of inclusive Yichud, the experience of fullness and the experience of absence, the manifestation of contentment and the manifestation of longing, are one and the same greater dynamic, as you cannot have one without the other.

A COMPLETE SHABBOS

A *Chol* / void is an emptiness that needs to be filled. By its very definition, work operates in a dynamic of emptiness and fulfillment. To work is to strive to complete what is lacking. Something is missing, and your work is a movement to fill that abyss. Movement itself suggests that something is not yet perfect, there is a *Cheser* / lack, and there is a trajectory toward satisfying that lack. Shabbos, on the other hand, is beyond any polarity of lack and fulfilment, beyond any possibility of Cheser or destruction. Not only does Shabbos complete the emptiness of the week, Shabbos itself is called "complete" (*Zohar* 2, p. 88b). Our greeting on Shabbos is *Shabbat Shalom*, which means 'A peaceful Shabbos,' but also 'a complete Shabbos.' Shabbos is a completion beyond the place of incompleteness. It radiates its unconditional wellbeing and fulfilment.

There is a world of *Cheser* / lack, and there is a world of *Sheleimus* / completion. Weekday is fundamentally the world of Cheser (*Arvei haNachal*, Bereshis, Drush 5). In the words of our sages, *HaOlam Chasar Menuchah; Ba Shabbos, Ba Menuchah* / "The world was lacking rest; Shabbos came and rest entered." In truth, not only *was* the world missing something, but by definition the world *is* a state of 'missing.' Shabbos, by contrast, is the world of *Shalem* / completeness. Shabbos is called *Shalom* / peace and wholeness (*Zohar* 3, 176b).

Shabbos completes the emptiness, the void of the week. Shabbos is the fullness that completes the desiring and yearning of Chol. The work we do during the week in order to fill a lack is, by nature, still related to the category of 'lack.' As work involves filling a lack, work remains existentially in a state of lack. Only by stopping work and 'not doing' can the core existential lack be filled. Only the *Menuchah* / rest, the 'beingness' of Shabbos, can fill our emptiness.

HEALING IS A RETURN TO WHOLENESS

Shabbos completes the week and brings healing to our past, returning us to wholeness. When we say a prayer for someone, on Shabbos, that needs healing, we say, "It is Shabbos, and we should not cry out; healing is close at hand" (*Shabbos*, 12a). Shabbos heals all sickness and brokenness, physical, emotional, mental and spiritual. The *Pasuk* / verse (Shemos, 21:19) says, רק שבתו יתן ורפא ירפא, which homiletically (and in a different context) can mean, "All he needs to give is rest, and then healed, he shall be healed.' Healing comes through the mere act of resting on Shabbos (*Likutei Levi Yitzchak*, p.60). Shabbos completes and makes whole, not only the week, but all of our deficiencies and illnesses. Shabbos is that missing piece which returns us to our missing peace.

Adam and Chava spent their first Shabbos in *Gan Eden* / Paradise, even after they sinned. In other words, after sinking into a paradigm of duality and separation, Shabbos allowed them to remain in their primordial state of unity, bliss and purity. Their exile only ensued after Shabbos ended.

The root word of Shabbos also means *return*, and on Shabbos we too return to Gan Eden, our primordial state; even if our deeds have been splintered and separative.

Paradise is a reality in which everything is perfect, whole and complete. The paradisiacal nature of Shabbos allows us to realize that everything of our past can be healed, fixed and integrated, and that all mistakes can be repaired. From this perspective of wholeness, you can realize that there are no 'mistakes.' What you thought may have been purposeless, or a wrong move, was actually Divinely orchestrated and *meant to be*, with the purpose of propelling you to return to the state of Shabbos.

Shabbos completes the past, and even deeper than that, it reveals the wholeness (and holiness) that is always-already present within the past.

SHABBOS AT THE BEGINNING, GIVING FOCUS

The House of Hillel conceives of Shabbos not as a place to reach, rather, as a place to come from. In this way, Shabbos blesses the entire week that follows (*Zohar*. See also *Aruch haShulchan*, Orach Chayim, 242:2). Shabbos is the *Mekor haBerachos* / source of blessings. Shabbos is the fountain and foundation of all blessings; כי הברכה ביום השבת היא מעין הברכות / "...for the blessing on Shabbos is the source and fountain of all blessings" (Ramban, *Bereishis*, 2:3). Even our material and financial blessings for wellbeing are drawn down on Shabbos. (Shabbos is called a *Chok* (*Shemos*, 15:25 *Mechilta*, ad loc. *Sanhedrin*, 56b), and material livelihood and sustenance is called a *Chok* as well (*Mishlei*, 30:8. *Beitza*, 16a). Shabbos is the source of all blessings of sustenance. *Markeves HaMishnah* on the Mechilta, ibid). On Shabbos we receive from Above all the potential blessings that will be revealed during the course of the week. Whereas on Shabbos these blessings are in the realm of the spirit, during the course of the week these blessings become manifest in physical reality (Ohr haChayim, *Shemos*, 16:25).

If Shabbos is just the destination and culmination of our week, then Shabbos remains Shabbos and *Chol* / weekdays remain weekdays. However, when we regard Shabbos as the foundation and source of the coming week, then the Kedushah of Shabbos begins to permeate the weekday and elevates the whole week into Kedushah.*

Hashem "rested" on the Seventh Day, on Shabbos (Shemos, 20:11). What does "resting" mean for the Creator? "Hashem rested," say our sages, "means that Hashem *created* rest" (*Medrash Rabbah*, Bereishis, 10:10). On the Seventh Day, Hashem created the reality of rest — in this way, rest is not merely inaction or non-activity, as in resting *from* activity, rather it is a positively existing inner rest, a fullness of being, harmony and tranquility. This kind of rest does not necessarily follow work, rather it can also precede work and even co-exist with work. Pre-Creation was (or is) only be-ing. The rest that was created and introduced to the 'doing' of Creation is not merely a means to attain a state of pre-Creation being, rather, it is a being state that includes and embraces doing, and is thus the root cause and context of all our doing.

---

* There is a prohibition to destroy or erase any of the Seven Names of Hashem, such as the Name, Hashem, (Yud-Hei-Vav-Hei) or Ado-noi, or Elo-ha. Upon this prohibition, the Rambam rules (*Hilchos Yesodei haTorah*, 6:3), "All (the letters) which are connected to the Name by being placed before (the Name itself), may be erased. For example... the letter Beis in *b'Elokim*, and the like. They do not possess the same degree of sanctity as the Name. All (the letters) which are connected to the Name by being placed after (the Name itself), for example, the final Chaf of Elo'ke**cha**... and the like, may *not* be erased. They are considered like the other letters of the Name, because the Name conveys sanctity upon them." In other words, whatever comes *after* the Kedushah is also Kadosh (on some level). This also applies to Shabbos and the week.

Beis Shammai's and Beis Hillel's polar perspectives on Shabbos are also reflected in another debate amongst the sages, illustrated within the following scenario. A person is traveling in the desert and forgets which day of the week it is and therefore does not know when Shabbos is (See also *Shulchan Aruch*, Orach Chayim, 344:1). What should he do? "Rav Huna said, he must count six days (from today) and observe the Seventh Day as Shabbos. Rav Chiyya bar Rav said, He must observe the first day as Shabbos and count afterward six 'weekdays' until the next Shabbos." What is the basis of their argument? One opinion holds that the traveler must follow the sequence of Creation, first the Six Days of Creation and then Shabbos.*

The other opinion holds that the traveler must follow the order of the creation of Adam, who was created on the Sixth Day of Creation, and soon thereafter began the Seventh Day, Shabbos (*Shabbos*, 69b. The Gemara sides with the opinion of Rav Huna).

Either we follow the order of the Creation of the Universe — six weekdays and then Shabbos, or we follow the creation of Adam — first Shabbos and then six weekdays.

---

* The created, manifest world of Tikun, is connected to the seven (lower) attributes, from Chesed to Malchus, Sunday being Chesed, Monday being Gevurah and Shabbos Malchus. Yet, there is also a higher dimension of Shabbos that is connected to Keser / Chochmah / Binah / Da'as. This higher dimension is the Shabbos that 'precedes' Creation (although deep within the Shabbos of Creation itself is the Shabbos that 'precedes' Creation). Shabbos comes before the creation of the six days (Rabbi Shabtai Donolo, *Chachmoni*, on Sefer Yetzirah, end of Chap. 4). If Creation begins on what is now called the 25th of Elul, the Shabbos before Creation must have been on the 24th of Elul. The Rashash reveals an even deeper level of Shabbos. The Creation of our world (of Tikun) begins on the 25th of Elul, yet, there is also a 'Creation before Creation,' a week of the World of Tohu, which begins on the 18th of Elul, and the "Shabbos" before the Creation of the World of Tohu is the 17th of Elul.

Whichever way, in the above scenario when we do not know when the actual seventh day of the week is, and we count and dedicate a day as Shabbos, that Shabbos is not merely 'symbolically' Shabbos, it actually *is* Shabbos for us. According to Torah law, it is in fact the real Shabbos (*Teshuvos haRadbaz* 1, Siman 76. This also seems to be the opinion of *Rabbeinu* Bachya, Bamidbar, 15:32). Through our counting and dedicating days we create the 'existence' of Shabbos. In the image of the Creator, we too can *create rest*.

THE 'EXISTENCE' & THE KEDUSHAH OF SHABBOS

There is the מציאות השבת / *Metziyus haShabbos* / the Existence of Shabbos, and there is the קדושת השבת / *Kedushas haShabbos* / the Sanctity of Shabbos. Kedushas haShabbos is gifted to us from Above, without our work or prayers (*Zohar* 3, 94a. *Pri Eitz Chayim*, Sha'ar 20:1). Shabbos is מקדשא וקיימא / *Mikadsha v'Keima* / Sanctified and Established (*Beitzah*, 17a. *Chulin*, 101b); it does not need the *Kiddush Beis Din* / sanctification of the High Court (*Baba Basra*, 121a), as does *Rosh Chodesh* / the first day of the lunar month.

A Yom Tov, in contrast to Shabbos, is sanctified by the high courts of man. Yom Tov follows a lunar cycle. Pesach, for example, is the 15th day of the month of Nisan, and the 15th day is based on Rosh Chodesh Nisan, which is established by the testimony (and today by the calendar) of man. If two witnesses came to the High Court in *Yerushalayim* / Jerusalem on Tuesday and testified that they had seen the new moon last night, the Courts would *Mikadesh* / sanctify Tuesday as Rosh Chodesh, the first day of the month, and fifteen days later would be the first day of Pesach. Theoretically, if no witnesses showed up on Tuesday, then Wednesday would be declared the first day of the month and Pesach would be fifteen days from that Wednesday. Human beings thus sanctify Rosh Chodesh, and by extension sanctify and establish the days of that month's Yom Tov. So much so, that midrashically speaking, when the angels on high ask when will be Rosh Hashanah, Hashem tells them, "You are asking Me? Let us, Me and you, go ask the courts below" (*Yalkut Shimoni*, Tehilim, 831).

Yom Tov liturgy uses the phrase, *Mikadesh Yisrael ve-haZemanim* / (Hashem), Who sanctifies Israel — and through Israel, the times"; as it is only through Israel that the day is sanctified. Whereas on Shabbos the liturgy uses the phrase *Mikadesh haShabbos* / ...Who Sanctifies Shabbos (*Pesachim*, 117b). The Kedushas haShabbos is not dependent on us. When the seventh day of the week ensues, the Kedushah of Shabbos descends without our involvement.

Yet, in order for there to be a Kedushah of Shabbos, there needs to be *Metziyus* / an 'existence' of Shabbos, and that existence comes from our conscious observation and honoring of Shabbos in time.* Through our observation and counting of days, we create the Metziyus of Shabbos and then the Kedushah of Shabbos can descend into it, as it were. Perhaps this is what the Rambam means when he contrasts the sanctification of the new moon and Shab-

---

* Writes the Magen Avraham, regarding the scenario of a person who is lost in the desert and does not know when Shabbos is, ואף על גב דרוב ימים הם חול זה מקרי קבוע. So although the majority of the week is mundane, since he does not know when Shabbos is, there is a *Safek* / doubt. Regarding such a Safek, the Halachah is to follow according to the majority. Thus, since the majority of days are weekdays, why keep one day of Shabbos at all? Says the Magen Avraham, because Shabbos is קבוע / *Kavua* / established, and the Din is that קבוע is not *Batel* / nullified.

bos, "The (establishment of Rosh Chodesh) based on the sighting of the moon is not the province of every individual, as is the Shabbos. (In the latter instance,) everyone counts six days and rests on the Seventh Day" (*Hilchos Kidush haChodesh*, 1:5. "Shabbos is given over — to count — to each individual." *Teshuvas haRadbaz*, 1, Siman 76. *Chayei Adam*, beginning of Hilchos Shabbos). We need to count six days so there can be the seventh day. Sunday is always Sunday whether we are aware of it or not. On the other hand, if hypothetically we all lost count of the days of the week, the Kedushah of Shabbos would not have a specific 'seventh day' upon which to descend. There cannot be a Kedushah of Shabbos without the Metziyus of an actual day of Shabbos. Shabbos is 'the holy day of Shabbos' because it is the seventh day that we count and observe from Sunday.*

This is the reason that when one is lost in a desert (or in a more modern analogy, orbiting the earth in a spaceship), his counting is what creates the seventh day, the Metziyus of Shabbos; he establishes when the Metziyus of Shabbos is, and then the Kedushah of Shabbos descends from Above *on its own*, as it were.

---

* This is the reason why there is a *Hava-mina* / original thought in the *Mechilta*, that if all the Jewish people 'desecrated' Shabbos (according to law, for example, in a time of war, or maybe even if a war ends on Shabbos), there is no Shabbos (*Mechilta*, Shemos, 31:14). Why is there such a Hava-mina? If it is because all of Shabbos is "one unit of 24 hours," and once broken, the entirety is broken (as the *Tzafnas Paneach* learns), then why does the Mechilta offer such a far-fetched example, where everyone desecrated Shabbos, and not simply say if an individual desecrated Shabbos? The Rebbe understands the Mechilta as saying that perhaps there would be no Kedushah of Shabbos if there was no Metziyos of Shabbos, as in a case when the entire community 'desecrates' Shabbos (*Likutei Sichos* 8, p. 49-60). Perhaps these two ideas of Shabbos are related to the two concepts of Shabbos; our 'creating Shabbos' (giving it Metziyus) and 'observing the laws of Shabbos' (receiving its Kedushah) (*Chidushei haGriz*, (the back of the *Beis haLevi*) 202).

This scenario of either counting six days then observing Shabbos or first observing Shabbos then counting six days, seems to play out in our lives as well, every week. If Shabbos is the culmination of the week, then we should follow Beis Shammai and put aside all superior foods or enjoyments for Shabbos. If Shabbos is the source of the week, impregnating the week with Holiness, then we should follow Beis Hillel and enjoy the Kedushas Shabbos that manifests each day. The truth is, however, these approaches are not mutually exclusive, rather they work together.

THE REWARD IN THE PRESENT

When we *combine* the approaches of Beis Shammai and Beis Hillel, Shabbos is both the completing culmination of the week and the guiding inspiration for the week. In this dynamic construct, work and rest balance and complete each other. Our rest completes our work, as work without rest is physically, psychologically, mentally and spiritually depleting. Our rest also nourishes our work, giving it focus and intentionality.

The effects then snowball, as our work improves our Shabbos, our Shabbos improves our work, which then improves our next Shabbos even more, and so on.

When we rest from materialistic preoccupations we open time to engage in matters of the spirit. Free from labor we can concentrate on intellectual and spiritual issues, as well as on our families and loved ones, without any expectation of outcome. In a 'doing' modality we are always thinking about results; if I work x amount of hours I will take in x amount of money. This is result-oriented, purpose-driven 'movement,' with an intent to change the status of being.

Shabbos is being without a goal, without trying to make a change or profit. In fact, there is no need for movement or transformation at all in this state. This non-doing is *not* assuming a glazed, hollow-emptiness and apathy; rather, it is an existential freedom from the compulsion to change or manipulate life as it is in the moment. When we focus for one day on just being in the moment, with no reference to a future or past, Shabbos reveals that "the reward of a Mitzvah is the Mitzvah itself." The journey itself is the destination. Shabbos is the World-to-Come, and the *S'char* / positive consequence of our Mitzvos, radiating in the eternal present for us to access and experience now.

Shabbos is not merely a מעין עולם הבא / *Mei'ein Olam haBa* / taste of the World-to-Come, rather, מעיין עולם הבא / *Ma'ayan Olam haBa* / A Wellspring of the World-to-Come; a spring from the future that irrigates the present. And we are blessed with the opportunity to immerse and drink from this infinite wellspring of the future in the here and now.

When we properly enter the Kedushah of Shabbos the sensation that, "All your work is done" / *Kol Melachtecha Asuyah* (*Mechilta d'Rebbe Yishmael*, Yisro, 7), is truly felt; in terms of both physical and spiritual work. We bask in the light of Olam haBa sensing the reward in the present. Then when we re-enter the world of doing/movement/journey/noise, we retain a רשימו / *Reshimu* / an imprint of Shabbos, and that imprint of the Infinite illuminates and blesses the coming week (*Zohar* 2, 63b). In this way, we continue to feel the *Tachlis* / purposeful end, the reward, the destination of our journey, even as we walk through the week.

SHABBOS IN THE MIDDLE OF THE WEEK

As Shabbos is both the culmination and the foundation of the week, another way of perceiving Shabbos is that it is in the middle of the week. From this perspective, Shabbos is the center of the week, with Wednesday, Thursday and Friday being the three days preceding Shabbos, referred to as קמי שבתא / *Kamei Shabbata* / before Shabbos, and Sunday, Monday and Tuesday being the three days following Shabbos, called בתר שבתא / *Basar Shabbata* / after Shabbos (*Pesachim*, 106a. *Gitin*, 77b). Shabbos is like the central pole of a Menorah, with "six branches coming out on each side; three branches to the right and three to the left" (Shemos, 25:32). In this way, the focal point of every week day is Shabbos, as the flames atop each of the six branches incline toward the center. Shabbos simultaneously impregnates and completes each day, as each branch of the Menorah simultaneously emanates from the central pole, and inclines its light towards it.

Rav Eliyahu De Vidas (16th Century, Tzfas, Israel) creates a diagram to illustrate the centrality of Shabbos during the cycle of the week, where he places Shabbos in the innermost circle, and the days of the week surrounding it (*Reishis Chochmah*, Shaar haKedushah, Chap. 2). Shabbos is, in this way, the essence of the week, with traces of its *Koach* and *Chayus* / energy and vital life-force emanating out into the three days that follow, as well as traces of its Koach and Chayus embraced by the three days which preceded.

This notion of Shabbos overflowing into the first three days of the week, and retroactively irrigating the three days prior, has practical *Halachic* / legal applications.

As mentioned, three days before Shabbos it is forbidden to undertake a journey by sea (*Shabbos*, 19a) or schedule a significant medical procedure, if there is no emergency. Since in general it takes at least three days to become acclimated to the sea, and the same amount of time to recover from certain procedures, we need to plan for that adjustment period properly, so we can ensure that our Shabbos will be restful. According to this perspective, we would not need to worry about the effects of such actions on Shabbos when it is still Sunday, Monday or Tuesday, since these three days are part of the Shabbos that precedes. But from Wednesday forward we need to guard Shabbos, as it is already 'beginning.' The construct of *Erev Shabbos* / the Eve of Shabbos, the accepting of Shabbos, already begins on Wednesday, writes Rabbeinu Bachya (Shemos, 1:2-3).

Every day we recite a particular Psalm, called the *Shir Shel Yom* / Song of the Day, in our prayers. These are the songs that were sung by the *Levi'im* / Levites in the Beis haMikdash. On Wednesday we recite Chapter 94 of *Tehilim* / Psalms, however, we conclude the song with the first three verses from chapter 95, לכו נרננה / "Come, let us sing praises to Hashem; let us shout to the Rock of our Salvation..." These are the verses with which we open *Kabbolas Shabbos* / the acceptance of Shabbos. And so, on Wednesday, when a glimmer of the upcoming Shabbos begins to enter, we joyfully 'begin' the service of Kabbolas Shabbos.

AN EXTRA SOUL

As mentioned earlier, on Shabbos we are gifted with an "extra soul" (*Betiza*, 16a). Rav Yitzchak / Isaac Luria (1534-1572), universally known as the Arizal, an acronym for "the G-dly Rabbi Isaac of blessed memory," revealed (*Sha'ar Hakavanos*, p. 61a) that we need to start thinking more seriously about Shabbos on Wednesday, not just because in three days it will be Shabbos, rather, because on Wednesday we already receive something of the Nefesh-level of the extra soul of the coming Shabbos.

Within the 'extra soul' that we receive on Shabbos there are three levels: Nefesh, Ruach, and Neshamah. The Nefesh level of the soul is associated with our blood, with our liver, and with our digestive system. On an elementary level, Nefesh is our subtle bioenergy. Nefesh is the animating 'intelligence' of the physical body, organizing the cells of the body and all its functions, instincts, and sensory experiences. Our survival instincts are an expression of our Nefesh. This is part of our 'sustaining' and 'vegetative' aspect of soul. The Nefesh ensures survival, expanding and growing the body.

Ruach is more subtle than our tangible, perceived physicality. Emotions, devotional expressions, and creative self-expressions are part of our Ruach consciousness. Ruach is associated with the heart, the expansiveness of feeling and the ability to sense something greater and beyond ourselves. Ruach is our emotional reality.

Neshamah is our rational self, the place of free choice. Neshamah gives us the ability to choose our life, and choose it according to the deepest resources of our deepest selves. Neshamah is our mental reality.

Accordingly, Nefesh corresponds to *Ma'aseh*, the world of action. Ruach corresponds to the world of *Dibbur* / speech; and Neshamah corresponds to *Machshavah*, the world of thoughts.

The extra spiritual boost that we receive on Shabbos is threefold; we are empowered to elevate 1) our Nefesh so that our physical actions are more holy, mindful and focused, 2) our Ruach so that our emotions are more holy, alive and dedicated, and 3) our Neshamah so that our mental state is more holy, sharp and focused. As the Even Ezra writes (*Bereishis*, 2:3), "on Shabbos we are blessed with extra intelligence."

These three levels — of Shabbos experience — enter in stages on Shabbos evening, but they already begin to assimilate into consciousness three days prior. On Wednesday, a measure of Nefesh of the upcoming Shabbos begins to enter. On Thursday, a measure of Ruach enters, and on Friday, a measure of the Neshamah enters.

On Wednesday, we are infused with the Nefesh quality of Shabbos so that our actions can become more elevated, and at the same time we should begin to pay extra attention to our actions. On Thursday, we are injected with an extra Ruach quality of Shabbos, so that our emotions can be more properly aroused, and we also need to pay more attention to our emotions. On Friday, we receive an extra Neshamah quality of Shabbos, so that our mental/intellectual state is potentially more elevated, and accordingly, we too need to be more cautious and aware of our thoughts on Friday.

This process is reversed during the days of *Basar Shabbata* / after Shabbos. The quality of Shabbos extends into the following three days after Shabbos to the extent that we are even allowed to recite

Havdalah / the separation service until Tuesday (*Pesachim*, 106a. According to our version in the *Yerushalmi* one can recite Havdalah until Thursday, the end of the week. *Berachos*, 5:2. Although see the *Chareidim*, ad loc). Just as the Nefesh, Ruach and Neshamah enter in stages, they also leave in stages. On Sunday, the extra Neshamah of Shabbos still exists in our consciousness. As Monday departs, the extra Ruach of Shabbos departs, and at the end of Tuesday the Nefesh of Shabbos expires; making way for the Nefesh of the next Shabbos to enter.

In this way, Friday and Sunday are days more connected with *Machshavah* / thought and our mental state. Thus, Sunday is a good time to think and plan the week ahead, and Friday is a good time to think about our spiritual, inner selves and lives. These are good days to pay extra attention to our thoughts.

Thursday and Monday are days more connected with Dibbur, corresponding to the Torah readings that are recited in Shul on Mondays and Thursdays. These days are good times to communicate and pay special attention to our speech.

Wednesday and Tuesday are more connected with Ma'aseh / actions; and are therefore good times to initiate projects and pay extra attention to our actions (*Pri Eitz Chayim*, Sha'ar haShabbos, 1)

Machshavah, Dibbur, and Ma'aseh, again, embodied in the days of Sunday/Friday, Monday/Thursday, and Tuesday/Wednesday, also correspond to the three inner worlds (which we will explore more fully later on), called *Beriah* / Creation, the world of thought, *Yetzirah* / Formation, the world of speech, and *Asiyah* / Doing, the world of action. For duality to emerge from the Oneness of Hashem there had to have been a progressive process (as the Creator 'chose' to create in a way that is comprehensible to man). First there was a Divine 'thought,' an inner 'movement' within the 'Mind' of the Creator, as it were, to externalize and bring Creation into existence. This is where conceptual time-space was created. The Divine 'thought' became further externalized until it was revealed as a 'word,' existing in the form of a 'vibration.' And then finally, the original thought became a tangible phenomenon of time and space, as the physical world of Asiyah.

Shabbos, again, pictured as the center of the six days, embodies the world of Atzilus, the world of Unity. Atzilus transcends time and space. It is a reality in which the 'vessels' (the potentiality of finitude corresponding to the eventually manifest creation of finite physicality) exist completely absorbed in the Light of Hashem, and thus there is only Infinity.

As the center of the week, Shabbos is the reality of Infinity that branches out into the six directions of space-time: right, left, front, back, up and down, with Shabbos symbolized as an elusive center point of the cube. The six directions correspond to the six days of the week: Wednesday/Thursday/Friday correspond to above, below, and to the right of Shabbos. Sunday/Monday/Tuesday correspond to the spaces to the left, behind, and in front of Shabbos.

As mentioned earlier, the conventional week begins on Sunday and leads up to Shabbos, yet, from another vantage point, Shabbos is the point in the middle which flows outward into Sunday, Monday and Tuesday, and begins to sparkle anew from Wednesday onward.

Just as the spiral of the week, with the days revolving around Shabbos at the center, includes a cycling through levels, there is also a sense of progression from beginning to end, building up from Sunday and culminating with Friday and then Shabbos. Just as "Hashem spoke one, and we heard two," we are able to experience both of these models simultaneously; on Sunday we begin to prepare for the next Shabbos while simultaneously descending slightly from the previous Shabbos.

WEDNESDAY	THURSDAY	FRIDAY	SHABBOS	SUNDAY	MONDAY	TUESDAY
Nefesh Enters	Ruach Enters	Neshamah Enters	Chayah & Yechidah	Neshamah Departs	Ruach Departs	Nefesh Departs
Action	Speech	Thought	Being	Thought	Speech	Action
Asiyah	Yetzirah	Beriyah	Atzilus	Beriyah	Yetzirah	Asiyah

IKAR / SHABBOS / HASHEM & TAFEL / CHOL (WEEKDAY) / ELOKIM

Weekday is called חול / *Chol*, from the root word *Chal* / empty, hollow. Every work day of the week has an empty core, an existential and spiritual sense of emptiness and lack, and this emptiness is filled with the sense of 'completeness' and 'oneness' when we actively engage Shabbos. For this reason, when the Torah speaks of the desecration of Shabbos, it is referred to as חילול שבת / *Chilul Shabbos*. The word *Chilul* comes from the word חלל / *Chalal* / empty tube. Desecrating the Shabbos is to take the 'center' of the week, the Infinity within the rhythm of the week, and render it as Chol, just another of the 'empty' days of the week. Via Chilul Shabbos, one is effectively emptying the source of energy not only from Shabbos but also from the entire week.

Insofar as Shabbos is just one day of the week, we might assume that instead of Shabbos being able to affect and elevate the week and transform the six days into a Shabbos-like state, perhaps the workweek has the power to overwhelm Shabbos. Indeed, there is a Torah principle of בטל ברוב / *Batel b'Rov* / a minority is nullified in the majority. According to Torah law, one item can be nullified in only two items — how much more so one in six.

There is, however, another principle at play, and that is עיקר / *Ikar* / primary importance and טפל / *Tafel* / secondary importance. Within the laws of carrying on Shabbos, this principle comes into focus. Say, for example, a person carries a sizable bowl from his private home into a public domain on Shabbos. He would be liable as he violated the prohibition of carrying and transporting an inanimate object from one domain to another. Now, suppose this same person takes a tiny piece of bread — less than the amount considered to be a food item — and places the bread in the exact same bowl, and then carries the bowl into a public domain. In this case, he is not doing Chilul Shabbos. Why? Because the intention was to carry the bread, which was the Ikar, and the person only carried out the bowl as a vessel to hold the bread, and the bread was too small to violate the prohibition of carrying. The bowl was Tafel, secondary, and a Tafel object is nullified to the Ikar object (*Shabbos*, 93b).

Shabbos is the *Tachlis* / end-intention, the ultimate purpose in Creation. It is the Ikar of Creation, to which all else is nullified. Shabbos, the center of the week, is therefore more in a position to affect and elevate all the days of Chol, rather than to be impacted by them. Through Shabbos, all life comes into focus. Certainly, in the future, when every day becomes Shabbos, the emptiness and strain of Chol will be nullified and we will bask in the 'reward' of millennia of toil as we sit and rest in the revealed Presence of Hashem.

Like the bowl and the piece of bread, the weekday is the vessel carrying the Ikar reality which is Shabbos. Similarly, the world is called the vessel of the Divine Name Elokim, and the Name Elokim is called the vessel of the Divine Name Hashem.

The mundane world is created via the Divine Name Elokim, as the Torah opens with the words, "In the beginning, Elokim created..." In fact, the Name Elokim appears 32 times in the Creation narrative. Elokim is the Divine attribute or expression that is connected to the physical and finite world. The natural world is governed by Elokim via the laws-of-nature, thus *Elokim* and *haTeva* / the Natural are equal in numerical value.[*] The creation of the physical, the dimensional and the dualistic world (Heaven and earth, night and day, upper and lower) emerges from Elokim and Elokim rules Heaven and earth (*Tur*, Orach Chayim, 5). Indeed, all sense of plurality is created through Elokim. That is why the Name Elokim is spelled in the plural, *-im* implying 'many.'

Elokim is the Divine flow sustaining the physical world, so in comparison to the animating and enlivening force, the world (*Olam* in Hebrew) is the Tafel, the secondary *Kli* / vessel that contains the light of Elokim. And thus, *Olam* in numerical value is 146,[**] which is the same as the word *Kli Elokim* / vessel of Elokim.[***] However,

---

[*] *Elokim:* Aleph/1, Lamed/30, Hei/5, Yud/10, Mem/40 = 86 *haTeva*: Hei/5, Tes/9, Beis/2, Ayin/70 = 86

[**] Ayin/70, Vav/6, Lamed/30, Mem/40 = 146.

[***] *Kli:* Kuf/20, Lamed/30, Yud/10 = 60 *Elokim* (86). 60, 86 = 146.

in comparison to the higher Divine Name, Hashem or Yud-Hei-Vav-Hei, Elokim is merely a Kli. The numerical value of *Elokim* (86) is exactly the value of the phrase, *Kli Hashem* (60 + 26 = 86) / the Vessel of the Name. In this way, the Olam is the Kli of Elokim, and Elokim is the Kli of Hashem.

Chol, the mundane weekday and world of duality, is connected to the Name Elokim, while Shabbos is connected to the Name Hashem, *Yom laHashem* / "a day of ('to') Hashem" (*Devarim*, 5:13). Shabbos is the center of Creation and its inner point of Infinity. The Name Hashem represents the utterly Transcendent One. These four letters, Yud-Hei-Vav and Hei, when rearranged, can spell out the words *Hayah* / it was (past), *Hoveh* / it is (present) — and when you exchange the Vav for another Yud (the Vav is understood to be an elongated Yud) it spells *Ye'hiyeh* / it will be (future). This Name, then, represents the simultaneous totality of all past, present and future — Infinite Transcendence, beyond any conception of time; extending from before the past, into the present moment and on into the future and 'beyond.'

Experientially as well, the weekdays are an Elokim reality, as the Name Elokim represents rulership (*Medrash Rabbah*, Shemos, 3), dominion (Even Ezra, *Bereishis*, 1:1), and mastery (Rashi, *Bereishis*, 6:2). During the week we are busy mastering the world around us, manipulating nature, whether planting, sewing or exercising. One way or another we are working to gain mastery over the world around us and trying to push the present along to make it into a 'better' future. On Shabbos, we are gifted with a taste of infinity, a reality beyond time or progress, an ability to just be present, without the urge to manipulate. To experientially be beyond movement, and tap into our already and always 'perfect' soul — this is the transcendent space of Shabbos, beyond all manipulation, duality and movement.

When we are able to experience Shabbos on this higher/deeper level of 'perfection' and transcendence, we can then step beyond it into the essential level of Shabbos, which is simultaneously transcendent and yet all-inclusive of immanence. This level includes and even embraces Chol and 'work.' It is not only beyond duality, but beyond being beyond duality. It is a transcendence and unity that includes within it, as it were, duality and multiplicity.

YOM SHEKULO SHABBOS / A DAY ON WHICH ALL IS SHABBOS

We have described three levels of experiencing Shabbos: 1) as the culmination of the week, 2) as the source of the week, and 3) as the center and Ikar of the week. These three levels of experience are accessible to us within the day of Shabbos itself. However, the fourth dimension of Shabbos is only revealed after Shabbos, on Motzei Shabbos, especially during the meal of *Melaveh Malkah* / the escorting of the Queen.

After Havdalah, the prayer ritual that separates Shabbos from Chol, we sit down and eat the Melaveh Malkah meal. While this meal is eaten after the conclusion of Shabbos, after Havdalah, it too is in honor of the Shabbos Queen. It is celebrated on a weekday, yet it is also an extension of Shabbos, and thus it represents a quality of Shabbos that is beyond Havdalah, beyond the distinction of weekday and Shabbos. The Arizal teaches that until midnight on Motzei Shabbos there is a *Ha'aros Shabbos* / ray of the light of Shabbos that still permeates the world, and thus we should not recite prayers of penitence or lack until after midnight (See Bnei Yissachar, *Ma'amorei Shabbos*, Ma'amar 2:4). During this period in general, and especially with the celebration of the Melaveh Malkah, we are extending the light of Shabbos into Chol.

This is a level of Shabbos that permeates all of Chol. It is the Tree of Life, of Oneness, and there is no longer any *Havdalah* / separation. This is a state of the ultimate *Hamtakah* / sweetening, in which there is only Yichud and everything without exception is revealing the oneness of Hashem; all time is Shabbos, the Yom laHashem.

As the Melaveh Malkah is connected with the Tree of Life, beyond any form of duality, it embodies the quality of immortality, beyond death and disintegration. There is a tiny and indestructible bone in the body (*Medrash Rabbah*, Bereishis, 28:3), called the *Luz* Bone or *Nisko*, from which the eventual Resurrection of the body will occur (*Midrash Rabbah*, ibid. Vayikra, 18:1. Koheles, 12:5. *Zohar* 2, p. 28b. *Siddur Beis Yaakov*, Melaveh Malkah, p. 206). This bone is located either at the base of the spine or on the back of the skull (*HaAruch*, Erech Luz. *Avodas haKodesh*, 2:40. *Likutei Torah*, (Arizal) Nach, Shoftim), and although it is a finite creation, it does not succumb to the ravages of worms or any other natural putrefaction or disintegration. It is said that this bone receives nourishment and pleasure from the Melaveh Malkah. It is the only meal from which this 'immortal' part of the body receives sustenance (*Beis Yoseph*, Orach Chayim, 300 in the name of the *Shibolei haLeket. Kaf haChayim*, 300:1-2. *Shulchan Aruch haRav* and the

Mishnah Berurah, 300:2 quoting the *Taz*). Although a bone, by definition, is a finite structure, the essence of the Luz Bone is immortal, timeless and 'infinite,' and it is nourished by the meal that embodies 'inclusive transcendence,' the infinity of Shabbos that embraces even the finite dimension of a weekday.

In the Luz Bone, is an expression of the ultimate Yichud; eternity, timelessness and infinity Davka revealed within the finite physical body. This bone represents a finite property that will not expire and disappear into eternity, rather, eternity will enter into and be expressed in dense physicality; Infinity within finitude. Similarly, the meal of Motzei Shabbos occurs in the liminal, unifying space that connects Kodesh and Chol, soul and body, and thus, represents an eighth 'day' or dimension that transcends, embraces and unifies the paradigms of six days and Seventh day.

SIX DAYS / CHOL / MUNDANE WEEKDAY / FINITE	SEVENTH DAY / KODESH / SACRED SHABBOS / INFINITE
'EIGHTH DAY' / BOTH CHOL AND KODESH / MOTZEI SHABBOS / BOTH FINITE AND INFINITE	

Once Shabbos 'ends,' we sit down for a hot meal (hot foods on Motzei Shabbos are healing, *Shabbos,* 119b), which is prepared and cooked after Shabbos, during the 'weekday' when cooking is allowed. We then eat from the Tree of Life, the reality of *Yichud / unity*. If this were merely a spiritual or meditative practice, it would not include physicality, and would remain in a category of duality.

'Inclusive transcendence' is manifested specifically in the act of eating which includes the physical plane. This essential level embraces and includes the lower levels of reality (even the 'workweek' and the 'body') within holiness, without separation.

This paradigm of unity is similar to the ultimate state of the world, *Olam haBa* / the World-to-Come, and indeed, Shabbos is like Olam haBa (*Berachos*, 57b. *Mechilta*, Shemos, 31:13). Olam haBa is the peak of history and existence, when the 'reward' of all our toil in *Olam haZeh* / this World will be manifest. The Ramban writes that Olam haBa will be experienced when our souls are joined (or rejoined) with our bodies, in the time period of Resurrection (*Toras haAdam*, Sha'ar haG'mul. *Targum Yonasan*, Yeshayahu, 58:11. See also Rabbi Menachem Recanti on Bereishis. *Magen Avos*, 3:4. *Ohr Hashem*, 3:1:4. *Beis Elokim*, Sha'ar haYesodos, 53). The peak of goodness and spiritual delight will be experienced when body and soul are re-joined as one, in total harmony and unison. The ultimate transformation, of all 'things' of this world, will become apparent in the state of Olam haBa, when the body will also participate in the greatest of spiritual revelations and become an equal partner in receiving, absorbing, and in turn, projecting the light of the Infinite. The meal of Melaveh Malkah is the glow of Olam haBa; when the holiness of Shabbos has transformed the weekday and body into something that has the *Kedushah* / sacredness of Shabbos itself. As such, it is an opportunity for us to practice and experience a bit of what life will be like upon Redemption; it is an infinite moment for us to live *as if moshiach has already arrived.*

Weekday, Chol is a manifestation of the Tree of Knowledge of Good and Evil — of duality, opposing desires, friction, movement and toil. Shabbos is the Tree of Life — unity, harmony and a space of rest beyond all toil and the onrush of time.

Adam and Chava were created on Friday, placed in the Garden of Eden and told that they could eat from *all* the trees of the Garden, just not from the Tree of Knowledge. The Arizal reveals that the prohibition not to eat from the Tree of Knowledge was temporary, pertaining only to Friday until Shabbos ensued. Once Shabbos began they would have been permitted to eat from the Tree of Knowledge (see also Shach *al-haTorah*, Bereishis. Ben Ish Chai, *Halachos second year*, Parshas Bereishis). This helps explain an apparent contradiction in the statement, on the one hand they are told that they can eat from all the trees, from 'everything,' and yet, the next sentence says that they cannot eat from the Tree of Knowledge. Now we can understand that they could eat from 'everything' once Shabbos arrived, but could not eat from the Tree of Knowledge before Shabbos arrived.

Adam and Chava — and truly us as well — need to first exclusively 'eat' or identify with the Tree of Life, the Oneness of Hashem, the Shabbos mode of being, and then from that basis, proceed to eat and internalize *knowledge*, meaning *distinctions*. In other words: they needed to include duality within the context of unity. They needed to set the foundation of human life in a paradigm of 'Oneness expressed in the many' and 'the many included within the One,' within the *Alma d'Yichudah* / World of Unity.

This scenario demonstrates that there is a level of integration in which the Tree of Knowledge is subsumed and enfolded within the Tree of Life. We can reach a state in which *Chol* (physicality) and duality are embraced within a context of Unity. This state is 'prior to' the *Chet* / sin of eating from the Tree of Knowledge; and the whole world will again be in this integrated state during Olam haBa. Today, 'after' the eating from the Tree of Knowledge, the closest reflection of this dynamic is Motzei Shabbos and the meal of Melaveh Malkah. On Motzei Shabbos we eat a 'Shabbos' meal even after Shabbos. We are still in a Gan Eden state of being — precisely at the point when Adam and Chava were ejected from Gan Eden. This is a *Tikun* / healing of the root of human suffering and mortality, performed at the nexus of the apparent division between soul and body.

The visceral sensation of a person who experiences 'Shabbos' when it is already Motzei Shabbos is that of a paradoxical calm, a relaxation amid opposing energies. For example, one experiences a desire to act, to do a Melachah, yet, this desire for action comes from a place of deep stillness. The Melachah performed is rooted in a deep state of being. It is as if a desire to create sound forms within silence, and the sound itself then arises from within that silence. This is a time of *Etzem* / Essence, simultaneous transcendence and inclusion of all.

Shabbos is completion, Sheleimus. Yet, Shabbos is not only an opposite to the weekday, it is of a higher dimension entirely. Shabbos is *Etzem* / Essence, and thus it includes both the 'Yesh' of weekday struggle, imperfection, and the 'Ayin' of rest, wholeness and perfection.

To be clear, it is not that Motzei Shabbos in its own right is higher or deeper than Shabbos. Rather, it is the converse: the Kedushah and power of Shabbos is so overwhelming and expansive that it overflows into Motzei Shabbos and transforms at least part of Chol into *Kodesh* / sacred. This is the deeper reason why this meal is connected to King David, the grandson of a convert. The *Ger* / convert is someone who was (on a manifest level) on the 'outside,' in the category of Chol, and entered into the 'inside,' into the Kedushah of Klal Yisrael. The convert is the absorption of Chol within Kodesh, or a Kodesh that expands and embraces Chol.

Centuries back, the wise men of the West asked of an illustrious Yemenite sage who was then living in Israel, the Rashash, Rav Shalom Sharabi (1720-1777), an intriguing question (*Nahar Shalom*, 31b). The preface to the question is as follows: It is written in a Kabbalistic text (*Mishnas Chassidim*, HaAtzilus Arvis, Perek 6:2), that during the *Ma'ariv* / evening service of Motzei Shabbos — during the fourth blessing of the Amida — there is the final "coupling" of the metaphysical Bride and Groom (the 'bride' also represents K'neses Yisrael, i.e. us, the physical world and the body). This is why we say in that fourth blessing אתה חוננתנו / *Ata Chonantanu* / You have gifted us... *Chonantanu* has the same letters as חיתון / *Chitun* / marriage. This means that on Motzei Shabbos there is a 'marriage' between the Bride and the Divine Groom. Friday evening is all about the Bride, Shabbos day it is about the Groom, and the ultimate coupling and joining together only occurs on Motzei Shabbos. On Friday evening we say, during the Amida, *Atah Kidashta* / You have betrothed, referring to the time of *Kidushin* / betrothal. During the morning Amida we say, *Yismach Moshe b'Matnas* / Moshe rejoices with the gifts... This represents the gifts that are brought to the wedding (Rashi did not know the reason why we should say Yismach Moshe on Shabbos, and he deleted it from Shacharis. *Sefer haManhig*, 1. p. 150). In Musaf we say, *Atah Konanta* / You have prepared... This is the meal of the wedding. During the Minchah Amidah we say,

Atah Echad / You are One... This represents the unity under the *Chupah* / wedding canopy. And then, on Motzei Shabbos, in the blessings of *Da'as* / knowing (as in Adam 'knew' Chava), we recite *Atah Chonantanu* which is the actual intimacy of the Divine Bride and Groom.

Here is the question posed to the Rashash: insofar as the actual wedding is after Shabbos, how can Shabbos be merely a preparation, laying the groundwork for what will occur on Motzei Shabbos? How can the effect (Motzei Shabbos) be greater than the cause (Shabbos itself)?*

The answer is the following: it is not that Shabbos is a preparation for Motzei Shabbos, rather it is the other way around. The Kedushah of Shabbos is so powerful that it pierces through the wall separating it from the weekdays, spilling into the weekdays, transforming and imbuing them with a Shabbos-like quality. In other words, a unity is created when there is an 'other' that becomes unified. As such, the ultimate unity of the Kedushah and power of Shabbos is one that embraces and enfolds the weekday within the context of Shabbos.**

---

* Perhaps, since in *Kodshim* / the laws of holiness and the Temple, 'the night follows the day,' the meal of Melaveh Malkah is actually part of the meals of Shabbos (see *Assara Ma'amaros*, Ma'amar Chikur Din, 1:21). Or this can be attributed to the concept of the Rashbam on *Bereishis*, 1:15, that before Matan Torah, the night followed the day. And 'principally,' although not in actual post-Matan-Torah Halachah, since Shabbos is connected to a reality of pre-Matan-Torah (and was given, in fact, before Matan Torah, at the encampment in Marah (*Sanhedrin*, 56b)), there is some residue of this idea, and Melaveh Malkah is part of the 'day of Shabbos.' Although, see *Ohr haChayim*, Vayikra, 19:3, at the end.

** Perhaps this explains why שדקמב ויא תובש / there are no Rabbinic decrees enforced in the Beis HaMikdash, as the Gemara in *Eruvin*, 102a -104b, discusses. And this explains why specifically, by Divine providence, אל השבכנ וריחו אלא בשבת / the beginning of conquering and settling the Land of Israel was (specifically) on Shabbos (Yerushalmi, *Shabbos*, 1:8).

Today, for us to experience the Tree of Life, we need to refrain from work on Shabbos; we need to stop 'doing.' It is a negative — a cessation of all 'Tree of Opposites' activity — that allows us to enter the higher being state of Shabbos. Non-doing gives us access to higher being. Yet, Shabbos today is only a 'glimmer' of the World-to-Come, since the highest and deepest state of the world, the actual World-to-Come, includes all doing within being, and all bodily expression within the infinite ground of the soul. Indeed, it is the meal of the Melaveh Malkah which sustains our Luz Bone. And with the Luz bone all those who have passed from their bodies will be resurrected and live on in Olam haBa, in *Neshamos b'Gufim /* souls joined with bodies, eternally. This joining and unifying of all apparent opposites and dichotomies is the essence of Shabbos and the ultimate goal of all creation. "And on that day Hashem will be one and His name will be One."

This also has practical application (Yerushalmi, *Moed Katan,* 2:4. *Gittin,* 8b), as buying land is similar to the process of conquering (*Eglei Tal,* Tochen, 38:6). All of this expresses the "inclusion" of a type of "work" on Shabbos, or of the inclusion of Shabbos into what is normally considered "work." See also, Yerushalmi, *Shabbos,* 1:5.

08

FOUR LEVELS OF SHABBOS REST

AS EXPLORED, THERE IS A NEFESH, RUACH AND NESHAMAH of Shabbos, and these levels of Shabbos slowly begin to enter our consciousness from Wednesday onward. Again, Nefesh corresponds to our functional reality, the world of action, Ruach to our emotional position, the world of feelings, and Neshamah to our mental state, the world of thought.

Nefesh is action and Neshamah is thought. Ruach, our emotion (what 'moves us' and the way we 'move' towards others) is also connected to speech. Ruach literally means wind, and speech is manipulated, contextualized and formalized wind/breath.

After the 'new' Shabbos consciousness enters us from Wednesday through Friday, we experience another leap in consciousness on Shabbos itself. Besides those three levels of soul becoming more deeply integrated within us, we receive an even higher level of Soul from the World of Atzilus.

To review the correspondences between the levels of soul and the Four-Worlds: Nefesh corresponds to the world of Asiyah, Ruach is the world of Yetzirah, and Neshamah is the world of Beriah. The soul level of the world of Atzilus is called *Chayah* / life force, and is reflected in our deeper will and desire.

Shabbos is called a *Yom laHashem* / a day 'of' or 'to' Hashem. The Name Hashem has four letters, Yud-Hei-Vav-Hei. These four letters or expressions are refracted into the Four-Worlds (the four levels of Soul):

YUD	Aztilus, World of Unity	~Chayah -Transcendent Will or Desire*	Right Brain
UPPER	Beriyah, World of Thought	~Neshamah -Soul of Higher Intellect	Left Brain
VAV	Yezirah, World of Emotions	~Ruach -Emotional Spirit	Heart, Gut
LOWER HEI	Asiyah, World of Action	~Nefesh -Physical Energy	Body

*In *Mispar Katan* / the small numeric value, Shabbos is 72. Shin/3, Beis/2, Tav/4 = 9, then being divided into 7+2, alludes to 72 and the Divine Name *Av*. The Name Av is the Name of Hashem when the four letters are filled with Yuds, as in; Yud/10, Vav/6, Dalet/4 = 20. Hei/5, Yud/10, Hei/5 = 20. Vav/6, Vav/6 = 12. Hei/5, Yud/10, Hei/5 = 20. The sum of 20, 20, 12 and 20 is 72. Shabbos, on the level of Atzilus, is particularly connected to the Yud within the Name of Hashem.

Given these four experiential realms of Shabbos, we can map out the four progressive degrees of *Menuchah* / rest to which we can aspire. These four types of rest are connected with the four 'purposes' of Shabbos: 1) זכר למעשה בראשית / *Zeicher l'Maaseh Bereishis* / remembering Creation, 2) זכר ליציאת מצרים / *Zeicher l'Yetziyas Mitzrayim* / remembering the going out of Egypt, 3) מעין עולם הבא / *Me'ein Olam haBa* / a taste of the World-to-Come, and 4) יום שכולו שבת / *Yom sheKulo Shabbos* / a day when all is Shabbos. The four levels of rest are as follows:

1) Menuchah of the physical World of *Asiyah* / action and actualization, corresponding to the lower letter Hei of the Divine Name and the soul level Nefesh; it is experienced by 'not doing' certain purposeful activities. This is Shabbos as *Zeicher l'Maaseh Bereishis*, just as the Creator 'rested' from creating the physical world, we too rest from physical activity.

2) Menuchah of the emotional World of *Yetzirah* / Formation, the realm of speech, corresponding to the letter Vav of the Name, and the soul level of Ruach; it is experienced by resting from certain types of speech. This is Shabbos as *Zeicher l'Yitziyas Mitzrayim*, also called the Shabbos of the Revelation of Torah. As the Divine medium of Revelation is Speech, we ensure on Shabbos that our speech too is holy and positive.

3) Menuchah of the mental World of *Beriah* / Creation, the realm of the higher intellect, corresponding to the upper letter Hei of the Name and the soul level of Neshamah; it is resting from turbulent, negative, worrisome or mundane thoughts. This is Shabbos as *M'ein Olam haBa* / a glimpse of the World-to-Come, a time of ultimate perfection, free from worry, here on earth.

4) *Menuchah* on the spiritual World of *Atzilus* / Nearness or Oneness, corresponding to the letter Yud of the Name and the soul level of Chayah; its experience is one of total inner peacefulness and *Deveikus* / clinging unity with Hashem.* This is related to Shabbos of *Yom SheKulo Shabbos*, which is total and unending Deveikus with Hashem.

Before looking in even greater detail at these four levels of rest, let us revisit the ideas of *Shamor* / guarding the Shabbos and *Zachor* / remembering the Shabbos.

ACTIVE AND PASSIVE

Overall, there are two aspects to Shabbos: passive rest and active rest. *Zachor* is an active form of 'remembering.'**

---

*There is a fifth-level of soul called *Yechidah*, which is the crown of the Yud, the inner World of *Adam Kadmon* / Primordial Man. On the Yechidah level there is no duality whatsoever, and so there can be no 'rest,' as rest suggests an opposite posture of non-rest.

** The Mitzvah is not just to 'remember' Shabbos mentally, but to verbally declare that you are remembering it. In the words of the Rambam, "It is a positive commandment from the Torah to sanctify the Shabbos day with a *verbal statement* (as implied by *Shemos*, 20:8), "Remember the Shabbos day to sanctify it" — i.e., remember the Shabbos and do so with Kiddush, sanctifying it" (Rambam, *Hilchos Shabbos*, 29:1). Our sages (*Pesachim*, 106a) instituted that Kiddush needs to be over a cup of wine. Again, in the words of the Ramban, "It is a Mitzvah (instituted by) our Sages to recite Kiddush over (a cup of) wine (*Ibid*, 29:6). The understanding that on Shabbos we perform an active form of remembering answers a puzzling Rambam (see *Likutei Sichos*, 21, pp. 68-73). The Rambam in the laws of Pesach writes, "It is a positive commandment of the Torah to relate the miracles and wonders wrought for our ancestors in Egypt on the night of the fifteenth of Nisan, as *Shemos*, 13:3 states, 'Remember this day, on which you left Egypt,' just as *Shemos*, 20:8 states, 'Remember the Shabbos day'" (Rambam, *Hilchos Chametz u'Matzah*, 7:1). The questions are obvious. Why does the Rambam need to draw a parallel between the two verses that say "remember"? What does the verse regarding Shabbos add? Why isn't the verse "remem-

Shamor is a passive non-doing; simply by not working (as well as following the intricate laws of Muktzah*), we are demonstrating, to ourselves and everyone around us, that today is Shabbos.

These two dimensions of Shabbos are expressed and experienced on all four experiential levels of Shabbos; *Ma'aseh* / action, *Dibbur* / speech, *Machshavah* / thought and *Kavanah* / intention, the existential Shabbos mode of being.

Each of these four progressive levels of observing Shabbos is more subtle and inward than the next. For example, keeping Shabbos on the practical and external level of Ma'aseh, in terms of Shamor, means refraining from Melachah. As prohibited by Torah Law. Shamor, on the level of Dibbur, means not speaking about Melachah or mundane activities; this is prohibited by Rabbinic Law. More subtle is Shamor on the level of Machshavah. Thinking about Melachah on Shabbos is technically permitted by Torah as well as Rabbinic Law, since there is no manifest manipulation or observable change made in the physical world. Yet, it is clearly ben-

ber this day... leaving Egypt" sufficient? Why bring proof that there is a Mitzvah to relate the miracles on Pesach night "just as (it states) remember the Shabbos"? The answer is that there are two forms of remembering, passive and active. We learn from Shabbos that there is an active Mitzvah of remembering (Kiddush (and by our sages over wine)) and thus, on Pesach, we need to actively "declare" and speak about the miracles and wonders.

---

* Why was Muktzah instituted? Writes the Rambam, "(Another reason for this prohibition is) that there are some people who are not craftsmen and are always idle — e.g., tourists and those that stand on the street corners. These individuals never perform labor. Were they to be allowed to walk, talk, and carry as they do during the week, the result would be that their cessation of activity on (Shabbos) would not be discernible" (Rambam, *Hilchos Shabbos*, 24:13. דאין זה היכר שבת במה שיושב ואינו הולך. *Tosefos*, Shabbos, 69b). In other words, by adding the laws of Muktzah, it becomes discernible that today is Shabbos, and not simply that we are resting on a Tuesday.

eficial to one's Shabbos observance when one rests from thoughts of Melachah. There is an even more subtle and unobservable inner state of the person, his or her general sense of being, the individual's existential reality, which we are calling *Kavannah*. Shamor on this level involves resting from any sense of anxiety or inner noise, and ultimately, from any departure of/from the Gan Eden state of Shabbos.

LEVEL ONE: PHYSICAL REST
SHABBOS OF ASIYAH / ACTION / NEFESH

On the level of Action we need to actively pursue rest and choose to refrain from doing work on Shabbos. In the active Zachor mode of Shabbos we need to seek out physical forms of pleasure and Oneg Shabbos that bring us a deeper sense of physical rest.

For example, there is a special Mitzvah to eat finer foods on Shabbos (*Shabbos*, 118b) and (perhaps as an effect of eating more) to sleep a little extra on Shabbos night (Remah, and *Shulchan Aruch Harav*, Orach Chayim, 281:1), or even during the day to take a nap (*Mishna Brurah*, 4:36. See also *ibid*, 290:2). There is a well-known adage that the word *Shabbos* is an acronym for *Shina b'Shabbos Ta'anug* / the sleep of Shabbos is pleasurable (*Yalkut Reuveini*, Vaeschanan). Certainly for one who is a Talmid Chacham, a person who throughout the week toils in Torah learning, taking a nap on Shabbos is a positive expression of the rest of Shabbos (Meiri, *Shabbos*, 118b. *Shulchan Aruch haRav*, 290:5). So much so, that some sources write (*Peleh Yoetz*, Shina) that a person should declare, before taking a nap, "I am taking a nap in honor of Shabbos."

In addition to the special things we do on Shabbos, such as the extra delighting in food, sleeping a little longer, having intimacy, and even things we normally do such as taking a walk— the *way* we do them on Shabbos should be different. Everything we do on Shabbos should be more subtle, more restful and more mindful. "Our walking on Shabbos should be dissimilar to our walking during the week" (*Shabbos*, 113a). We should not run (*Berachos*, 6b), or jump, and in general we should not walk in a rush on Shabbos (*Shulchan Aruch*, Orach Chayim, 301:1). This is not just a restriction on how far we walk, rather, it is relating to the manner and the *way* in which we walk. All our activities on Shabbos should be specially elevated, and permeated with a Shabbos-like quality.

Our mindset should be that everything we do on Shabbos should be *Shabbosdik* / in the spirit of Shabbos. Before we do anything on Shabbos we ought to think about whether what we are going to do enhances our focus and attention, our experience of Shabbos, or the opposite. With a little ingenuity, one can discover many technical loop-holes within the basic laws of Shabbos. As a very colloquial example, say one takes a 'Shabbos elevator' to a roof bar party, has paid for the drinks before Shabbos, and sits down to enjoy the live music, which is being played by non-Jews for non-Jews. Perhaps it could be construed that no basic laws of Shabbos have been violated, but this is certainly not Shabbosdik activity.

In the modality of Asiyah, for us to genuinely be in a Shabbos state and truly reap the benefits of Shabbos, we need to ensure that everything we are doing on Shabbos is Shabbosdik. We also need to ensure that we do not get bogged down in the minutiae of law in an attempt to figure out loopholes that seem to justify non-Shabbosdik activities. To the contrary, when our general sentiment is restful and Shabbosdik, we will naturally only seek 'actions' that will enrich and expand these sentiments.

In the more 'passive' mode of *Shamor*, we need to ensure that we refrain from all the Thirty-Nine Melachos prohibited on Shabbos with all their derivative actions. This includes all the laws of *Muktzah* / objects for which we have no use on Shabbos, and thus should not be moved (in a normal way) or even touched.

All the activities that we rest from on Shabbos, both the prohibitions from the Torah and those from our sages, are part of the Mitzvah of the Torah to rest on Shabbos (*Ramban*, Vayikra, 23:24. *Sifra*, Acharei, 7. However, the Rashba, *Yevamos*, 6a, is of the opinion that the Mitzvah of *Tishbos* / rest only embraces the *Avos* / main Melachos of Shabbos). The various 'do-nots' and the hundreds of derivative prohibitions are not at all meant to create a sterile or gloomy atmosphere. In fact, on Shabbos there is also a 'prohibition' to be sad or melancholy, or to engage in any form of mourning, assuming you have control over your moods (see *Shulchan Aruch*, Orach Chayim, 287-288). Rather, all the 'do-nots' allow us to transcend mundane activities, creating the context and parameters in which we can truly rest and be in the eternal moment of Shabbos.

On Shabbos, we take time off and rest from trying to master the world around us. We simply cease from trying to build up or improve Creation. We even let go of the restlessness of trying to re-create Shabbos in a way that we think will serve us.

We rest on Shabbos, as the Creator "rested" from creating, meaning that Hashem 'stopped' creating and let everything just be, no longer 'interfering' with Creation and allowing it to begin functioning on its own, as it were. "Resting" means essentially the same for us; stopping and letting go of creating, interfering with and mastering 'our world.' For six days of the week we manipulate, explore, innovate and dominate the world around us, mimicking Hashem's acts of creation during the six primordial days. On Shabbos, we stop and rest, as Hashem rested, relinquishing our active domination over the world around us.

On Shabbos there is a Divinely mandated peace between ourselves and nature. No longer are we trying to harness, exploit or fight against nature; any form of interference, even small or apparently trivial, is a violation of Shabbos rest. Clearly, plowing the land or building a shelter is a change in our relationship to nature, but even something like pulling up a single blade of grass or boiling a cup of water, is acting contrary to its natural state, and thus is contrary to Shabbos rest. We need to leave nature untouched. Rest is not merely rest from the hard labor of the six days of the week, deeper passive rest is resting from altering or exerting control over the world, or creating profit in any way.

In the 'Shabbos of Action' there is a strong sense of *Zeicher l'Maaseh Bereishis*, remembering and bringing closer to our consciousness that Hashem alone created the world. By resting from trying to fix or improve the world, we are declaring that Hashem is the Master of the Universe.*

* The numerical value of the word *Shabbos* is 702, which is 27 times 26. The Name of Hashem is 26 (Yud/10, Hei/5, Vav/6, Hei/5 = 26). There are 27 letters in the Aleph Beis: 22 regular letters and five end-letters. The Hebrew letters are the building blocks of Creation, thus Shabbos reveals how all of Creation (27) comes from Hashem (26).

From another perspective, the Name 'Hashem' itself equals 27: the four letters, which are 26, plus the *Kolel* / 1 for the word itself. In this way, 27 times 26 is an illustration of Hashem resting in His Absolutely Simple Oneness, in Himself; Hashem's Attributes 'resting' or

We may work the whole week to "perfect" the world, for that too is the will of Hashem — "Six days you shall work..." However, by our non-doing on Shabbos, we demonstrate that this is HaKadosh Baruch Hu's world.

To summarize, 'remembering and guarding Shabbos' in the physical world of Asiyah is to actively enjoy pleasure from good meals, wine, sleep, intimacy, and to do all of it in a Shabbosdik way, refraining from prohibited Melachah and all other 'actions' that are not Shabbosdik.

'settling' into Hashem's Essential 'Self.' *Kolel* also means 'inclusion.' By means of Shabbos (702), Hashem 'includes' (27) all of Creation within this Self-rest (26).

LEVEL TWO: EMOTIONAL REST
SHABBOS OF YETZIRAH / SPEECH / RUACH

On the level of Speech, in the active mode of *Zachor*, we need to 'declare' Shabbos, and in the passive mode of *Shamor*, we need to rest from work-related and un-Shabbosdik speech.

There are seven orifices in the head: two ears, two eyes, two nostrils, and the mouth. The first six represent the six days of the week, and the fact that they come in pairs, represents the world of duality. The central, singular orifice of the mouth is connected to the center of the week, Shabbos. Speaking only when we need to, resting from combative or 'worldly' speech, and speaking lovingly and honestly, are forms of speech that are intrinsically bound to Shabbos.

מצות עשה מן התורה לקדש את יום השבת בדברים / "There is a positive commandment from the Torah to sanctify the Shabbos day with a verbal statement" (Rambam, *Hilchos Shabbos*, 29:1). Any declaration that it is now Shabbos is sufficient to fulfil this obligation, even just saying "Good Shabbos" (*Haga'as Rabbi Akiva Eiger*, Orach Chayim, 271:1. Although, see *Biur Halachah*, ibid, 2). For the most part, the best possible way to 'sanctify' Shabbos is to recite the liturgy of Kiddush over a cup of wine. This is the positive observance, the Zachor, of the Shabbos of Speech; to use the power of words, the creative power of speech that defines us as human beings, in order to declare the reality of Shabbos. Indeed, we should continuously use this power, for example, whenever we eat or partake in the pleasures of Shabbos, and even while preparing for Shabbos, to proclaim, "I am doing this to honor Shabbos," or, "I am acquiring this for the honor of Shabbos" (Magen Avraham, *Orach Chayim*, 250:1. *Kanfei Yonah*, 4. Shaloh, *Maseches Shabbos*, 1).

In the more passive mode of *Shamor* / safeguarding Shabbos through not-doing, we need to ensure that our speech and manner of communication is different on Shabbos than during the week. Not only should we not speak of work-related, wasteful, stressful, idle, or trivial words on Shabbos (*Shulchan Aruch haRav*, 307:2. *Tanya*, Kuntres Acharon, 9), but as the sages advise us, "Our speech on Shabbos should be dissimilar to our speech during the week" (*Shabbos*, 113b. ממצוא חפצך ודבר דבר (Yeshayahu, 58:13) Says the Gemara, חפצי אסורין שמים מותרין / "It is prohibited to deal with your weekday affairs and to speak about them, however, affairs of Heaven are permitted." ודבר דבר שלא יהא דבורך של שבת כדבורך של חול / "And (simply) speaking words, your speech on Shabbos should not be like your speech during the week.").

In other words, in terms of the 'active' mode of Shabbos speech, even the words we do use should be spoken with a different tonality and manner. There are sages who suggest that we should only speak when needed, and also to exclusively use *Lashon haKodesh* / the Holy tongue on Shabbos (*Mishnas Chassidim*, Maseches Leil Shabbos, 6:1). In general, our words should be softer, gentler, more subtle and sensitive, similar to the manner of a *Talmid Chacham* / wise student of Torah. A true Talmid Chacham is called "Shabbos" (*Zohar* 3, 29a), and speaks accordingly with a soft demeanor; "The words of the *Chachamim* / wise are heard (when spoken) softly" (Koheles, 9:17). On Shabbos, all can aspire to speak with a gentler, softer voice (*Kad Kemach*, Shabbos).

On Shabbos, when we do speak, it should be "Lashon haKo-desh" — words of Torah, of deeper meaning, or simply of necessity (these are three of the higher forms of the five types of speech illustrated by the Rambam, *Pirush haMishnayos*, Avos, 1:16). Says the Zohar, on Shabbos we should involve ourselves with words of Torah and songs of praise (*Zohar* 2, 205b). Certainly, we should rest from speaking about business or enclothing our *Ruach* / power of speech in empty words. When we do need to speak, for example, to ask someone to pass a dish, it should be politely and gently, not bluntly or unnecessarily loud. Imagine that you are a king or queen, and there is no need to raise your voice. Speak like a wise person.

If possible, as part of Shamor Shabbos, endeavor to speak less on Shabbos; try to use suggestion rather than speech. Our sages recount (*Vayikra Rabbah*, end of 34), that once Rabbi Shimon Bar Yochai, the Rashbi, noticed his mother speaking extra words on Shabbos, and he exclaimed, "Today is Shabbos!"* This story suggests that on Shabbos we should speak less in general, even about issues not related to work. שבות כאלקיך מה אלקיך שבת ממאמר אף אתה שבות מן המאמר / "Rest like your G-d. Just as Hashem rested from all speech, you too rest from speech" (*Pesikta Rabsi*, 23:1). Indeed, it was with great difficulty that the sages of old allowed us to even say hello to another person on Shabbos (Yerushalmi, *Shabbos* 15:3. Shabbos, *Tosefos*, 113b).

---

* *Pesikta Rabsi*, Parsha 23:3. *Tosefos*, Shabbos, 113b. Yerushalmi, *Shabbos*, end of chapter 15. Rashbi was, in general, careful with speech. See *Baba Metziya*, 58b, regarding causing another person pain through words. The carefulness of speech on Shabbos is being careful that others do not become lax with vows (*Nedarim*, 66b). Rashbi once said, that if he was at the giving of the Torah, he would have prayed (initially, although he changed his mind) that Hashem give man two mouths, one to speak Torah and one to speak mundane words. Yerushalmi, *Berachos*, 1:2

SHABBOS / SILENCE BEYOND THE WORLD OF SOUND

Shabbos is from another dimension, beyond sound. Shabbos is the silent aspect of the otherwise noisy week. The weekdays were created by Divine Speech — the Ten Utterances. On Shabbos, Hashem rested from 'Speech' and the world was sustained by Divine Silence, the meta-root of Divine Sound.

The Torah describes Creation as a process of Ten Divine Utterances which give rise to the universe. It is through these primary, primordial utterances that Creation emerges and is manifest. "G-d said let there be light, and there was light," there was a Divine saying and the creation of a phenomenon. All in all, there are only ten basic Divine declarations, creating light, celestial spheres, vegetative and animal life. However, there are of course trillions upon trillions — almost infinite numbers — of variations of physical phenomena. Even two raindrops are dissimilar. How do a mere ten utterances create all of this? These utterances are the roots of all that exist, and through *Tziruf* / letter combinations, all phenomena emerge and are given life to be sustained.

Speaking of how everything in this world is sustained by the Divine utterance, the life-force of all Creation, the *Tanya* says that even a stone is sustained by the Creator's utterance of the Hebrew word *Even* / stone; "Now, although the word אבן / stone is not mentioned in the Ten Utterances recorded in the Torah (how then can we say that the letters of the Ten Utterances are the life-force within a stone), nevertheless, the life-force flows to the stone from the Ten Utterances by means of combinations and substitutions of letters… so that ultimately, the combination of letters (that forms) the name אבן descends from the Ten Utterances… And so it is with all created things in the world" (*Shaar haYichud v'haEmunah*, 1).

The Hebrew word for 'thing' is *Devar*, literally 'word' or utterance, for everything in this world has a distinct vibration, resonating with a unique Divine frequency. The countless objects we observe in the world are physical manifestations of their corresponding Divine frequencies. Things are merely *Devarim* / words; a specific *Tziruf* / combination of Divine 'letters,' 'vowels' and 'sounds.'

Every moment from the time of Creation is a re-Creation. Every instant, a Divine vibration of speech is spoken into the world, which creates energy, and this energy solidifies into matter. Divine speech is the meta-physical vibration that triggers corresponding physical vibrations, which eventually become the objects in our lives. Everything is essentially a product and manifestation of a unique Divine vibration or 'word.'

Speech is a movement from the inside-out. Think about this in terms of human communication and speech. When we speak and communicate our feelings to another, we take something from inside us, and through speech, we reveal it to the outside, to another. Speech moves feelings, ideas, and whatever else is going on within the interior, to the exterior where others can apprehend them.

'Prior to' or deeper than the world of Speech, and the eventual manifest world, is the world the way it exists within the Mind of the Creator, as it were. There, 'within the interior' of the Creator, the world subtly exists in an inner world of Silence.

Again, using the analogy of human communication, first there is the conception of an idea, how it exists within your mind, and then you verbalize the idea, and move it from your inside to the outside. What's more, the way you see the idea in your mind — in your silence — is in its fully developed and *Tachlis* / end-result state. Say, you want to build a chair. You have an idea of how the chair is going to look in your mind, and then you go through the process of actually building it. This is why, סוף מעשה במחשבה תחילה / *Sof Ma'aseh b'Machshavah Techilah* / "The end result is present within the first thought." Once the project is completed, you have manifested the original image you had in your mind — more or less. This is the nature of Shabbos. Shabbos is the completion of the end of the week, yet it is the original conception of the world, the 'first thought,' the way the world existed prior to being externalized and formed.

On a deeper inner level, on Shabbos the world exists in the level of Divine thought, which is 'completion,' beyond the world of speech, which is 'process,' Weekdays are mostly connected with the World of *Dibbur* / Speech (Asiyah), although sometimes they vibrate higher, and connect with the World of *Kol* / Sound/Voice (Yetzirah). On Shabbos, the world is sustained by the World of *Machshavah* / Thought and we too function with an 'extra soul' that is rooted in the world of Divine Thought (*Likutei Torah*, Shabbos Shuvah, p.66). This gives us a glimpse into the world of Divine Unity (Atzilus) and a 'silence' beyond all forms of speech. Shabbos is Silence, a space beyond the cacophony of the week.

Our sages tell us a story (*Berachos*, 58a), Rav Sheshet was blind. Everyone was going to greet the king and Rav Sheshet stood up and went along with them. A heretic found him there and said to him, "The intact jugs go to the river, where do the broken jugs go? Why is a blind person going to see the king?" Rav Sheshet responded, "Come, see that I know more than you do." The first troop passed, and when the noise grew louder, this heretic said to him, "The king is coming." Rav Sheshet said to him, "The king is not coming." The second troop passed, and when the noise grew louder, this heretic said to him, "Now the king is coming." Rav Sheshet said to him, "The king is not coming." The third troop passed, and when there was silence, Rav Sheshet said to him, "Certainly now the king is coming." The heretic said, "How do you know this?" Rav Sheshet answered, "Royalty on earth is like royalty in the Heavens, as it is written (with regards to Hashem's revelation to Eliyahu haNavi), 'And Hashem said to him, 'Go forth, and stand upon the mount before Hashem.' And, behold, Hashem passed by, and a great and strong wind split the mountains and broke into pieces the rocks before Hashem; but Hashem was not in the wind. And after the wind an earthquake; but Hashem was not in the earthquake. And after the earthquake a fire; but Hashem was not in the fire. And after the fire a קול דממה דקה / Kol Demamah Dakah / still, thin voice. And when Eliyahu heard this still, thin voice, he wrapped his face in his mantle and went out, and stood in the entrance of the cave to await the revelation.'"

Wind, earthquake and fire, correspond to the three 'outer' worlds of Asiya, Yetzirah and Beriah (Biur haGra, Tikkunei Zohar, 13a). This is the 'noise,' the great sounds of the world, but this is still not where the King of the Universe is present. Shabbos is the קול דממה דקה / still thin voice.

This "still, thin voice" is the level of Atzilus. It is a totally inaudible voice, as there is no longer any reason for sound or speech — sound and speech suggest duality and separation and a desire to communicate and overcome a divide. Like Atzilus, Shabbos is a world of unity, and thus, silence, the *Kol Demamah Dakah*.

On Shabbos we enter the inner world of the Tachlis, the ultimate intention of Creation. This is why we need to practice more silence on Shabbos, so that we too are aligned with our interior, 'world of unity.' By practicing radiant silence or even just speaking more gently, with a *still, thin voice*, we are aligning our way of being with the cosmic reality of Divine Silence, as when Hashem 'rested from speech.'

THE INNER WORLD OF SOUND, THE SOUND OF REVELATION / TORAH

Shabbos is a world of silence, of inwardness. The Creator's 'resting' from speech revealed the 'inner' Divine world, as it were. Yet, even silence is an *expression* and even Shabbos is a *creation*. A creation of any sort, even one of pure being and Infinity, requires some type of Divine speech to bring it into being, albeit a higher/deeper form of speech.

Just as there are Ten *Ma'amaros* / Utterances of Creation, there are Ten *Dibros* / Words (or Commandments) of Revelation. There is an external, manifest world created by the Ten Utterances, and there is the inner world of Divine Revelation, the Torah, "the Blueprint of Creation," that is revealed to us through the Ten Dibros.

The inner sound of the Torah, the *Devar Hashem*, is the 'meta-root vibration' and deepest sound of all Creation. According to the refinement of our thoughts, words and actions, and their consistency with the spiritual precepts of Torah, we can experience a revelation of this Devar Hashem. We can 'hear' the inner sound of Creation, which was revealed at Mount Sinai through the Ten Dibros (*Sefas Emes*, Yisro, Tav/Reish/Lamed/Dalet). In fact, each of us have heard this before. Following our redemption from the physical-emotional-mental-spiritual constrictions of *Mitzrayim* / Egypt, we collectively attained a heightened spiritual sensitivity. As we stood at the foot of Mount Sinai we were opened to hear this inner sound of Creation, the silent-sound of Torah and Revelation.

Shabbos is like a Mount Sinai moment. As Shabbos is nearing, we get closer and closer to the Mountain. When Shabbos finally enters, all the noise and bustle of the world, all the cacophony and chaos of material existence, has quieted down. In this serenity and peacefulness, the weekday world of the Ten Utterances of Creation is less blatant. As the sound of commerce and interference with nature falls silent, we become more sensitive to hear the inner sound of Creation, the still, small sound of the Ten Dibros, the sound of Torah.

This is why the "Shabbos of Speech" is intricately connected to *Zeicher l'Yitziyas Mitzrayim*, the going out of Egypt, and the Revelation at Mount Sinai.

The 'emotional' level of remembering Shabbos in the world of Yetzirah includes experiencing *Oneg* / pleasurable, holy emotion, among good company, enjoying good conversation with friends and family, singing songs together in honor of Shabbos (*Tur, Remah,* Orach Chayim, 281), beautifying the *Tefillos* / prayer services, and so forth. Make sure that you are in a proper mood for Shabbos, a Shabbosdik emotional state, and do your best to refrain from engaging with any emotional stresses that are not in the spirit of Shabbos.

LEVEL THREE: MENTAL REST
SHABBOS OF BERIAH / THOUGHT / NESHAMAH

On the level of Thought, in the active mode of Zachor, we need to actively be mindful of Shabbos, and be creative in our learning of Torah, as will be explored. In the passive mode of Shamor, we need to refrain from even thinking about the past workweek, or planning what we will do during the upcoming week. Even if the future holds an activity that is not work related, such as travel, this too we should put to rest on Shabbos, and not even think about it.

Our Neshamah gives us our mental prowess. When we are invited by the Master of the Universe to celebrate Shabbos, we are asked to rest from our creativity in terms of trying to master our world, yet, we are not asked to rest from all mental/intellectual creativity. Denying ourselves mental creativity would mean being less human, and Shabbos is all about restoring us to our rightful place in creation, not entrenching us further in states of consciousness that betray our true purpose and potential. We are asked to cease using our creative abilities in the realm of *Maleches Mach'sheves* / intentional actions of harnessing or manipulating creation, but this does not mean we must stop thinking or being inwardly creative, to the contrary, when our minds and creativity are released from mere instrumentalization, they are able to reach ever unimaginably new heights, especially in realms of Torah and spirituality.

Shabbos is not a 'lazy' day or a vacation for sitting around and being idle. Neither is it a time to clean house, play chess or catch up on the news. On the level of Neshamah, it is a day to refocus our creativity from the realm of physicality, into the realm of spiritual intellect and creative contemplation in Torah thought.

Shabbos was given so that we can study Torah (*Yerushalmi, Shabbos* 15:3. *Pesikta Rabsi*, 23: 9). On Shabbos we ought to study Torah, for "Shabbos is all Torah" (*Tana d'vei Eliyahu*, 1). This is certainly true of 'laymen,' who do not have as much time to involve themselves with Torah learning during the week (Tanchuma, see *Beis Yoseph*, 290. *Shulchan Aruch haRav*, Ibid, 5). Shabbos is the 'wife' of the Torah, and this bond ensures that the Torah will always be studied, even by those who are occupied with other endeavors during the week (*Yalkut Shimoni*. See Tur, Ibid).

Ingenuity and innovation are the most important parts of being human and feeling alive. On Shabbos we rest from using our creativity to figure out how to secure another digit in our bank account or how to further research so we can land on Mars, and instead we use our creativity to *Mechadesh* / innovate in Torah. Shabbos, writes the Shaloh haKodesh (Rav Yeshayah Halevi Horowitz c.1555-1630), is the most opportune time to be Mechadesh in Torah, creating novel and innovative Torah thoughts (*Maseches Shabbos*, Ner Mitzvah. 61-66. *Asarah Ma'amaros*, Ma'amar Chikur Din, 3:12. See also *Mishnah Berurah* 290:3. Ibid, *Shaarei Teshuvah* 3). We rest from mundane, work-related and even trivial thoughts (*Reishis Chochmah*, Sha'ar haKedushah, 3), in order to focus our attention and ingenuity on holy and lofty thoughts.

THE TORAH OF DIRECT LIGHT VS. THE TORAH OF LIGHT THAT EMERGES FROM DARKNESS

Within the Oral Torah itself there is a *Niglah* / revealed aspect of the Torah, predominantly encoded and developed in the Gemara, the Babylonian Talmud, and there is the more esoteric, inner dimension of the Torah, which is also referred to, ever since the 11th Century, as Kabbalah or the *Nistar* / hidden secrets of the Torah. The most fundamental canonized text of Nistar is the *Holy Zohar*. Shabbos is an especially good time to learn the *Sod* / secret level of the Torah, the Arizal teaches, as Sod is connected to the world of Atzilus (*Pri Eitz Chayim*, Sha'ar haShabbos, 9:1). Atzilus is the deepest inner world, and, as will be shortly explored, corresponds to the highest form of rest on Shabbos.

Niglah tends to deal with how the Divine manifests within mundane, physical reality, such as the laws of how much one pays when one's animal gores another, for one example, or, how to divide equally shared properties, etc. Nistar tends to deal with lofty, spiritual themes, such as how does the world come into being, what is our soul, and how should we relate to the Infinite One. Another marked distinction between the Gemara and *Zohar*, for example, is that the Gemara is filled with arguments and counter arguments, disputes and resolutions, while the *Zohar* is more "straightforward," albeit often written in deeply encoded metaphors.

In Gemara, when the sages want to offer an idea or proof for an argument, they often begin with the phrase *Ta Shema* / "Come and hear," whereas the *Zohar* (and *Yerushalmi*) often begins with the phrase *Ta Chazi* / "Come and see." Seeing is immediate; you can take a single glance and 'see' a whole picture. Hearing involves a greater distance from the source, and it takes more work and time in order to gain clarity of perception. When you 'hear' information, it can take several steps before the full idea is assimilated; when you are able to 'see' something, it is revealed in its totality upon perception.

Babylonian Talmudic study uses a dialectical process: tension and resolution, question and answer and new question. It is the quintessential form of discovering answers through the arduous labor of probing and challenging; it is a path of light and redemption that passes through darkness and exile. Our sages tell us that the verse, "He placed me in darkness, like those who are dead forever" (*Eichah,* 3:6), refers to the Talmud of *Bavel* / Babylon (*Sanhedrin,* 24a. The sages of Bavel are connected to 'darkness' (*Zevachim,* 60b. *Bechoros,* 25b. *Ritvah, Yuma,* 57a), and (perhaps) 'light that comes from the darkness.' The *Yerushalmi* is called "light." *Zohar Chadash,* Eicha, 112b). It is a way of learning in which wisdom, clarity and resolution are attained via the toil of debate. It is the dimension of Torah where the light emerges from within, and indeed precisely because of the opacity of questions. This is called *Ohr Chozer* / reflective light, a light that bounces off the receiver, stimulating a generation from within. It is the world of *Ta Shema* / come and *hear.*

"The people who walked in darkness have seen a great light" (*Yeshayah,* 9:1). The "great light" refers to the great clarity that is attained by the sages of the Gemara, for through the 'darkness' of questions, Hashem enlightens their eyes in matters of ritual law and laws of purity (*Tanchumah*, Noach, 3).

The nature of such study and pondering is arduous and labor intensive; it can be mentally exhausting and even physically tiring (*Sanhedrin*, 26a). In fact, the mystics suggest that the purpose of such toil and questioning is to break all the *Kelipos* / husks of negativity that camouflage the Divine Light within the student (*Chesed l'Avraham*, 2:28).

A question arises when the resolution of an issue is 'concealed' and 'distant' from the questioner. There is a disconnect and a sense of alienation and exile from the 'light,' the answer, the clarity. This is conceptually similar, on an abstract intellectual level, to a literal concealment in life, a Kelipah, such as a hardship or struggle. By breaking open the question and toiling with it, 'a great light' is revealed. This kind of mental struggle breaks the Kelipah of the world, allowing the world to be a place where we see Hashem's Light and Presence in a more revealed, 'less-clouded' way.

A world where there is still toil, strife and ambition, of breaking Kelipah, of struggling with unfulfilled dreams and repairing physical, emotional, financial, mental and spiritual alienation can only appear in the realm of the six days of the week. This is the realm in which we are Divinely commanded, "Six days of the week you should work." We are asked to toil, strive and perhaps even struggle, in this world of Asiyah, Yetzirah and Beriah — the cosmic realm of 'separation.' In terms of our intellectual life, the weekdays represent *Safek* / doubt, uncertainty, questions, and mental restlessness. On Shabbos we enter a place of resolve, of certainty and clarity (כשאדם בא לידי הבנת איזה דבר חכמה נקרא שבת. *Divrei Chayim*, Bechukosai), we enter, as will be shortly expanded upon, the World of Atzilus, the inner world of Unity and Light.

In the course of the workweek we are connected to the *reflective light*, the light that emerges from the darkness, which is the paradigm of Gemara study and *Iyyun /* in-depth learning. In fact, the paradigm of the weekday itself is called *Maseches Chulin /* the Gemara's 'Tractate of Non-Sanctified Items' (Shaloh, *Maseches Chulin*, beginning), alluding to the relative darkness of 'non-sanctified' weekdays. Thus, during the week we should spend more time studying Niglah and *Halacha /* law. The word *Halacha* has the same root as the word *Melachah /* work and the root is *Hiluch /* moving. Participating in this dynamic movement of spiritual toil allows us to be in sync with the times and help facilitate the breaking of all Kelipah and the coming of Moshiach.

On Shabbos, it is the reverse; we should spend more time studying *Sod /* the mystical secrets of the Torah (*Midbar Kadmos*, Kuf, 11). We should involve ourselves in the study of Nistar, the Torah connected to the World of Atzilus, which is far beyond the realm of darkness, unresolved questions and uncertainties.* Shabbos is not so much a time for Iyyun. (*Siddur Ya'avetz*, Shabbos, 119b, regarding Rabbi Zeira. *Meiri*, Shabbos, 118. רבי זירא מהדר אזוזי זוזי דרבנן אמר ליה במטותא מינייכו לא תחללוניה. See Rashi, ad loc., Chasam Sofer, *Toras Moshe*, Vayakhel). Yet, elsewhere, the Gemara says, "Ravina said to Rav Pappa: 'Since you were not with us last night within the Techum Shabbos, you did

---

* Shabbos is a time to create *Yichudim /* Divine unifications, more than (the weekday type of) 'learning.' Baal Shem Tov, see *Tzafnas Poneach*, Mishpatim. *Keser Shem Tov*, 2:374.

not hear that Rava raised a contradiction between two Mishnayos and taught their resolution.'" (*Zevachim*, 2b. *Ben Ish Chai*, Shu't Torah Lishmah, Siman 110) This is the *Ohr Yashar* / Direct Light paradigm, and the world of *Ta Chazi* / come and 'see'; where the Light is revealed to all easily and instantaneously. (Shabbos is מוכן לכל השגה / open to all higher thoughts and wisdom. *Levush*, Orach Chayim, 281)

There are *Chidushim* / innovative Torah insights that arise from within the realm of Pilpul, dialectics, intellectual analysis, question and answers, and Ohr Chozer, and there are Chidushim that arise more from within the world of Ohr Yashar, intuition and inspired creativity. On Shabbos, not only are we encouraged to learn much Torah, but we are also positively encouraged to be Mechadesh in Torah, and specifically in the Nistar of Torah. Our Chidushim should also be made in the 'way' of Nistar; using our intuition and 'restful,' joyful creativity. 'What' we learn, but also 'how' we learn, should be aligned with the world of Ohr Yashar. Meaning that, even if we do learn Niglah on Shabbos, how we learn it should be conducive to Shabbosdik ease and pleasure, with an 'Ohr Yashar' spirit of ingenuity, rather than a weekday sense of 'labor.'

Not only *should* we endeavor to be Mechadesh in Torah, but it is *essential* that we *do so*. In the lexicon of the *Zohar* (*Zohar 3*, 173a), the 'extra soul' we receive on Shabbos ascends on High once Shabbos is over and is brought before the Master of the Universe and asked, 'What original *Chidushim* / innovative Torah insights did you reveal on Shabbos?' Any words of Torah which the soul communicates gives tremendous joy on high (for souls of deceased parents (*Machazik Beracha*, Orach Chayim, 290:4-5)), and the angels also receive life from these words.

If, for some reason, you do not feel you have the imaginative power to be Mechadesh on a particular Shabbos, you should at least learn a piece of Torah that you have never previously learned, and the learning itself will be a 'Chidush' for you (ibid, *Kaf haChayim*, 290:10-11. Although, if the student is totally new to this wisdom (or a child) it will cause more anxiety than pleasure and thus new ideas should not be learned. See *Nedarim*, 37a. Rambam, *Hilchos Talmud Torah*, 2:2). This is all part of the *Oneg* / pleasure of Shabbos on the level of Neshamah/Beriah, the world of intellect, learning and the mental pleasure that comes from creativity and unearthing new insights.

Oneg Shabbos in the world of 'action' is to enjoy a good meal; Oneg Shabbos in the world of 'speech' is to declare Kiddush; Oneg Shabbos on the level of 'thought' is to be Mechadesh in Torah (Shaloh haKodesh, *Maseches Shabbos*, Ner Mitzvah, 62). The latter is a higher, more refined and ethereal form of Oneg. The highest or deepest Oneg is that of pure Deveikus, as will be explored — although Deveikus can arise within any of these 'worlds,' even from within the simple Oneg of eating delicious food.

Celebrating the Shabbos of Thought, of Torah wisdom, is intricately bound with the Shabbos level of *M'ein Olam haBa* / a taste of the World-to-Come. Speaking about the time of Moshiach, the Rambam (*Hilchos Melachim*, 12:4- 5) writes, "The Sages and the prophets did not yearn for the Era of Moshiach in order to have dominion over the entire world... or to eat, drink, and celebrate. Rather, they desired to be free to involve themselves in Torah and wisdom without any pressures or disturbances... In that era (after Moshiach and later in, the World-to-Come), there will be neither famine or war, envy or competition for good will flow in abundance and all delights will be as freely available as dust. The occupation of the entire world will be solely to know G-d." Delighting in Torah on Shabbos is a taste of this future time.

RESTING FROM MUNDANE & WEEKDAY-RELATED THOUGHTS

Filling our thoughts with matters of Shabbos and creating new ideas in Torah, both relate to the positive, active 'rest' in the World of Thought. In the more passive modality of Shamor, we ought to refrain from all stress and work-related thoughts. The mental, Neshamah/Beriah aspect of Shamor is to refrain from all thoughts that are not Shabbosdik. This clearly includes certain thoughts about what we might do in the coming week.

Here is a tale from our sages. There was once a pious person who noticed a breach in one of the fences surrounding his field. At that point he (merely) thought to himself, "I will fix the fence after Shabbos." After Shabbos he chose not to fix the breach, reasoning, I should have not pondered such matters on Shabbos. A short time later, miraculously, a *Tzlaf* / caper bush grew at the breach and from that very bush he secured a livelihood for his family (*Shabbos*, 150b. *Yerushalmi, Shabbos*, 15:3. *Pesikta Rabsi*, 23:3).

Technically, merely thinking about doing a Melachah in the coming week is not a violation of Halachah or Shabbos rest on the level of action. Yet, this pious person desired to keep the 'spirit' of Shabbos on the level of 'resting from thoughts' and even intuited that the thought 'I will fix the breach' had not been appropriate and so he refrained from acting on it even during the weekday.

The *Mekubalim* / mystics reveal (Arizal. See Shaloh haKodesh, *Maseches Shabbos*, Ner Mitzvah, Chap, 66. *Ben Yehoyada*, Shabbos, 150b) that the pious person in the above narrative was a *Gilgul* / reincarnation of the Biblical character Tzlafchad. The Torah tells us a story about the first desecration of Shabbos, following the giving of the Torah, "When the children of Israel were in the desert, they found a man gathering wood on the Shabbos day" (Bamidbar, 15:32). The Torah itself intentionally conceals the name of this man, yet, Rabbi Akiva disclosed that he was Tzlafchad, whose daughters feature prominently in the Torah (*Shabbos*, 96b). By 'resting from thoughts' on Shabbos and keeping Shabbos on a higher level, the pious man was able to bring a Tikun to the soul of Tzlafchad. And as a sign that the Tikun was complete, a *Tzlaf* / caper bush grew and protected his field and brought him and his family nourishment.

Tzalafchad's intention, his mindset in gathering wood on Shabbos, was actually *l'Shem Shamayim* / for the sake of Heaven, for a higher purpose. He reasoned that since, following the episode with the *Meraglim* / scouts / spies, the adults of the People of Israel were given a harsh verdict that they would not enter into the Land of Israel, perhaps they would erroneously think that they no longer had to keep the Mitzvos. Thus he decided that he would desecrate the Shabbos and be appropriately punished, so that everyone would know clearly that Shabbos is still Shabbos (see Tosefos, *Baba Basra*, 119b). In other words, Tzalafchad desecrated Shabbos physically, in *Ma'aseh* / action, but in his *Machshavah* / mind and thoughts, he had holy intentions.

In the episode of the pious man there was never any Chilul Shabbos in Ma'aseh, and there was not even a thought to do a

Ma'aseh of Chilul Shabbos, all he 'thought' was that after Shabbos he would build a fence. But because he did not follow through with this un-Shabbosdik thought, a Tikun was created. In fact, there is a perfect symmetry in this; Tzalafchad's prohibited act, sourced in a subtly 'pure' intention, was countered by his Gilgul prohibiting himself an act sourced in a subtly 'impure' intention.

All Melachos of Ma'aseh are strictly forbidden by the Torah. Dibbur, speaking about Melachah is forbidden by the laws of the sages. Thinking, having a Machshavah of Melachah, such as the thought of this pious man, is technically permitted, yet, if we are able to go beyond the 'letter of the law' and keep with the spirit of 'rest' and *Oneg* Shabbos, it is better not to think such thoughts (*Orach Chayim*, 306:8). Perhaps we can even perform a Tikun by avoiding them. Certainly, we should refrain from thoughts that cause anguish (*Beis Yoseph*, ibid, 306, in the name of R. Yonah).

Our mental state on Shabbos should be, כאילו כל מלאבתך עשויה / "As if all your work is done." The word כאילו / *as if* is appropriate; it does not necessarily mean that you are actually effortlessly feeling this way, rather, you are choosing to adopt a certain mindset, considering ourselves "as if" all our work is done. As the Baal Shem Tov teaches, "You are where your thoughts are"— the act of thinking this way actually allows us to *Mamash* / literally experience, on some level, a glimmer of the reality in which everything is "done," thereby accessing the spiritual realm where everything is, in fact, perfectly complete. Deeper still, the underlying *Cheshek* / desire to feel such inner calmness, the yearning to experience the eternal perfection of Shabbos, is in fact the *Kav* / line that connects us to this possibility.

In the world of *Adam Kadmon* / Primordial Being, which is the Blueprint of all of Creation, the world exists in a perfect state. This means, prior to being created, the world existed in a state of complete crystallization. Furthermore, this is the state the world will reach at the end of time; the beginning and end are intricately bound together in a state of timeless perfection. When we cultivate the mindset and experience of "everything is done and perfect," we tap into this world of perfection at the 'beginning' and 'end' of time. In fact, with more and more practice, we can truly experience the full sensation of *being done*, with nothing to worry about, and nothing even to plan.

Everything that *could* have been done before Shabbos was done. This is a fact. Therefore, we do not *need* to think about business, or anything else that we may want to do after Shabbos. We should aspire to just be present, in Shabbos. Be here now, in the moment, without following any restless ruminations of what could have been or what might be in the future.

Any project that you begin or are in the middle of, any book you have started writing, or business proposal you have not yet completed — from the perspective of Shabbos, it is *done*. There is nothing left to do now. It is all 'perfect,' and there is not one iota to change.

Practicing Shabbos on this level inculcates us with the fundamental understanding that Hashem is the Master of the Universe. Once a week, as we totally surrender, unplug and let go of both our past and future, we are showing ourselves and the world around us that we deeply sense that, *Yesh Ba'al haBayis l'Birah Zu* / "there is an Owner of this home," this world.

"He who observes the Shabbos is regarded as having observed the entire Torah, and vice versa" (Yerushalmi, *Nedarim*, 1:9). This is because, by letting go on Shabbos, we demonstrate to ourselves and to those around us our complete faith that Hashem is the Master of the Universe. Six days a week we are playing the role of an active partner, but on the seventh day, we turn everything over to Hashem, we give Hashem our *Pekel* / baggage, our lives and our dealings in this world, and say, 'It's all Yours!'

QUIETING THE MIND OF THE TENUAH / MOVEMENT OF RUSHING THOUGHTS

Just as there is *Tenuah* / movement in physical action, which constitutes Melachah, there is a subtle movement in *Dibbur* / speech, which too can be a form of Melachah. Thus, we need to rest from mundane and prohibited speech. There is an even more subtle Tenuah in the area Machshavah; every thought is a type of movement within the mind. On the first level of 'mental rest' on Shabbos, we should aspire to cease thinking all thoughts that are related to Melachah, and certainly all thoughts that normally plague a person or cause anxiety. To accomplish such a cessation, we must first and foremost choose to do so.

On Shabbos we ought to try and lovingly control our conscious thoughts, so that our thoughts do not control us. This will help us focus our energy and mental resources on Torah, on our purpose in life, and on our deep connection to ourselves, others and Hashem. In other words, Shabbos is a time to engage the mind in higher pursuits.

We should aspire not to have any *Hesech haDa'as* / interruption of awareness of Shabbos. A spiritual novice can seek to not have Hesech haDa'as while eating on Shabbos. One can always keep in mind while eating that 'today is Shabbos and I am eating in honor of Shabbos.' The more experienced in spiritual practice and the Talmid Chacham should attempt to not have Hesech haDa'as in *Dibbur* / speech, in addition to action, throughout Shabbos. One can keep in mind before speaking, that, 'today is Shabbos; what I say, and the manner in which I say it, should be Shabbosdik.' As a student of the Baal Shem Tov writes (*Toldas Yaakov Yoseph*, Parshas Noach, Parshas Beshalach), a Tzadik (and truly, "all of Israel are called Tzadikim") should aspire to not have Hesech haDa'as even on the level of Machshavah.

All of the above disciplines are within the realm of our choice and ability, but the question remains, how should we actually achieve the instruction of the Mekubalim to rest from weekday Machshavah altogether? And what does it really mean to rest from 'thoughts,' to leave the world of the six days and everything it encompasses, and think only higher, more noble thoughts? Also, when mundane (or worse) thoughts do rise up without our 'consent,' how can we address such an occurrence?

Indeed, this second and higher level of 'mental rest' is more than just engaging our thoughts in higher subjects. It means to completely quiet the mind from the onrush of negative or work-related or mundane thoughts. It means to have no *Machshavah Zarah* / foreign thoughts at all, nothing unrelated to Shabbos, spirituality, Torah, and deeper meaning.

Human beings experience a challenging phenomenon that the Russian and Polish Rebbes called 'horse-thoughts.' Horses were abundant in Eastern Europe, inspiring this phrase. To the best of our knowledge and estimation, a horse is always thinking about what is in front of him at that very moment. Whether it is a basin of water or a pile of hay, the horse is always thinking of the basin of water or the pile of hay. Sadly, the vast majority of some people's thoughts are horse(type) thoughts; they only extend to what is right in front of their face, and mouth, at any one moment.

Imagine you decide to think over a particular idea on your walk to work. As you step out of your house you bring the thought into your mind's eye, but immediately the first thing you see, hear, smell or touch pops into your train of thought. Let's say you hear a siren going off in the distance and your mind instantly wonders about the reason for the siren. Then you notice the clouds, so you begin to calculate if it's going to rain soon. This sets off a whole chain of thoughts: where's my umbrella? Umbrellas are so expensive. I should really make more money. I don't like my boss, and so on and so forth. The horse thoughts begin to gallop and they take over the driver's seat of your mind. In a short time, your mind has traveled on a wild ride of loosely connected associations, leaving you effectively nowhere. The unifying point of them all is that not one of them was chosen and not one of them was the original thought you decided to think about on your way to work.

"I think, therefore I am," is not as true as, "I am what I think." Most people think they choose their thoughts, when in truth, their thoughts choose them. When our minds are without clear focus, thoughts can jump around like kernels of corn in a popcorn machine. As a result, our words and deeds too become unfocused, unintentional and haphazard. A scattered mind creates scattered words and actions. How many times do people say something out loud, and then only a moment later say, "I am so sorry! I said that, but didn't really mean it." It seems as if the mouth has a mind of its own. The same is true with actions — one does something only to regret it a second later.

'SHABBOS BRAIN' VS. 'WEEKDAY BRAIN'

This scatteredness of the brain, and the rushing and jumping around from one thought to the next, is a malady of the world of the 'six-days,' the world of *Perudah* / separation. Part of the reason that the Machshavah of a person is constantly moving and popping around is because the brain 'fills' itself up with stimulation, and then immediately feels empty. Right away the brain looks for another stimulus to fill the void, the *Chalal* / hollowness. This is a manifestation of *Chol* / weekday consciousness, with its existential sense of *Cheser* / lack, as explored earlier. A weekday consciousness runs about, grasping for fulfilment, but never attains real satisfaction or completion, and never senses that it has a stable center.

In this 'scatter-brain' mode, there is great *Pizur haNefesh* / diffusion of one's energy and soul. Every moment is something new, and no two thoughts are deeply related, only tangentially or associatively juxtaposed. 'Shabbos-brain,' by contrast, is centered, focused and unscathed by surroundings. To paraphrase Rav Moshe Alshich (1508-1593), "To have a level of *Da'as* / awareness that is settled, in a state of completion with nothing missing, is the highest level of *Oneg Shabbos* / Shabbos pleasure" (*Toras Moshe*, Ki Tisa, 31:13). Shabbos is the world of *Yichud* / unity, and is the 'center' of time and reality. A Shabbosdik brain has the ability to stay with one thought for a long period of time, pondering all its details without any distraction. To be in a Shabbos mode is to *Sheiv* / settle or sit (a term which shares the root of the word *Shabbos*). You can settle into a single idea and deeply think it through without any unwanted intruding thoughts grabbing your attention, guiding it onto an aimless path.

A majority of people operate ineffectively because they are not settled in a stable place of mental integrity and therefore cannot orchestrate their own physical, mental and spiritual energies. They function from a 'weekday brain,' always at odds with themselves and lacking a sense of alignment with their center. They are always living in the Chol paradigm of *Rav* / a lot, as explored earlier — a lot of superficial movements going on internally. As a result they are not nourished by the sense of *Kol* / everything, which is the state of *Yichud* / unity and Shabbos-consciousness.

Shabbos is the center of time, the center of the week, the center of the world, but it also has a centering quality on consciousness. On Shabbos, the entire world is in a state of *Shuv* / returning; all of time, space and consciousness is returning to its Source (*Likutei Torah*, Shabbos Shuvah, 66b). We too, by the cosmic force of return, and by our conscious choice to 'let go' of the external world, return and come into direct contact with our true inner self. We rest from the world of dramatic external stimuli and noise. We move away from our sense of lack, and the part of self that derives its identity from the externalities of life, such as material possessions, titles, honorifics, and public approval. In this way, we become more silent, secure, centered and focused.

Ideally, Shabbos would arrive and we would snap right into 'Shabbos-brain.' Ideally, we would have such control over our thoughts that we could simply will ourselves to be more centered and present, without any distracting thoughts. Unfortunately, while we all would love to live within a Shabbos paradigm at all times, or at the very least on Shabbos itself, this desire itself does not create the reality. How then do we get there? What practice will help us quiet the scatteredness and desperate grasping for fulfilment in the world of separation. What can we do that will allow us to enter the world of Unity and Silence?

A PRACTICE TO ENTER A
'SHABBOS-BRAIN' CONSCIOUSNESS

Sit comfortably, and allow yourself to just be present.

Invite all of yourself into this space.

You do not need to close your eyes,
but it may be helpful.

As you sit, various sounds, sensations,
thoughts and feelings may arise.

Allow them to surface without the need to hold onto,
internalize or judge them.

As they come, so they go.

Gently bring your awareness to your thoughts.

Are they random? "Foolish"? Incessant?
Just observe them without judgment or analysis.

As you are observing the thoughts that are coming up,
very softly recite to yourself a short teaching by our

sages or a verse in the Torah.

Allow the phrase or sentence to repeat —

not in an automatic or hypnotic way, but mindfully and thoughtfully.

Let this sentence serve as the focal point, returning your mind to center when it wanders off.

The repetition of the sentence diffuses distraction and clarifies your focus on the content of the teaching or verse.

With gentle awareness you may sense that your mind is becoming more empty and quiet; less thoughts are intruding.

If your mind wanders, as it may tend to do, gently return to your focal point, the teaching or verse.

Allow inner experiences to arise and resolve.

You are the unmoving center of them all.

Try not to work yourself up in excitement or tension, rather assume a 'Shabbosdik' posture of ease and pleasure.

Continue as long as you wish to focus on your teaching or verse, with gentleness and calm.

This is a very simple and straightforward path to help quiet the chaos of the 'weekday brain' and enter into a more Shabbos-like consciousness. This is all part of the higher, second level of 'mental rest' that we ought to aspire to attain on the holy Shabbos.

LEVEL FOUR: EXISTENTIAL REST
SHABBOS OF ATZILUS / DEVEIKUS / CHAYAH

On the level of Deveikus, in the active mode of Zachor, we aspire to achieve a revealed sense of total existential rest and tangible
closeness to HaKadosh Baruch Hu. On the level of Atzilus, there
is very little to be done, all we need do is make sure we do not
stand in the way of Hashem's imminent presence. On Shabbos,
"something completely new, something that does not exist during
the week, is birthed within the People of Israel, and that is a love
and desire to connect to Hashem beyond our comprehension or
contemplation" (Alter Rebbe, *Torah Ohr*, Vayakhel). The passive mode of
Shamor is reflected in our *Bitul* / negation of all ego-based wills
and desires. *Shabbos* of course means *rest*, but can also mean 'to
nullify' (Shemos, 12:15. Bamidbar, 26:6). This alludes to the nullifica-
tion of our splintered sense of separate self, resulting in the *Bitul* /
negation or subjugation of the egoic 'I,' and its eventual integration
within the 'I' of Hashem, as it were.

Everything in this world is רוצה בקיומו / *Rotze b'Kiyumo* / wanting to exist. The nature of the world is to strive for survival, whether of the self or the species. Survival is tantamount to existence
because the inner world of the *Chayus Eloki* / Divine animating
force, that creates and sustains Creation itself, 'wants' to continue to
create and sustain and to exist — this is the natural expression of
the Six Days of Creation. After the Six Days of Creation, there is
a moment of *Dai* / "Enough!" (see *Chagigah*, 12a. *Dai* is numerically 14,
perhaps corresponding to the elevation of 14 levels of the world on Shabbos.
Sha'ar Ma'amorei Rashbi, Kedoshim) At that moment, the inner desire to
create and exist recedes back into its Source. The inner life force

sustaining Creation no longer wants to exist and express itself as being separate from its Source, as it were. Klal Yisrael, who are in sync with the innermost workings of Creation, also want to cease to exist, in a manner of speaking, and to return to their Source, on Shabbos. As mentioned numerous times, *Shabbos* shares a root with the word *Shavas* / return. This illustrates the powerful yearning of Klal Yisrael to return to their original state of Bitul, in which soul and body and Creator are joined in a comprehensive unity. Shabbos awakens this will and desire to return to the limitless space of perfect stillness and fullness.

Just as external noise resolves into external silence, an absence of our internal noise can resolve into a deep existential silence and stillness, beyond all noise. Shabbos, on a higher level, is this inner rest, silence and stillness. Yet, often it is the external silence, the simple absence of noise, that allows us to get to the place of inner silence. The 'Shabbos of Speech,' as explored earlier, is connected to the practice of external silence, simply speaking less. The 'Shabbos of Thought' is connected to quieting the cacophony of random/ unwanted thoughts. And then there is the 'Shabbos of Existence,' the Shabbos of Atzilus, which is the silencing of the separate self, a silencing of our sense of self-centeredness, allowing a deep existential rest and silence to emerge and settle.

There is a mental *Hashkatah* / quieting of the mind from intruding thoughts, and there is a more existential Hashkatah, quieting of the ego itself. The Mishnah tells us, "The Early Chasidim would wait one hour and then they prayed, so that their hearts (minds) would be directed to their Father in Heaven" (*Berachos*, 5:1). The language the Mishnah uses for "wait" is שׁוֹהִין, in transliteration spelled,

Sho'in / the act of being still. In other words: They would stop speaking, quiet their thoughts for a full hour, and only then commence to pray (Rambam, *Pirush haMishnayos*, Berachos 5:1).

On this level of Hashkatah, being still is not merely silencing one's speech and thoughts, but also silencing the whole constructed voice of the limited individual self. Through this practice, the Early Chasidim would experience a *Hispashtus haGashmiyus* / divestment of materiality. This is a spiritual state wherein they were detached from their bodily sensations, allowing them to meditatively enter into a state removed from the limitations of physical form. They surrendered any psychic ties to the constrictions of their physicality. This is a lofty stage analogous to prophetic consciousness (Tur, *Orach Chayim*, 98. Mechaber, *ibid.* Shaloh, *Asarah Hilulim*, p. 319. *Nefesh haChayim*, Sha'ar 2:14). This divestment from the physical can be experienced via visualization of separation from one's body (*Sha'arei Kedushah*, 4), as well as by internally silencing one's *Yesh* / egoic sense of self. These Early Chasidim would regularly free themselves of attachment to all outer physical sensations and experiences, and would thereby attain a measure of divestment of all materiality and sense of being a separate entity (*Pri haAretz*, Vayakhel-Pekudei. See also *Avodas Yisroel*, p. 164. *Shearis Yisroel*, p. 3).

At least once a week, on Shabbos, we too should aspire to proactively divest ourselves from materialism and materiality and live for the 25-26 hours of Shabbos as if we have no material needs whatsoever. Imagine how we would live if our ego was not the dominant driving force in our lives. Perhaps, we would still need a diminished, natural ego-self to ensure that we eat, drink and sleep, house and protect our family and provide for their needs. But without the *exaggerated* ego, our selfish desires for honor, power and fame, would dissipate and vanish.

For the 25-26 hours of Shabbos do not think, 'What can I gain?' 'What could I get out of this?' 'How does this or that experience make me feel?' Rather, one dominant thought should be your template, and that is, 'What does Hashem want from me?'

Take the 'I' out of the equation of your activities and interactions. Once the obstacle of the inflated ego is put aside, the deeper part of yourself, your soul, can shine forth and dominate, and you can live in Deveikus, a tangible sense of unity with Hashem and your bigger purpose of life.

Some indications that we are authentically living in a posture of Deveikus are the following: 1) You feel free from worry and anxiety of what *will be*, and also emptied from the nagging unrest of what *could have been*. 2) You are living with very little fear of the world and its challenges. Instead, you feel empowered with *Emunah* / faith in Hashem and *Bitachon* / trust in Hashem's goodness. 3) Your mind and heart are open with awe and love towards the Creator and all of His Creation. All of these are experiential indicators that you are living from a place of Deveikus, the epitome of Shabbos consciousness.

'I need this,' 'I want that,' 'I am so worried about what will be,' 'I am consumed with regret over not doing what I could have done' — all of this is egoism, plain and simple. And when the ego rules supreme, deep fear sets in, and fear is the most crippling and devastating emotion there is. Every fear, whether real or illusionary, is rooted in the ego. Every anxiety is the ego resisting its annihilation. From the greatest fear, the fear of death and extermination, to the slightest one, the fear of being embarrassed, all fears have an element of the fear of partial or total extinction. From the fear of being physically hurt, or losing a limb, to the fear of being crushed mentally, all are manifestations of the fear of losing the ego, and they are all the result of the ego's cunning schemes to secure its survival and perpetuation.

On Shabbos we are empowered by the 'extra soul' that we receive to enter a state of *Yiras Hashem* / fear or awe of the Creator (*Sefer Yerei'im*, 410). The higher Yirah, the awe and sense of humility and nothingness in the presence of the infinite majesty of the Creator, banishes all lower forms of fear, and consumes them all, whether they are petty or not. This Yirah is part of the *Shamor* / protecting of Shabbos, to ensure that the anxious ego is checked, and that one is firmly immersed in the Deveikus of Shabbos.

When we function from a place of Yirah, humility and Deveikus, we are living out the truth that everything, all of life, is in the hands of Hashem. Throughout the week we are asked to be co-creators in bettering Hashem's Creation, but on Shabbos we simply rest and surrender; we thereby give everything back to Hashem. Shabbos is a day we function with little or no ego-driven ambition. Once the ego is tamed and rendered transparent to Hashem, our true selves, our souls, shine-forth and we are *Shomer Shabbos* in the truest sense.

For the 25-26 hours of Shabbos, we are given extra *Koach* / power to overcome our *Yesh* / ego-self, and surrender our worries or fears to Hashem. This worry-free zone is also free of material wants and desires. We even need to let go of our spiritual drives and ambitions, as it were. When our sages tell us that on Shabbos we should vividly imagine that "all our work is done," this means, say the Chassidic Rebbes (*Meor Einayim*, Miketz, and Ki Tisa. *Sheim M'shemuel*, Bamidbar, Chasuna. See also: *Likutei Torah*, Balak, p. 71), even our spiritual work. We need to envision ourselves as perfect Tzaddikim, and live from that perspective.

This is truly a *Chidush* / novel idea, that even our spiritual work is considered 'done' on Shabbos, and there is truly nothing more to do or achieve. But encoded into the very word *Shabbos* is the word *Shav* / sit or settle, into stillness. Primarily, the approach of 'sitting' is to observe your life and simply accept 'what is,' both on a physical and a spiritual level. Shabbos is *Menuchah* / rest and the absence of all *Tenuah* / movement (although, there is also the possibility of *Aliyah* / rising higher even from, paradoxically, a place of total Menuchah (the Rebbe, *Toras Menachem*, Hadranim, p. 308. Note 65), similar to the idea of מהלך כעומד דמי / "One who walks is like standing" (*Shabbos*, 5b), i.e. walking and standing together). Shabbos is *Shalom* / peace, wholeness and perfection. On Shabbos there is no internal strife or struggle, as there is no *Yetzer haRa* / negative, ego-based inclination (*Sefas Emes*, Yisro). The external world is perfect, and we too, in our internal world, are 'perfect' as well, aligned with the One.

We each have an inner 'perfect-self'; a sliver of the Ultimate Being of Infinite Unity, this is the self that is whole, present and just is. We also have an 'imperfect self'; a self that strives, longs, yearns and aspires. The part of us that is always whole and perfect is the 'Shabbos' point within our *Nefesh* / soul. The part of us that is 'imperfect' and fragmented, in a constant state of becoming, is the 'weekday' aspect within our soul. Shabbos reveals, if we allow it to, our deeper dimension of self in which we are always-already 'perfect' and in a constant state of unity with the Creator. Keeping Shabbos on this level of inner perfection is connected to *Yom sheKulo Shabbos* / a day when all will be Shabbos, as is clear for those with understanding.

On Shabbos, there should be a sense that we have arrived; there is nowhere else to go and nothing else to do. We are home. We are princes and princesses who have returned to the Palace of our Father, the King. "There is nothing *Cheser* / missing in the palace of the king" (כלום חסר לבית המלך :*Shabbos*, 153a). We, who dwell in the Palace of the King of Perfection, cannot help but feel this perfection and wholeness.

Shabbos is the 'Promised Land.' When Shabbos arrives, and we enter deeply into it, we have attained our destination, both physically and spiritually. *Klal Yisrael* / the Community of Israel began as a people with a Divine command to move forward, to journey and progress. When Hashem chose Avraham and first communicated with him, Hashem told him, "Go forth from your land and from your birthplace and from your father's house, to the land אשר אראך / that I will show you" (*Bereishis*, 12:1). He, and by extension all of us, are told to journey, to move forward, to not stand still, until we reach "the land that I will show you." The word אראך / *I will show you*, in numerical value is 702 (Aleph/1, Reish/ 200, Aleph/1, final Chaf/500 = 702), which is the same value as the word *Shabbos*. Throughout the week, in the world of Tenuah, movement, we too need to strive, aspire and journey, elevate ourselves and move forward in a perpetual state of motion. Comes Shabbos, and we stop; we recognize the inner perfection that is always-already present, and declare, "I have arrived and all my work is done."

PLEASURE & THE LOSS OF THE SEPARATE SELF WITHIN SOMETHING OR SOMEONE ELSE

On Shabbos there is a Mitzvah of *Oneg* / pleasure. Oneg Shabbos is to *feel* what you do and, even more importantly, to deeply feel a connection with the Source of all Life; this is a level of Deveikus.

Most people think that pleasure is gained by self-indulgence, such as relishing a delicious dish, enjoying music, alcohol or physical intimacy. If this would be the case, Oneg would be the total opposite of Deveikus, as Deveikus is the total absence of self and ego. Yet, throughout the ages, many great Tzadikim have confirmed that there is no greater pleasure than Deveikus. "If the great sinners of the world, those who indulge in the pleasures of the world, would know the pleasure of Deveikus," the Alter Rebbe once quipped, "they would let go of all the pleasures in this world and run towards spirituality."

To experience Deveikus and spiritual Ta'anug is one of the reasons we were created and placed within this world.*

---

* There are various 'reasons' (and 'reasons' suggest 'separation' and movement away from the space of Unity) that the world came into being. For example, "The nature of the Good is to give goodness" (*Emek haMelech*, Sha'ar 1:1. *Da'as Tevunos,* 18). Hashem, the Source of Goodness, creates a Creation in order to bestow 'goodness' upon it. Or, alternatively, the reason the finite, multi-faceted Creation came into being is to "reveal the complete array and perfection of His powers and deeds" — i.e., to reveal that the Infinite One can create a finite world (*Eitz Chayim*, Sha'ar 1. Derush Igulim v'Yosher). Or, possibly, the Creation exists "so that we shall know Him" (*Zohar* 2, 42b), and "know that He exists" (*Ramban*, Shemos, 13:16).

The 'difficulties' with each of these reasons are: a) if the Creator merely created angelic, celestial beings, they too would be a sufficient creation upon which to bestow goodness, and they, more than human beings, for example, would be more appreciative of the Infinite's power, and certainly they "know Him" better; and b) any 'reason' given suggests a 'need'

"Our souls descend to this world to experience delight with Hashem and to have pleasure from the light of the Shechinah" (*Mesilas Yesharim*, in the beginning). This is especially true on Shabbos. In the words of the Alter Rebbe, "The service (of Hashem on Shabbos) is not (accomplished) via hard (spiritual) work, rather, only by experiencing delight with Hashem" (*Likutei Torah*, Balak, 71a). This is the *S'char* / reward of our actions in *Olam haZeh* / this world, which we will only experience fully in *Olam haBa* / the World-to-Come.

Still, the question remains: how do Oneg and Deveikus function in unison? Pleasure seems to be all about the self; "I am enjoying the music," "I am delighted by these foods." Whereas Deveikus is all about the 'other,' be it binding oneself to another person or to Hashem.

Pleasure is actually a peculiar phenomenon. It may seem counterintuitive, but the peak of pleasure is the collapse of self within something else.

---

and need suggests a 'lack'; something that is 'missing' and can be 'completed.' The Creator does not lack anything.

The Alter Rebbe quotes the Medrash (*Tanchumah*, Naso, 16) that the purpose of this Creation is that "Hashem *desires* to have a dwelling place (a *Dirah* / home) in the *Tachtonim* / the lower realms (*Tanya*, Chap. 36). This is the 'ultimate' purpose of the Creation of this physical, lower, world. This is a 'reason' beyond rational reasons, as the nature of desire is beyond reason (see Rashab, *Hemshech Samach Vav*, p. 7). Desire is not a 'need,' rather it is a 'want.'

And in fact, all of the above, 'revealed reasons' for the Creation (see Rebbe, Rashab, *Hemshech Ayin Beis*, p. 70. Rebbe Rayatz, *Tav/Shin/Beis*, p. 32) complement the root desire for a *Dirah b'Tachtonim* / dwelling place in the lower realms (see the Rebbe, *Likutei Sichos*, 6, p. 21. Note 69). When we 'know Hashem,' when we receive and thank Hashem for His goodness, we appreciate Hashem's power, and we ensure that the Dirah is illuminated with Hashem's revealed Presence. Our actions and Mitzvos create the dwelling place for Hashem in this world, and our conscious recognition of Hashem's presence illuminates the dwelling.

The ultimate pleasure of food or music, for example, is not when you are self-aware and enjoying the food or music, because this self-awareness actually separates you from the experience. If you are listening to music and are aware of yourself as a person who is listening to the music, it is a barrier for your total enjoyment. But the moment you stop thinking about yourself and lose yourself in the music, you experience true pleasure and become lost in the experience. In fact, only afterward will you become aware that 'you' had the experience. Another example would be marital intimacy. The ultimate bliss is when the two partners lose themselves within each other, merge completely and lose consciousness of being separate selves, as they become *Basar Echad* / one flesh. In this way, the peak of pleasure is in fact Deveikus, as Rashi writes (*Sanhedrin*, 58b), אין כאן דבק שמתוך שאינה נהנית בדבר אינה נדבקת עמו — to paraphrase, 'If there is no pleasure in it, it is not Deveikus.' The sensation of pleasure can bring one to an experience beyond an isolated awareness of sensation, and is thus a path to experience Deveikus, which is the ultimate pleasure.

Physical pleasures are called תענוג מורכב / *Ta'anug Murkav* / blended pleasures, meaning, there is a you and there is 'another' element — for example, the other person you are with or the music you are listening to — and in the pleasure the *two* become 'blended' into a composite unity. Spiritual pleasure, by contrast, is when the 'you' becomes utterly submerged in the Infinite Unity of Hashem, which in reality is never separated from you in any way. This is called *Ta'anug Pashut* / simple, pure pleasure; you are not losing yourself in 'something' that is separate from you, rather, you are losing yourself in the Presence of HaKadosh Baruch Hu, which is always with you and deeply within you without separation.

In the realm of physical pleasure, the 'separate' objects that give us pleasure are limited and finite. A certain piece of food, for example, temporarily stimulates the vessel that 'receives' the pleasure, our taste buds. When our finite ears are enjoying a certain 'finite' piece of music, usually only our ears, along with other parts of our nervous system and brain, are enjoying it. These parts of the body are in general only enjoying the *music* and the effect that it stimulates. If we do succeed in losing ourselves via a finite musical experience, it is only fleeting and ephemeral. Abiding or transformative pure pleasure is not accessed, as there is no complete, full body consciousness and immersion. When the music ends, the vessel and experience of pleasure fades, revealing again its status as a finite entity, remaining separate from us. As a result, we need to listen to the piece of music again and again to access the stimulation we desire. With repetition, the pleasure often fades, and if the stimulation were to be perpetual, the pleasure would quickly vanish, as our sages teach, "Constant pleasure is not called pleasure at all" (*Likutei Amarim* (the Maggid) 168, in the name of the Baal Shem Tov).

In a 'weekday' or 'Tree of Knowledge' reality, every pleasure that we receive comes to us through two constricting 'garments': 1) the physical, finite garment of the object of pleasure — the thing or person which is 'giving' the pleasure, and 2) the physical, finite garment (or vessel) of the subject of pleasure — we who are receiving the pleasure (Leshem, *Sefer haDe'ah* 2, Derush 4, 11:4). When we taste a fruit, for example, it is only the flavors and physical consistency of the fruit that give us pleasure, and no other aspects of the fruit. We do not procure pleasure from the entirety of the fruit because its multi-dimensional wholeness and supernal spiritual roots are restricted to us; not all of it is available to us. This is a limitation within the object of pleasure. The same is true with the recipient of the pleasure. When we eat a tasty fruit it is only with our taste buds, our mouth and specific parts of the brain with which we sense the pleasure, and not with the entire body and soul.

Whereas the depth of all pleasure is the 'losing' oneself in something or someone else, in 'weekday,' finite pleasures there are barriers and limitations, they do not elicit a full body and soul surrendering within the totality of something or someone. The Shabbos, Tree of Life, spiritual-level of pleasure is total and all consuming. It is where we lose our total self within the Ein Sof, the Infinite Light of Hashem, that which is not a separate object.

Shabbos is a 'taste of the World-to-Come'; it is other-worldly. This world is defined by action, *HaYom l'Asosam* / "Today we need to work," to act, to move forward, and relatedly, to move the world around us forward. Only in the World-to-Come will we bask in the *S'char* / reward or effects of our work, which is called *Oneg* / pure spiritual delight. The World-to-Come is defined by integral Unity, while our world is defined by the perception of duality. And yet, on Shabbos we are privy to the spiritual Oneg, a glimpse from the World-to-Come. As we enter the world of Unity we get to live the future in the present.

On this level of Oneg, the place of S'char and Olam haBa, we access pleasure without the intermediary of *Levushim* / garments or limitations within the object or within ourselves. The essence and the entirety of even a fruit will 'touch' the essence and entirety of our being.

Experientially speaking, this means that our entire self, not just our taste buds, stomach or certain parts of the brain take pleasure in the Divine. Once we have lost our finite self, even our feet partake in the unmitigated pleasure of the Divine Glory. Only by losing our entire selves in the Infinite Source of All Life, and actively living in unison with It, can we experience a perpetual 'peak' of pleasure. This is the Deveikus and pleasure of Shabbos, a spiritual pleasure beyond all pleasures of the world, the total-loss of self-awareness within the Infinite expanse of the Ein Sof.

In addition to the 'temporary experience' of spiritual pleasure with the whole body and soul, the after-effects dramatically differ from those of physical pleasure as well. In physical pleasure, if it is unconnected to spiritual pleasure, even if one loses oneself temporarily in the expanse of the pleasure, in the end the effects are that one feels empty, depleted or exhausted. There is no immediate desire for more of the same. One's thirst has been quenched. Spiritual pleasure — for example, the pure spiritual pleasure of Deveikus in prayer, or even a physical pleasure that contains a depth of spirituality, such as eating on Shabbos in order to gain Deveikus within Hashem's delight — contrasts strikingly with limited physical pleasure. In spiritual pleasure, you lose yourself deeper and deeper in the Ein Sof, and following the experience you feel more alive, empowered, energized, and you also have a visceral hunger for more and more *Yichud* / connection and ever-deeper levels of Deveikus.

ONEG VS. NEGA: EDEN / NAHAR / GAN

This qualitative contrast of pleasures is expressed in the mystical teaching of *Sefer Yetzirah* / the Book of Formation (one of the oldest published works of Sod), "There is nothing higher than Oneg and nothing lower than *Nega* / affliction" (*Sefer Yetzirah*, 2:7). *Oneg* and *Nega* have the same letters, just arranged differently. The Nega of the spiritual skin disease called *Tzara'as* comes about through acts of *Pirud* / separation, such as speaking *Lashon haRa* / 'negative' or separative speech against another person (*Erchin*, 16a Keep in mind that "Nega is not a natural occurrence, rather it is a sign and a wonder prevalent among the Jewish People to warn them against undesirable speech." Rambam, *Hilchos Tzara'as*, 16:10). As a consequence of speaking Lashon haRa, the speaker must spend time *Badad* / alone, or isolated from the community, to realize the extent of the affliction caused by his words. Oneg, on the other hand, is Unity. Oneg Shabbos, says the Zohar (*Tikkunei Zohar*, 58a), is the exact opposite of Nega. And one who does not experience Oneg on Shabbos experiences Nega (Radbaz, *Metzudas David*, Mitzvah 91).

Nega and Oneg are two completely different concepts. However, on a deeper level, the Nega spoken about in this context comes from a type of negative Oneg (the distorted, selfish pleasure of speaking Leshon haRa) which is felt in the moment as pleasure or release, but which leads to greater 'separation' and spiritual depletion. Nega is physical or psychological pleasure for its own sake, not for the sake of Deveikus with the Creator of pleasure.

To explain: both of these words have three letters, Ayin, which stands for *Eden*, Nun which stands for *Nahar* / river, and Gimel for *Gan* / garden. In the word *Oneg*, first comes Eden, then the river, then the garden; this is Shabbos (*Tikkunei Zohar*, 12a).* In fact, this is the way the Torah describes the Garden of Eden, "And a *Nahar*

---

* Shabbos is Oneg. *Oneg* is spelled Ayin, Nun, Gimel, an acronym for *Eden-Nahar-Gan*. The last letters of *Eden, Nahar, Gan* (Nun-Reish-Nun), are an acronym for *Nefesh*, **R**uach and *Neshamah*, the extra levels of soul energy that enter on Shabbos. The middle letters of

went forth from Eden, to irrigate the garden" (*Bereishis*, 2:10). Thus, the Nahar comes from Eden and then it flows into the Gan — the sequence being Eden, then Nahar, then Gan, which forms the acronym, *Oneg*. In the concept of *Nega*, first comes the Nahar then the Gan, and then Eden. What is the inner difference between Eden-Nahar-Gan, which is the highest form of pleasure, and Nahar-Gan-Eden which is the lowest form of affliction, sometimes masking as pleasure?

First we need to take a closer look at what these three elements mean and represent (See Rashab, *Yom Tov Shel Rosh Hashanah*, Samach Vav, p. 11). In terms of the Sefiros, the cosmic and inner map of reality, Eden is generally *Chochmah* / higher wisdom (*Zohar* 1, 247b. 3, p. 290a. *Tanya*, Igeres haKodesh, 5. *Koheles Yaakov*, Eden), or *Binah* / understanding (or *Keser* / Transcendence. *Tikkunei Zohar*, Hakdamah, 12a. *Zohar* 2, 90a. *Pardes Rimonim*, Sha'ar 23:16, Eden).

Eden, Nahar, Gan, (and the word *Gan* only has two letters, so it is omitted) are Dalet/4 and Hei/5 = 9. Nine is the *Mispar Katan* / small numerical value of the word *Shabbos* (Shin/3, Beis/2, Tav/4 = 9).

Besides the two Mitzvos from our Sages, the Four Cups of wine on Pesach night and Chanukah candles (which are both done for *Pirsumei Nisa* / publicizing the miracle), the only other Mitzvah where a poor person is commanded to go collect money to help perform the Mitzvah, is for the lighting of candles Friday evening before Shabbos. This, the Rambam writes, is because lighting candles is part of Oneg Shabbos (Rambam, *Hilchos Shabbos*, 5:1). Although, in general, with the Mitzvah of Oneg one can fulfil the obligation with the bare minimum, as one can gain Oneg from a simple stew (Rambam *Hilchos Shabbos*, 30:7). Or even from fasting (Alter Rebbe, *Shulchan Aruch*, Orach Chayim, 288:2); yet, without seeing what you are eating there is no real Oneg, pleasure, enjoyment and satisfaction (*Yumah*, 74b). Indeed, Shabbos is Oneg and 'without Oneg there is no Shabbos.' Even the Oneg of eating delicious foods itself, simply having pleasure in the foods one eats, is Oneg Shabbos. *Beis haLevi*, Torah, Terumah. See however, *Aderes Eliyahu*, Yeshayahu, 1:12.

Nahar is the river of our emotions (the six Sefiros from Chesed thru Yesod), and Gan is Malchus, the outward expression and material-ization of all that preceded it. In this way, the movement of Oneg is from the Source, the *Mashpiah* / Bestower (Eden), to the *Shefa* / medium of bestowal (Nahar), to the *Mekabel* / recipient of the Shefa (Gan).

Another way of explaining this movement is that it is from Chochmah (the Bestower) to Malchus (the receiver). In simpler language, water represents desire, therefore *Nahar* represents our emotional desires. *Gan*, a lush garden represents a place of pleasure, the actual partaking in the pleasures of the world, the Mekabel. Eden, then, indicates an abstract space devoid of water, vegetation and fruit, and so it represents the 'emptiness' and mindful detach-ment out of which the river emerges, like an underground spring.

In exclusively physical pleasure, unrelated to any spirituality, and thus connected to Nega and the world of separation, the move-ment is as follows; at first there is a strong desire to attain and indulge in the pleasure, be it what it may be. This is the Nahar, the waters of desire. Then, one goes ahead and indulges in the pleasure, say, food, for example. The individual partakes in the delicious 'fruit' of the garden, and 'loses himself' in the food (without trying to connect to anything deeper). This is the garden. Then, at the end of an overindulgence of this type of selfish physical pleasure, one feels the 'emptiness' of *Eden*, although in this case it is felt as depletion, tiredness, and existential emptiness, with no wish to go back for seconds. Perhaps there is even a level of disgust with the pleasure just indulged. This is a collision with the *Klipah* / impure 'shell' of Eden. Pleasure should thus begin from a place of Ayin, not end there.

When a desire is quenched in a non-holy, non-ethical, or even just exclusively physical way, the end feeling is literally the opposite of pleasure. There is a disturbing story in Tanach which poignantly illustrates this point. There was a beautiful woman named Tamar. "...And Amnon, her half-brother, fell desperately in love with her. Amnon became so obsessed with Tamar that he became ill," and he devilishly devised to trick Tamar into his bedroom. And so, he pretended to be sick, and asked that his sister Tamar come prepare food for him. When she came with the food, he said to Tamar, "Now bring the food into my bedroom and feed it to me here." So Tamar took his favorite dish to him. But as she was feeding him, he grabbed her and demanded, "Come to bed with me, my darling sister." "No, my brother!" she cried. "Don't be foolish! Don't do this to me! Such wicked things aren't done in Israel..." But Amnon wouldn't listen to her, and since he was stronger than she was, he raped her (Heaven forfend). Then suddenly Amnon's love turned to hate, and he hated her even more than he had loved her" (Shemuel 2, 13:1-15).

Sadly, when a person who has a terrible urge and desire, a tremendous amount of Nahar, and then indulges it in a perverse expression of pleasure, the forbidden fruit of the *garden*, they may gain momentary satisfaction, but are then left feeling empty and despondent, the Kelipah of Eden, which can deepen into hate and disgust (although, see *Sanhedrin*, 21a). The above story is an extreme example of Nahar leading to Gan and then to Eden, but all purely physical indulgences follow the same pattern; initial desire and eventual disgust for a particular food or person. Indulging in desires with no mindfulness and simply being guided by raw, 'animal' passion, leaves a person repulsed by one's own hunger, selfishness and lack of control.

Imagine, you yearn to relish a particular food, say a piece of meat, and you go ahead and stuff yourself until you are bloated, nauseous, sick, and disgusted. Afterwards, you promise to yourself that you will never eat meat again in your life. This is the trajectory of all physical desires that are not rooted in a higher spiritual context or a yearning for Deveikus; first desire, then fleeting pleasure, then a collapse into the Nega of afflictive emptiness.

With real Oneg, the movement is the opposite. One begins with a sense of Eden, a holy emptiness, a mindful detachment and healthy observation that channels the Nahar/desire so that one can partake of the fruit of the garden of eternal delight.

The process of entering into spiritual pleasure is different than that of entering into physical indulgence. One begins with *Choch-mah* / higher wisdom, and some measure of *Binah* / understanding of what is about to transpire and what is the objective, and then one can act with *Daas* / practical intelligence and an ability to choose whether to pursue the desire or to reject it. And so is the result; the effect of the Oneg is profoundly different than the effect of mindlessly indulging a craving. The more one loses their 'self-awareness,' their identity as a separate self, and merges deeper and deeper into the Ein Sof, the Infinite expanse of the Divine, the more alive, empowered and energized they feel following the experience. There is, as a result, almost a visceral, tangible hunger for more *Yichud* / connection and more Deveikus. The exalted spiritual pleasure of Deveikus and Oneg Shabbos is pleasure beyond all pleasures of the world, resulting in a total loss of ego-self within the Infinite Divine Self.

In fact, Oneg Shabbos elevates even our animal cravings. When one's domesticated animal rests on Shabbos, the animal is elevated spiritually, as Rashi says, allowing an animal to rest brings it to Kedushah (צריכי דאי תנא לוקח ה"א משום דקא מייתי לה לקדושה אבל מוכר דקא מפקע לה מקדושה אימא ליקנסימייתי לה לקדושה — שתהא שובתת בשבת וכיון דמצוה עביד ליכא למיקנסיה Bechoros, 2a, although see Tosefos, ad loc). In other words, insofar as the Kedushah of Shabbos is applicable to animals, if an animal rests on Shabbos, there is a spiritual elevation for the animal, not just the animal's owner. This means that our physical desires, including eating, sleeping and intimacy, when indulged on Shabbos with a concomitant desire to connect with HaKadosh Baruch Hu, become vessels for Oneg as well. Shabbos thus has the power to transform Nega into Oneg.

SHABBOS IS NECHMAD / PLEASURABLE BEYOND THE WORLD OF TOV / GOOD

The Vilna Gaon (*Ideres Eliyahu*) points out that the word *Tov* / good is found in the Torah with regard to each of the Six Days of Creation. Even though on Day Two the Torah does not explicitly say the word *Tov*, on Day Three the word *Tov* appears twice, once for the completion of Day Two and once for completion of Day Three. The only day of Creation where the word *Tov* does not appear at all is Shabbos, the Seventh Day. This is because Shabbos is beyond the quality of 'good,' as good implies duality, as in the opposite of bad. Shabbos is a time of *Oneg* / pleasure and delight, and Shabbos itself is Oneg, as we say in the liturgy of morning prayers, *Oneg Kara l'Yom haShabbos* / "You called Oneg for the day of Shabbos."

Essentially, *Tov* is connected to the mundane workweek reality. Physical reality is tied to a utilitarian notion of *Tov*, as was the fruit of the Tree of Knowledge, "And the woman (Chava) saw that the Tree was 'good' for food" (Bereishis, 3:6). Tov means a type of wholeness in which things maintain their current status (thus, the word *Tov* was added to Birchas haMazon, when the sages saw that those killed in Beitar did not 'decay' (*Baba Basra*, 121b)), or function properly (preparing the Menorah so that it can be properly lit is called *haTovah*). Shabbos, however, is beyond 'good.' 'Good' functions in the world of duality, as distinct from 'bad' or 'evil' and the possibility of *Cheser* / absence; whereas Oneg represents a higher form of *Chayus* / life, beyond the world of Cheser (in the words of Tosefos, בורא נפשות רבות וחסרונם - כמו לחם ומים שאי אפשר בלא הם ועל כל מה שברא להחיות בהם נפש כל חי כלומר על כל מה שבעולם שגם אם לא בראם יכולין העולם לחיות בלא הם שלא בראם כי אם לתענוג בעלמא (Tosefos, *Berachos*, 37a)). Shabbos is a time of *Oneg* / pleasure and delight (*Yeshayahu*, 58:13).

Tov is a part of the functionality of this world, connected to the 'lower' more revealed 'aspects' of the Divine, represented by the lower Sefiros. Oneg is connected to the higher, deeper, more concealed and Transcendent 'aspect' of the Divine, namely the Sefirah of *Keser* / crown; before which the manifest world is like *Ayin* / nothing-ness, subsumed and enveloped entirely by the Divine Unity.

On Shabbos, there is an elevation of all the Tov of the week to the level of Nechmad. We have the power to elevate everything we have done during the week — even our *Tov* / good deeds, thoughts, and words — to an even higher, deeper level of pleasure, the world of Keser. This dynamic of elevation is beautifully illustrated by the *Gematriyah* / numerical value of the word *Tov*, which is 17. Six days of *Tov* (6 x 17) equal 102, which is the numerical value of the word *Nechmad*. On Shabbos we elevate the Tov of the week to the level of Nechmad.

During the week we are more connected with Tov, the utilitarian aspect of life, the functionality of existence, which is the Tree of Knowledge. On Shabbos, we are connected with Oneg, the Tree of Life.

As we step back from our weekday activities of constructive creativity, engagement with the world to better the world and efforts to further the *Tov* / goodness and progress in the world, we reveal the inner space and time we need to take pleasure in the inherent radiance and beauty of Hashem's Creation. Through that pleasure, we attain pleasure with Hashem Himself. On Shabbos, the world and our vision of the world transforms before our very eyes from being a finite deposit of raw materials for our further manipulation (Tov), into a unified Creation that is complete within itself.

Throughout the week, we act as artisans, constantly tweaking and tinkering with the world's constitutive elements. On Shabbos we shift into the role of the 'audience,' with front-row seats at the multi-sensory symphony of Hashem's delightful Creation. The world, in all of its dimensions, becomes a work of art that contains the hidden signature of the Ultimate Artist, Hashem. This dynamic, the world being manifest as *Tov* during the week and *Nechmad* on Shabbos, mirrors the dual potential of the single Tree of Reality, the fruit of which can manifest as either the Tree of Life or the Tree of Knowledge, depending on how and why we eat it. On Shabbos, we have the enhanced spiritual ability to partake in the Tree of Life and take pleasure in Hashem's Creation and in Hashem Himself.

09

THE SECRET OF ONE

"THE SECRET OF SHABBOS IS SHABBOS; THAT IS UNIFIED WITH THE SECRET OF ONE" (*ZOHAR*, 1, 135).

THERE IS A MYSTICAL TRADITION TO RECITE THIS PASSAGE AS Shabbos begins. It is a declaration that Shabbos is *Echad* / One. Every number is part of a sequence; one comes before two, two comes after one and before three, etc. Every number is also a *Murkav* / construct that can be added to other numbers, for example, two is twice one, and twice two is four. Yet, *Echad* represents a singularity that is not part of a sequence nor a Murkav. The word *Echad* means the 'oneness' that stands singular and unified, beyond the dimension of sequence and 'combining' with others.

As explored earlier, the six days of the week represent the plurality and multiplicity of Creation, the world of the many, the world of sequence and separation. The six days correspond to the six directions (up, down, right, left, front, back) and the fullness of dimensionality. Unity in this context of 'six days' (what the Maharal calls the *Tzurah* / form (*Tiferes Yisrael*, 40)), would mean adding all the various directions and separate pieces together, into a single, unified cube or construct. This is the world of Murkav, one thing is added to the next; 'I have this and that going on in my life,' or 'I have a body as well as a soul, and they are joined.' Echad suggests a radically different way of living. Shabbos is Echad.

Let us understand this a little better. There is an Echad worldview which is Shabbos-consciousness, and there is a Murkav worldview which is weekday consciousness. In the world of Murkav and separation, there is me and there is everything outside of me; people, objects, time, and so forth. In this way of living, whatever we acquire, say a new watch or car, or whatever happens to us, whether winning the lottery or breaking a leg, the object or event is something outside of ourselves that we are acquiring or that is happening to us.

During the six days, the world around us is *Mikrah* / an occurrence that is happening to us. We are separate from objective reality. Everything that is not part of our inner subjective reality — objects, people and occurrences — are all outside of ourselves, 'blending' with our life.

Everything in this experience is a *Murkav* / blending of myself and the world around me. Because of this way of experiencing and thinking, there is much conflict, friction, resistance and pain. If something challenging happens to you, the first question you ask is, 'Why did *this* happen to *me*?' But inherent in this type of question is the assumption that the things that are happening to you are not 'related' to you, not inherently part of you or your life, rather they are things that are thrown at you. These 'intrusions' create friction, and resistance to such friction is the root of pain.

This dynamic is also present within 'positive' events. Say a person earns a million dollars, wins the lottery, or finds their perfect *Bashert* / spouse. When they live in a paradigm of Murkav, thoughts arise like, 'How did I ever deserve this? Is this a dream? Am I going to lose everything tomorrow?' Again, such thoughts come from their sense that what happens to them, the money they make, the objects they acquire, and even the people they have in their lives, are not part of them.

There is also another way to think in terms of *Etzem* / essence, Echad, Shabbos. In this context, everything that happens to you, and everything and everyone in your life, your wife or husband, parents, children, friends and associates, are all part of your essence, part of you. Just like 'you' have legs, and your legs are part of you, the same is with your wife/husband, parents and children, friends and even possessions, they are all part of your extended being.

Observing your life and the events that occur 'to' you, you can dismiss them as mere happenstance, but if you do so you are denying a basic tenet that your actions have consequences and there is reward and punishment (Rambam, *Hilchos Ta'anis,* 1:1-3). Or, alternatively, you can ask, 'What is the cause of these events?' While this is certainly deeper than dismissing them as happenstance, it still suggests a subtle separation, that HaKadosh Baruch Hu is apart from Creation and guiding events from afar. The deepest way of living is from the place of total *Yichud* / unity, in which the world and everything in it is a unified expression of Divinity. In the world of Yichud, the question is not, 'What is the cause of this event?' rather, 'What is Hashem telling me through this event?' This is much like a person who feels pain in his toe, and asks, 'What is my body telling me through this pain?'

When a person lives in a Shabbos state of mind, aware that everything is Echad, one with Hashem, and everything in their life is one with life itself, they understand that not only is there no happenstance or coincidence, and that אלקות אין אלץ אלי / everything is Divinity, but they too are included in this unity. Everything that you have and everything that is happening to you in your life is an absolutely necessary part of life, part of you. There is no resistance or second guessing, nor even ruminating that perhaps this money, this circumstance or this person, comes from outside of your reality. Everything is from you and part of you.

There are 'big' things in life, such as important interpersonal connections, and there are 'smaller' things in life, such as the type of watch you have, or the types of food you prefer. Yet, all things big and small are part of who we are. Every detail in our life is actually an essential part of our life and an expression of our very existence. Our 'self,' in the fullest sense, includes all the people we are connected with, and also expands and includes even the seemingly insignificant objects in our lives.

When we live in this consciousness, everything in life is welcomed and embraced as part of our existence, as Echad. We clearly understand that everything is meant to be and there is no resistance to whatever and however life manifests. Life flows freely and everything feels like Shabbos.

On Shabbos, says the Zohar, there is no waste (*Zohar* 2, 88b. Alter Rebbe, *Torah Ohr,* Chayei Sarah, p. 15. *Derech Mitzvosecha*, Lo Sivaru Aish). Our eating on Shabbos is like the eating of the *Mon* / Manna in the desert, which was completely absorbed within the body, leaving nothing left over, no rejection or waste (*Yuma*, 75b. *Pri Tzadik*, Kedushas Shabbos, 6. *Torah Ohr,* Beshalach. *Derech Mitzvosecha*, Ibid). On Shabbos, the Echad manifests itself even in the foods we eat. Our eating is infused with an awareness of Echad, thus, there is no resistance and no waste. Everything eaten is integrated and becomes part of us; we recognize that it was already part of our soul. This may be more vividly felt than with other objects, as we physically internalize what we eat and it literally becomes part of our flesh and blood.

ONENESS & מחוייב המציאות / NECESSARY EXISTENCE

Our Creator is called the מחוייב המציאות / Necessary Existence, while the Creation is called אפשרי המציאות / 'possible' or contingent existence. Creation exists, yet, before it existed there was a possibility that it would not exist. Why does it in fact exist? Only because the Creator desired and chose to create it. It is contingent upon the Creator's desire. However, once there is a Divine desire to create it, the 'possible existence' becomes 'part' of the Necessary Existence, as it is now part of the Divine desire, and the desire of the Creator is one with the Creator.

What if the creation is not openly revealing the Divine desire? Is the world still part of the Necessary Existence or does it return to the state of possible existence? The more our lives are expressing the Divine intention and desire, and the more deeply and inwardly we understand that the entirety of our reality is Necessary Existence, the more we do in fact live in Divine Existence and understand that our lives are Necessary, in an actual, non-theoretical way. The reverse is also true.

The *Nekudah* / point of Shabbos is Yichud, living with the awareness that we and everything in our lives is an expression of Necessary Existence as 'part of us.' Echad-consciousness creates the ontological and very real condition that everything in our lives is a מחויב המציאות / Necessary Existence and absolutely part of who we are and part of our Divine purpose. As a result, we actually begin to live in the world of Unity.

A possible existence is something that relies on an exterior reason for its being. Shabbos is called Chok, a law that transcends reason (*Shemos*, 15:25, *Mechilta*, ad loc. *Sanhedrin*, 56b). Logic and reason are in a sense extraneous to Unity; they imply that there is a lack or a need for validity that can be fulfilled by relying on something else. Shabbos (as the essence of all Mitzvos*) is rooted in the Absolute Simplicity of Hashem's Unity, and thus it is 'beyond reason.'

* All Mitzvos must be beyond reason — reason cannot be the cause of a Mitzvah, as it is Hashem who caused the Mitzvah. The world is preceded by Hashem's Torah and is created through Hashem's Torah, not the other way around. Having a real 'reason' for a Mitzvah would suggest that the world precedes the Torah, and that the world's needs stimulate particular responses from Above. But the Mitzvos actually exist prior to any worldly reason or stimulus.

A Chok is therefore 'an end unto itself,' rooted in the Oneness of Hashem which is the ultimate End unto Itself — the absolutely Necessary Existence. The Nekudah of Shabbos is this reality.

INTEGRATING OUR ENTIRE PAST WEEK INTO ECHAD

Shabbos gives us the gift of thinking differently about our entire life, with all of the people and objects in it. We begin to think of them in terms of Echad and מחויב המציאות / Necessary Existence, and to include our entire lives, with all of our weekday pursuits, as a vast Murkav construct, merging seamlessly into the context of Echad.

A special liturgy called *Kabbolas Shabbos* / greeting Shabbos was added to the evening prayers on Friday night, to help us accept the Shabbos state, but also to include the entire past week within the deeper context of Shabbos. A future volume of this text will be specifically dedicated to Friday night, and these ideas will be explored in greater length there. Here, however, a few points will be mentioned regarding the inclusion of the weekday into the context of Shabbos.

Today, the prevailing Friday evening custom is to begin *Ma'ariv* / evening prayers with Kabbolas Shabbos. Kabbolas Shabbos includes reciting or singing six chapters of *Tehilim* / Psalms, Chapters 95 through 99, and then Chapter 29. On a most simple level, Shabbos is celebrated as a testimony that Hashem created the world, that there is a Creator and there is a purpose to Creation.

The common theme that runs through all these six chapters is that Hashem is the Master of the Universe and there will be a future time when all people will recognize Hashem's all-pervading presence and mastery. On a deeper level, these six chapters correspond to the six days of the previous week.*

Each one of these six chapters expresses the spiritual character of another day of the week. As we are reciting, singing or chanting them, we are putting closure on these days, sealing and incorporating their disparate energies, in preparation to "go greet the Shabbos Queen." We finally greet the Queen with the recitation or singing of the poem called *Lecha Dodi* / "Come My Beloved."

LECHA DODI: COME MY BELOVED

In Talmudic times a custom of some of the sages was to dress up in their finest attire and exclaim, "Let us go greet the Shabbos Queen," or "Enter, O Bride, enter, O Bride" (*Shabbos*, 119a). In fact, there appears to be a Mitzvah to greet Shabbos by saying, "Enter, O Bride, enter, O Bride (*Semag*, Esei 30).

---

* Reciting these six chapters as a Kabbolas Shabbos service has its roots in the holy city of *Tzfas* / Safed, Israel, in the 16th Century. It appears that reciting chapter 29 is an older custom, dating back at least to the 12th Century, and this was also the custom of the Arizal. Today, most communities recite all six chapters, besides, for example, the Aleppo Jews. It was Rabbi Moshe Cordevero, known as the Ramak, who added the six chapters to the Siddur (see *Siddur* R. Yaakov Emdin). The custom to recite the six chapters is first recorded by R. Moshe Machir in *Seder haYom*.

During the medieval period, a custom developed to enhance the entrance and departure of Shabbos with song and dance, as would befit a royal bride (*Sefer haManhig*, Hilchos Shabbos).

In the 1500's, many sages and mystics of the holy city of *Tzfas* / Safed, Israel, would actually go out into the fields to greet the Shabbos Presence (R. Eliyahu Di Vidas, *Totza'os Chaim*, 21b. Although see, the Ramak, *Ohr Yakar*, Parshas Acharei. The Shaloh (in his Siddur) asks the reason for this, noting that Shabbos does not enter from the fields rather it 'descends' from Above). This was the custom of the Arizal, and many others of that generation. As the sun was setting over the hilltops, these sages and disciples would venture out into the open fields, or gather at one of the magnificent slopes, and open their minds and hearts in melodies of deep joy and longing, as they greeted the Shabbos Queen.

Going out into the fields represents moving into a *Reshus haRabim* / public domain, literally, 'domain of the many,' In this way, it represents going into the realm of the weekday, of multiplicity. When they would return to *Shul* / the synagogue, it represented the inclusion of the 'fields' of the 'many' into the *Reshus haYachid* / private domain, literally the 'domain of the Unified,' the place of Echad. (A Reshus HaYachid is a place ten *Tefachim* / handbreadths high or with a gate ten Tefachim high and four Tefachim wide (*Shabbos*, 6a). This measurement corresponds to the ten Sefiros within Malchus and the four letters in the Name of Hashem. *Tola'as Yaakov*, Sisrei Tefilos Shabbos uMoadim. *Tikkunei Zohar*, 12a).

During this same period there lived in Tzfas a famed Kabbalist, Rav Shlomo haLevi Alkabetz, who was the brother-in-law and teacher of the Ramak. R. Shlomo, like many in his circle, was also a poet and he composed the poem "Lecha Dodi." His name, Shlomo haLevi, is found in an acrostic of the verses — the middle eight passages begin with the eight letters of his name. The theme, "Come my Beloved," is a borrowed metaphor from the Song of Songs (7:12), where it says, "Come, my beloved, let us go into the field, let us stay in the villages, let us go early to the vineyards…" The sages and mystics of Tzfas were inspired by this imagery to go out into the open fields to welcome the Shabbos Bride. At the end of Lecha Dodi, we physically turn around and open ourselves to greet the Shabbos Bride.

TURNING AROUND

Lecha Dodi serves as a bridge between the six chapters of Psalms, representing the six days of the week, and the seventh chapter of Tehilim that follows, which is *Mizmor Shir l'Yom haShabbos* / "A song for the day of Shabbos." However, there is an important transition that we need to make before reciting the latter chapter. This transition occurs when we turn around at the end of Lecha Dodi.

When the entire congregation turns around and recites the final passage of the Lecha Dodi, all bow slightly to honor the entrance of our 'bride,' the presence of Shabbos.

On another level, as we are leaving behind the week and moving into a new sacred space, we are turning back for a moment to welcome our past, making sure we are bringing along all the events of the week, so we can integrate them into the 'Echad' of Shabbos. In this sense, the phrase *Lechah Dodi* is a call to gather together our past. And thus, as we chant the final verse, we bow in *Hachna'ah* / humble acknowledgment of our past, recalling where we have come from, and bringing all of us along into Echad. Then we can turn back around and allow our past week to merge into the light of Shabbos.

At the same time that we are greeting the Shabbos Queen, we also invite our past week to come along with us into Shabbos. We acknowledge that although misalignments may have occurred during the week, and our life may have been chaotic and scattered, we now have the ability to align all of the many disjointed parts of ourselves and fully enter the world of Echad.

On Shabbos we have the power to elevate everything of our past week, all our actions, words and thoughts. With proper intentions, we can even elevate the actions of other people.

Some suggest that when we are turning around, we're acknowledging the people who are sitting in the back of the Shul because they are in mourning, and we welcome them into Shabbos. Sensitive and beautiful as it may be, this reason seems very unlikely (Shu't, *Iggeres Moshe*, Orach Chayim, 3:45). Yet, it can nevertheless contain a symbolic meaning; we are turning around to our own selves, as it were, acknowledging the 'broken' parts that we left at the door, in the back of Shul. We are now compassionately welcoming all of this and bringing it into the deep wholeness and wellbeing that is Shabbos.

ERADICATING 'HAPPENSTANCE' / AMALEK

Our sages tell us that Amalek is the opposite of Shabbos (*Pirkei D'Rebbe Eliezer* 43:1. see also *Yalkut Shimoni*, Devarim 25:17). The archenemy of Shabbos is Amalek.

Amalek is the nation that attacked the People of Israel as they were traveling through the desert. And they attacked as soon as there was a *Chilul Shabbos* / desecration of Shabbos (*Shabbos*, 118b). The Torah tells us, "You shall remember what Amalek did to you on the way, when you went out of Egypt; אשר קרך בדרך / how he happened upon you on the way and cut off all the stragglers at your rear" (Devarim, 25:17-18). The word קרך / *Karcha* is a peculiar word choice, what does "happened upon you" mean? It seems to suggest some type of coincidence or happenstance.

Indeed, this is the worldview of Amalek. Amalek says 'things happen' — there is no design or providence in the world. Nothing is meant to be, everything is haphazard and a random chance of coincidence.

Amalek says, in the language of the Rambam, "What has happened to us is merely a natural phenomenon and this difficulty is merely a chance occurrence" / דבר זה ממנהג העולם אירע לנו וצרה זו נקרה נקרית (*Hilchos Ta'anis*, 1:3).

Echad is the radical opposite of *Karcha*. To say life is random (which is even worse than saying that 'outside objects, people and events' are mobilizing up against me), is the total antithesis of Shabbos and Echad.

Truly integrating the message of Shabbos includes understanding that "in six days Hashem created the world," and it is a completely intentional Creation; every speck of sand is Divinely orchestrated to be in its exact location. To live life from a place of Echad is to live with *Emunah* / faith, and thus to live a Shabbosdik life.

Living from a perspective of Echad, one truly grasps that nothing just happens to you. You do not just 'happen to' have this spouse, this family, these parents, or even this house or car or shoes. *Everything* is *part of you*, an essential part of your existence. Everything in your life is a part of your essence.

Recognizing this is part of "erasing (the memory) of Amalek." Truly celebrating Shabbos is part of the process of eradicating the very concept of Amalek (i.e. happenstance) from the world.

Shabbos is called a *Yom laHashem* (Devarim, 5:13), a hint that Shabbos is *haShem* / 'the Name' of HaKadosh Baruch Hu, the Yud-Hei-Vav-Hei. In contrast, with regards to Amalek, it says, "The Holy One, blessed be He, swore that His Name (Yud-Hei-Vav-Hei) will not be complete... until the name of Amalek is completely obliterated" (Rashi, *Shemos*, 17:16. *Tanchumah, Ki Teitzei*).

Through our connecting to the essence of Shabbos, the Echad, and choosing to live within it, we are bringing the world one step closer to the cosmic revelation of the full Name of Hashem, in which the whole world will recognize that Hashem is One and His name is One. May this day arrive speedily, in our days.

10

SHABBOS AS HOLY REST
VS. UNHOLY MELANCHOLY

S HABBOS IS A TIME OF JOY, LIGHT, AND EASE; A DAY OF
family, friends, introspection, devotion, pleasure, and Deveikus. In general, Shabbos feels like a 'light-filled' time. Of course,
it is a very serious time, but certainly not heavy or gloomy in any
sense. In the Creation narrative, after the description of each day,
the Torah says, "And it was evening and it was morning, Day One,"
or, "And it was evening and it was morning, Day Two," and so forth.
The only exception is the Seventh Day, Shabbos. The Torah never says, "And it was evening and it was morning, Day Seven." In
this narrative, even the word "evening" is never employed regarding

Shabbos, only "day." In fact, the phrase "day of Shabbos" appears three times in the Creation narrative, and these correspond to the three dimensions of Shabbos which were explored earlier. Each of these dimensions is thus called the "day" of Shabbos, even the evening.

Later on, when the Torah speaks of keeping Shabbos, the day of Shabbos is always referred to as *Yom haShabbos* / the day of Shabbos; the Torah never uses the phrase *Leil Shabbos* / the night of Shabbos. This is because all of Shabbos is 'day.' Shabbos is all light, intimating the time (says the Medrash, *Pirkei d'Rebbe Eliezer*, 19. See also *Resisei Layla*, 54) when, "it will be a unique day, a day known only to Hashem, with no distinction between day and night. When evening comes, there will be light" (*Zecharyah*, 14:7).

And yet, sometimes a light can be so intense that it causes blindness and darkness. Sometimes the very thing that is supposed to bring healing, light, comfort, and a respite from the toil of the week, can paradoxically be the source of heaviness, darkness and depression.

Shabbos is openness, freedom and soaring, transcending the world of work and movement. Yet, it can also seem to have a darkside, as it were. When not experienced correctly, Shabbos can appear to be the cause of constriction and gloom.

Shabbos, the Zohar teaches (*Tikkunei Zohar*, 70. See *Sheim Meshmuel*, Rosh Hashanah. *Shabbos*, 156a. Chasam Sofer, *Toras Moshe*, Bo), is connected to the influence of *Shabtai* / Saturn, a zodiac symbol that is connected to all forms of depression, darkness and 'wailing.' Indeed, historically, many ancient peoples (including, in a sense, the Karaites) who desired to tap into Shabtai energy, would sit in darkness on Shabbos and mourn. This was the practice of ancient civilizations such as Babylon, who dedicated every seventh day as an "evil day" or a "dark day." (Interestingly, the Jews that lived in Babylonian used to שובתין מתוך מריעין / rest after blowing a *Teruah* / wailing, mourning sound of the Shofar (*Shabbos*, 35b). Indeed, בבלאי דיתבי בארעא חשוכא אמרי שמעתא דמחשכא / "Babylonians, because they dwell in a dark land, state laws that are 'dark.'" *Zevachim*, 60b. *Berachos*, 25b) Indeed, many non-Jews erroneously thought that on Shabbos, Jews fasted or mourned. (Although, not only do we not mourn, we are not even allowed to publicly *appear* as if we are mourning or fasting on Shabbos. Mar the son of Ravina, who fasted all year long, even on (certain) holidays, ate on Shabbos. *Pesachim*, 78b, *Baal haMaor*, ad loc). The Roman emperor Augustus, was reported to have said to the future emperor Tiberius (the city Teveriya is named after him, although, it too has a Torah epistemology. See *Megilah* 6a), that he had fasted all day long, "more diligently than a Jew on Shabbos." Because of this potential negative influence, says the *Zohar*, the Torah instructs us to do the very opposite on Shabbos; to light candles, eat hot delicious foods, and be intimate with our spouse (to show that we are beyond this mournful and ascetic influence. See *Tola'as Yaakov*, Sisrei Tefilos, Shabbos uMo'adim, 15). We are therefore to experience Oneg on and from Shabbos. And when we choose to celebrate Shabbos, in a joyful and expansive manner, this 'negative influence' will have no dominance over us.

Let us unpack and understand this more deeply. What is this 'dark' side of Shabbos that needs to be countered, as if not celebrating Shabbos with joy and Oneg could cause one to fall into a negative influence.

OUTER WORLD OF MOVEMENT & INNER
WORLD OF STILLNESS

A dominant feature of our world is *Tenuah* / movement. Movement implies time, and an evolving or devolving of life. Everything is moving; even an inanimate object, such as a stone, is stirring with life and dancing particles.

Tenuah is an essential part of the fabric of this world, and perhaps paradoxically, even more so on Shabbos. On a simple level, in six days Hashem created the world and on the Seventh Day Hashem rested. Simply, this means that after six days of actively creating the world, on the Seventh Day Hashem rested from creating, and from then on the world started functioning on its own, as if 'without' the involvement of the Creator. In this way, as the Chasam Sofer points out (*Toras Moshe*, Likutim, p. 969), on Shabbos the world is in a more *advanced* state of Tenuah. On Shabbos the world is moving on its own, so to speak. Once Shabbos ensued, the world began to function 'independently.' For this very reason, if a person who is not commanded to 'rest' on Shabbos keeps Shabbos, he is violating the very essence of the reality of Shabbos.*

* Thus גוי ששבת חייב מיתה / "A non-Jew who keeps Shabbos is liable to death" (*Sanhedrin*, 58b), although this is not literal — מכין אותו ועונשין אותו ומודיעין אותו שהוא חיב מיתה על זה. אבל אינו נהרג (*Hilchos Melachim*, 10:9). As the Rambam rules, וכן עכו"ם ששבת אפילו ביום מימות החול אם עשאהו לעצמו כמו שבת חייב מיתה (Ibid). In other words, if he creates for himself a day like Shabbos, even just an entire day of resting from 'doing' (Rashi: אלא מנוחה בעלמא קא אסר להו שלא יבטלו ממלאכה), he is liable to death. This is because the world is defined by *Tenuah* / movement, growth, the continuous rhythm of seasons; "Day and night shall not cease" (Bereishis, 8:22). When a person of the world ceases from being in movement, progressing and creating, he ceases, as it were, from being. This prohibition thus exists prior to Matan Torah, and applies to every day of the week, as the Rambam rules. Alternatively, the Medrash (*Shemos Rabbah*, 25:16 and *Devarim Rabbah*, 1:18) explains another reason why "a non-Jew who keeps Shabbos is liable"; it is because Shabbos is a special gift of endearment from HaKadosh Baruch Hu to Klal Yisrael, and thus is only applicable post-Matan-Torah, and unlike the

Shabbos, from an external perspective, is even more active and alive with Tenuah than the weekday.

On Shabbos the world is stronger and more powerful, mimicking the first Shabbos of Creation. The external world actually began to function 'properly' on the Seventh Day, and ever since then, every Shabbos has this special quality, a sense of activation and alignment. This is also the reason why a proper time for rain is on Friday night, on Shabbos (*Taanis*, 23a). When the Pasuk says, "I will give your rains in their time" (Vayikra, 26:4), our sages tell us that 'in their time' means it will rain, for one example, on Shabbos eve (Rashi, ad loc).

Indeed, the 'external' world of nature, on Shabbos, is even more active, alive and pulsating with movement. "On the Seventh Day Hashem rested," means that on the day of Shabbos, the Divine desire to create, the inner Life-Force that is emanating from the 'inner life' of the Creator, as it were, recedes and rests from creative expression, and returns back into itself, into the Source, Hashem. Thus, the strength of the 'outer world' becomes even more pronounced, as it is left to its own devices, so to speak.

On Shabbos, the 'inner life' of Creation rests and is elevated (*Eitz Chayim*, Sha'ar 40, Derush 3. *Pri Eitz Chayim*, Sha'ar haTefilah, 6), while the activity of the 'outer life' is more dominant. And therefore rain

Rambam, it applies only to resting on Shabbos (see Rav Yoseph Engel, *Beis HaOtzer*, Avos). Interestingly, the Avnei Nezer teaches that the laxity of Klal Yisrael in keeping Shabbos created the possibility for the nations of the world to actually experience some form of Shabbos (*Shem MiShemuel*, Shemos, Shabbos, Chol haMoed, Sukkos. Note also *Ohr Chadash* (Maharal), in the beginning. *Medrash Rabbah*, Esther, 1:10). Clearly the Avnei Nezer's is a negative statement, but perhaps, paradoxically, in terms of Hanhagas haYichud, it indicates the movement of the entire world towards the world of Yichud.

falls on Shabbos, whereas the *Mon* / Manna ceased to fall on Shabbos, as Mon represents an inner Divine *Shefa* / flow.

We are connected with the inner life of the Creator (*Kaviyachol* / as it were), as our soul is "part of the Divine Above, literally." We too rest, and return with that inner life force 'into Hashem,' and this is what gives us deeper, spiritual, transcendental experiences on Shabbos. In this way, on Shabbos, our body and its appetites are more assertive in a pronounced way, yet so too is our soul, paradoxically enhancing our potential for spirituality.

Just as there are 'two worlds,' an inner world and an outer world, we have a dimension of self that is part of the external natural world, and a dimension of self that is "part of the Divine Above," part of the 'Innermost' Cosmic Reality.

In our outer self, we are part beast, a member of the animal kingdom. This includes our body and all its functions and needs: eating, drinking, procreating, and growing, progressing, being ambitious and wanting more and more, including more money, power or fame. From this perspective, we too are part of the Tenuah of the world. We are driven to grow, expand, desire and move.

Yet, the innermost part of us is beyond Creation, beyond the animal kingdom, beyond desire and movement. This dimension is hooked into the Inner Reality of the Creator, as it were, here we are at one with the Divine Inner Desire and Will for Creation. From this paradigm, we are always 'perfect,' one with the world of *Menuchah* / rest and interiority, and unscathed by the world of Tenuah.

The nature and needs of our body are much like the nature and needs of the entire world of movement. Sitting "idly with no work brings boredom" (*Kesuvos*, 59b). Being passive or stagnant causes irritability, cantankerousness (Rashi, ad loc), and even depression and eventual death (*Avos d'Rebbe Nason*, 11. See *Torah Temimah*, Bereishis, 8:22). The nature of the human body is to move and be active — "Man is created to toil" (*Iyov*, 5:7. The lower type of toil is actual 'work.' *Sanhedrin*, 99b). Furthermore, we need to be active not only in our physical actions but also in our thoughts: solving problems, planning, strategizing, learning, dreaming, hoping.

Sameach, the Hebrew word meaning "happiness," is closely related and phonetically connected to the Hebrew word for growth, *Tzomeach*. Despite the discomfort that often accompanies a growth spurt, we are most happy when we are in the process of moving towards some meaningful goal. This is because when we are engaged in motion we are being true to the nature of life, to the rhythm of being alive. All of Creation is in a constant state of flux and transformation, even something as seemingly still as a mountain.

Work, self-exertion, creativity and a sense of accomplishment are essential needs and integral qualities of the human condition; they are what keep us alive and vital. To create, to move, to achieve is part of our existential self. In contrast, idleness leads to all types of emotional and physical imbalances.

The Mishnah (*Kesuvos*, 59b) teaches that a man who vows that his wife is prohibited from doing any type of work, must divorce her and give her the payment for her *Kesuvah* / marriage contract since idleness leads to שיעמום / boredom and eventual immorality (Rambam, *Hilchos Ishus*, 21:3). One cannot enter into a relationship with another human being with a precondition of idleness, because boredom leads to a sense of lifelessness. Lifelessness, in turn, leads to licentiousness, because one is in such dire need to feel alive, that one would do anything to regain that visceral sensation of vitality. Another Mishnah tells us that one who plays with dice, meaning someone who gambles, is disqualified from being a witness (*Sanhedrin*, 24b). What is the reason? Rami bar Chama says that he is disqualified because gambling is a transaction with an אסמכתא / *Asmachta* / inconclusive consent. This means, one who gambles does not have conclusive consent to pay when he loses since he plays under the assumption that he will win. And as an אסמכתא does not affect acquisition, the one who wins a gamble takes money that is not legally his, and is considered a thief. Rav Sheishes says, this is not the reason, rather the reason is, "because they are not involved in settling the world" / לפי שאין עסוקין ביישובו של עולם (this is also the reason the Rambam offers. *Hilchos Eidus*, 10:4).

Man is created to toil. We need to work to feel worthy, and idleness leads to a sense of unworthiness. On a deeper level, mankind was created to "work and protect" creation and to be involved in ישובו של עולם / settling the world.

For six days of the week we are asked and invited to be co-creators with the Creator; to settle and 'improve' this world. Our purpose is innovating positive change and advancing the wellbeings of the world, whether by creating cures for diseases, developing new technologies that ease the life of the world's inhabitants and environments, spreading spiritual wisdom widely, or even just contributing to a healthy economy. This we do for six days of the week, each individual on their own level, and in their own way.

However, if on Shabbos we are simply resting from workweek activity, merely resting our bodies from labor, we may feel happier and lighter for the first few hours of Shabbos evening, but after too long, we may end up feeling restless, confined and even depressed. A person may even erroneously think, "Hashem gave me Shabbos to make my life miserable" (*Medrash Rabbah*, Devarim, 3:1). They may form the impression that keeping Shabbos just holds them back from achievement and gets them down, *Chas veShalom* / G-d forbid.

Indeed, there is a type of melancholy or tiredness that can set in on Shabbos afternoon, when one's practice of Shabbos is merely the absence of work and activity. The reason why these sentiments may arise is because this passive type of rest is contrary to the movement-driven nature of outer life.

When Shabbos is no more than inactivity and resting the body/ mind, it will eventually feel empty or like a heavy burden. "Shabbos is a day of the soul, and not a day of the body at all" (*Zohar* 2, 205b. 3, 174a). If your Shabbos is only about catching up on sleep, enjoying delicacies that you normally do not eat, and sitting around chatting, it will be counterproductive and leave you feeling less rested, less nourished, and less joyful. Indeed, to experience authentic Shabbos rest, which is freeing, liberating, and joyful, which is conducive for introspection, spiritual subtlety and mindfulness, we need to allow ourselves to tap into our own inner dimension, the part of ourselves that is always beyond the world of Tenuah and ambition. Shabbos calls us not only to rest from work and activity, but to enter a place beyond the pendulum of work and rest entirely. Cosmically, on Shabbos, the inner quality of Creation returns to its Source, and microcosmically, we too are given the opportunity to enter our Inner-World of Stillness beyond the dichotomy of activity and inactivity altogether.

Shabbos is, therefore, not merely a day off, a day to rest from work; if someone practices Shabbos this way, there is actually no *Geder* / definition of 'Shabbos' in it. The definition of Shabbos is *Yom laHashem* / "a day to Hashem."*

When our practice of Shabbos is *laHashem*, intrinsically linked to the *Elokim Chayim* / G-d of Life, Shabbos leaves us feeling more alive, free, 'perfect' and 'light.' When our Shabbos practice is linked to the dirge-like despondency of Shabtai, Shabbos leaves us feeling 'imperfect' and 'endarkened.'

Observing Shabbos as 'the Shabbos of Shabtai' is like taking an active person and forcing him to sit still and do nothing for no apparent reason, it's inevitably a source of frustration and anxiety. In fact, this type of inactivity can feel like a death sentence to a

---

* נהרג זה שהעידו עליו ואחר כך החמו אינן נהרגין מן הדין שנאמר כאשר זמם לעשות ועדיין לא עשה ודבר זה מפי הקבלה אבל אם לקה זה שהעידו עליו לוקין (*Hilchos Eidus*, 20:2). "If the *Eidim* / witnesses were refuted after the (court's) execution of the (accused) person against whom they had testified, they are not put to death through an (*a fortiori*) inference. As it is written, 'You shall do to him as he (the dishonest witness) schemed to do...' (Devarim, 19:19) — implying, 'but has not yet done.' This interpretation is based on tradition. However, if the accused against whom they had testified was lashed, (the scheming Eidim) are lashed." With regards to *Malkus* / punitive lashing, why do we not say, כאשר זמם לעשות / "as he had schemed to do"? and if *Malkus* was already given, the *Eidim* / witnesses do not receive *Malkus*? Rav Chayim Brisker (on the Rambam) answers, this is because if the person gets Malkus based on their testimony and it turns out that they were liars, then it was not a Geder of Malkus that was given, rather merely a hitting. Malkus has to be in front of Beis Din, Rav Chayim proves, and if it is outside Beis Din, then it is not Malkus, but rather just hitting, and since this was a false witness, there was no Din of Beis Din, and thus it was mere hitting. Furthermore, if the Eidim wanted to give Malkus and turned out to be only hitting, the Eidim themselves then get Malkus. Regarding Shabbos there is a parallel idea. Shabbos must be *Lifnei Hashem, laHashem* / 'in front of' and 'to' Hashem; if a person merely takes a day off from work it is not Shabbos, rather just resting.

vibrant person, and could cause him to lose his mind, as it were. (מועד לשבתות ואינו מועד לחול) says the Mishnah. Why? Says Rashi, לפי שהוא בטל ממלאכה חחה דעתו עליו (*Baba Kama*, 37a). An animal that takes on the status of a *Mu'ad* to gore on Shabbos, is not a Mu'ad to gore during the week, because if an animal does not work on Shabbos, he loses his mind and is restless.)

Shabbos, the Day to or for Hashem, is not just rest 'from' work, it is rest 'beyond' work. It is a day to tap into our Inner-World, to connect with the dimension of our Soul beyond Tenuah and to actively connect with the Source of Infinite Aliveness. The Day to Hashem is a time of inner-joy, a time of releasing our 'outer' ambitions, desires and strivings, to immerse in the dynamic, celebratory rest of prayer, study, song, introspection, silence and Deveikus. We can let go of trying to control everything that is going on in our lives and just live with total *Emunah* / faith and trust in Hashem. This letting go is not 'giving up,' G-d forbid, rather it is an experience of becoming unburdened, alive and free.

The choice is ours. We can choose the external or the internal Shabbos, to rest 'from' work or to rest 'beyond' work. We can use Shabbos for passive relaxation or for actively going inward. To ensure that our Shabbos is truly transformational we need to deliberately open ourselves up to the depths that are the gifts of Shabbos. We have to ensure that we have prepared properly for Shabbos so that when we enter Shabbos we can shift into our deeper self that is beyond the world of Tenuah. We need to engage Shabbos with holiness, with life, vigor, and active anticipation.

To help us enter Shabbos correctly we need to create the proper mindset. In addition, we need to internalize the practices that will assist us in making the transition from a weekday, aggressive, ambitious mode of movement, into a Shabbosdik mode of peaceful perfection. (G-d willing, the next volume in this series on "How to Enter Shabbos" will explore these transitional techniques.)

To truly understand what Shabbos is all about, we need to let go completely of the weekday and everything that the weekday paradigm represents, all ambitions and work, all worry and doubts, all struggle and duality. We need to enter fully into Shabbos and experience the Divine depths of Shabbos bliss.

Indeed, Shabbos is not just another Mitzvah that adds more Kedushah to our lives and our world. Shabbos is a Mitzvah that is essential to being a Jew. There are Mitzvos that are meant to add Kedushah to Klal Yisrael, such as those of the Beis haMikdash, and there are Mitzvos that are essential to Klal Yisrael and without these Mitzvos a person is not, so to speak, part of Klal Yisrael (*Beis haLevi*, Ki Tisa. According to Halacha, העובד כוכבים ומזלות ומחלל שבתות בפרהסיא הרי אלו מומרין לכל התורה כולה והרי הם כעכו"ם גמורים (*Chulin*, 5a). In the words of the Rambam: השבת ועבודת כוכבים ומזלות כל אחת משתיהן שקולה כנגד שאר כל מצות התורה והשבת היא האות שבין הקדוש ברוך הוא ובינינו לעולם. לפיכך כל העובר על שאר המצות הרי הוא בכלל רשעי ישראל. אבל המחלל שבת בפרהסיא הרי הוא כעובד עבודת כוכבים ומזלות ושניהם כעכו"ם לכל דבריהם. *Hilchos Shabbos*, 30:15). Shabbos is essential to who we are.

Shabbos is who you really are.

AFTERNOTE

Sof Davar / in conclusion, after all is said and done, what is Shabbos? *Shabbos is...*

BEING
REST
CALM
ELEVATION
SOUL
TRANSCENDENCE
FOCUS
CLARITY
REVELATION
REDEMPTION
UNITY
SILENCE
STILLNESS
WHOLENESS
COMPLETION
EVERYTHING
BLESSING
JOY
PLEASURE
TACHLIS
DEVEIKUS

And, ultimately,

SHABBOS IS SIMPLY *SHABBOS.*

On Shabbos, as we sing songs in honor of this most holy day and all it represents, quite often we simply sing, over and over again, the words, "*Shabbos, Shabbos!*" or "*Shabbos Kodesh!*" There is simply nothing like this on any other day of the calendar. On Pesach, we do not sit at our Seder singing, '*Pesach, Pesach,*' nor do we sit in our Sukkah and sing, '*Sukkos, Sukkos.*' Yet, many do sing this way on Shabbos. It is like the sweet whisper, or ecstatic exclamation, of a beloved's name.

On Shabbos we just want to sing, call out, and declare, *Shabbos! Shabbos!*

Indeed, "The secret of Shabbos is *Shabbos.*"

OTHER BOOKS BY THE AUTHOR

RECLAIMING THE SELF
The Way of Teshuvah

Teshuvah is one of the great gifts of life. It speaks of a hope for a better today and empowers us to choose a brighter tomorrow. But what exactly is Teshuvah? How does it work? How can we undo our past and how do we deal with guilt? And what is healthy regret without eroding our self-esteem? In this fascinating and empowering book, the path for genuine transformation and a way to include all of our past in the powerful moment of the now, is explored and demonstrated.

THE MYSTERY OF KADDISH
Understanding the Mourner's Kaddish

The Mystery of Kaddish is an in-depth exploration into the Mourner's Prayer. Throughout Jewish history, there have been many rites and rituals associated with loss and mourning, yet none have prevailed quite like the Mourner's Kaddish Prayer, which has become the definitive ritual of mourning. The book explores the source of this prayer and deconstructs the meaning to better understand the grieving process and how the Kaddish prayer supports and uplifts the bereaved through their own personal journey to healing.

UPSHERNISH: The First Haircut
Exploring the Laws, Customs & Meanings of a Boy's First Haircut

What is the meaning of Upsherin, the traditional celebration of a boy's first haircut at the age of three? Why is a boy's hair allowed to grow freely for his first three years? What is the deeper import of hair in all its lengths and varieties? What is the meaning of hair coverings? Includes a guide to conducting an Upsherin ceremony.

A BOND FOR ETERNITY
Understanding the Bris Milah

What is the Bris Milah – the covenant of circumcision? What does it represent, symbolize and signify? This book provides an in depth and sensitive review
of this fundamental Mitzvah. In this little masterpiece of wisdom – profound
yet accessible —the deeper meaning of this essential rite of passage and its eternal link to the Jewish people, is revealed and explored.

REINCARNATION AND JUDAISM
The Journey of the Soul

A fascinating analysis of the concept of Gilgul / Reincarnation. Dipping into
the fountain of ancient wisdom and modern understanding, this book addresses
and answers such basic questions as: What is reincarnation? Why does it occur?
And how does it affect us personally?

INNER RHYTHMS
The Kabbalah of MUSIC

Exploring the inner dimension of sound and music, and particularly, how
music permeates all aspects of life. The topics range from Deveikus/Unity and
Yichudim/Unifications, to the more personal issues, such as Simcha/Happiness
and Marirus/ sadness.

MEDITATION AND JUDAISM
Exploring the Jewish Meditative Paths

A comprehensive work encompassing the entire spectrum of Jewish thought, from the sages of the Talmud and the early Kabbalists to the modern philosophers and Chassidic masters. This book is both a scholarly, in-depth study of meditative practices, and a practical, easy to follow guide for any person interested in meditating the Jewish way.

―――――

TOWARD THE INFINITE

A book focusing exclusively on the Chassidic approach to meditation known as Hisbonenus. Encompassing the entire meditative experience, it takes the reader on a comprehensive and engaging journey through this unique practice. The book explores the various states of consciousness that a person encounters in the course of the meditation, beginning at a level of extreme self-awareness and concluding with a state of total non-awareness.

―――――

THIRTY – TWO GATES OF WISDOM
into the Heart of Kabbalah & Chassidus

What is Kabbalah? And what are the differences between the theoretical, meditative, magical and personal Kabbalistic teachings? What are the four paths of interpreting the teachings of the ARIzal? What did Chassidus teach? These are some of the fundamental issues expanded upon in this text. And then, more specifically, why are there so many names of G-d and what do they represent? What are the key concepts of these deeper teachings?

The book explores the grand narrative of the great chain of reality, how there was and is a movement from the Infinite Oneness of Hashem to a world of (apparent) duality and multiplicity.

―――――

THE PURIM READER
The Holiday of Purim Explored

———————

With a Persian name, a masquerade dress code and a woman as the heroine, Purim is certainly unusual amongst the Jewish holidays. Most people are very familiar with the costumes, Megilah and revelry, but are mystified by their significance. This book offers a glimpse into the hidden world of Purim, uncovering these mysteries and offering a deeper understanding of this unique holiday.

———————

EIGHT LIGHTS
8 Meditations for Chanukah

What is the meaning and message of Chanukah? What is the spiritual significance of the Lights of the Menorah? What are the Lights telling us? What is the deeper dimension of the Dreidel? Rav Pinson, with his trademark deep learning and spiritual sensitivity guides us through eight meditations relating to the Lights of the Menorah, the eight days of Chanukah, and a fascinating exploration of the symbolism and structure of the Dreidel. Includes a detailed how-to guide for lighting the Chanukah Menorah.

———————

THE IYYUN HAGADAH
An Introduction to the Haggadah

In this beautifully written introduction to Passover and the Haggadah, we are guided through the major themes of Passover and the Seder night. This slim text, addresses the important questions, such as: What is the big deal of Chametz? What are we trying to achieve through conducting a Seder? What's with all that stuff on the Seder Plate? And most importantly, how is this all related to freedom?

PASSPORT TO KABBALAH
A Journey of Inner Transformation

Life is a journey full of ups and downs, inside-outs, and unexpected detours. There are times when we think we know exactly where we want to be headed, and other times when we are so lost we don't even know where we are. This slim book provides readers with a passport of sorts to help them through any obstacles along their path of self-refinement, reflection, and self-transformation.

THE FOUR SPECIES
The Symbolism of the Lulav & Esrog

The Four Species have inspired countless commentaries and traditions and intrigued scholars and mystics alike. In this little masterpiece of wisdom both profound and practical - the deep symbolic roots and nature of the Four Species are explored. The Na'anuim, or ritual of the Lulav movement, is meticulously detailed and Kavanos,, are offered for use with the practice. Includes an illustrated guide to the Lulav Movements.

THE BOOK OF LIFE AFTER LIFE

What is a soul? What happens to us after we physically die?

What is consciousness, and can it survive without a physical brain?

Can we remember our past lives?

Do near-death experiences prove immortality?

What is Gan Eden? Resurrection?

Exploring the possibility of surviving death, the near-death experience and a glimpse into what awaits us after this life.

(This book is an updated and expanded version of the book; Jewish Wisdom of the Afterlife)

THE GARDEN OF PARADOX:
The Essence of Non - Dual Kabbalah

This book is a Primer on the Essential Philosophy of Kabbalah presented as a series of 3 conversations, revealing the mysteries of Creator, Creation and Consciousness. With three representational students, embodying respectively, the philosopher, the activist and the mystic, the book, tackles the larger questions of life. Who is G-d? Who am I? Why do I exist? What is my purpose in this life? Written in clear and concise prose, the text, gently guides the reader towards making sense of life's paradoxes and living meaningfully.

BREATHING & QUIETING THE MIND

Achieving a sense of self-mastery and inner freedom demands that we gain a measure of hegemony over our thoughts. We learn to choose out thoughts so that we are not at the mercy of whatever belches up to the mind. Through quieting the mind and conscious breathing we can slow the onrush of anxious, scattered thinking and come to a deeper awareness of the interconnectedness of all of life.

Source texts are included in translation, with how-to-guides for the various practices.

VISUALIZATION AND IMAGERY:
Harnessing the Power of our Mind's Eye

We assume that what we see with our eyes is absolute. Yet, beyond our ability to choose what we see, we have the ability to choose how we see. This directly translates into how we experience life. In a world saturated with visual imagery, our senses are continuously assaulted with Kelipa/empty/fantasy imagery that we would not necessarily choose. These images can negatively affect our relationship with ourselves, with the world around us, and with the Divine. This volume seeks to show us how we can alter that which we observe through harnessing the power of our mind's eye, the inner sanctum of our imagination. We thus create a new way to see and experience the world. This book teaches us how to utilize visualization and imagery as a way to develop our spiritual sensitivity and higher intuition, and ultimately achieve Deveikus/Unity with Hashem.

SOUND AND VIBRATION:
Tuning into the Echoes of Creation

Through our perception of sound and vibration we internalize the world around us. What we hear, and how we process that hearing, has a profound impact on how we experience life. What we hear can empower us or harm us. A defining human capacity is to harness the power sound -- through speech, dialogue, and song, and through listening to others. Hearing is primary dimension of our existence. In fact, as a fetus our ears were the first fully operating sensory organs to develop.

This book will guide you in methods of utilizing the power of sound and vibration to heal and maintain mental, emotional and spiritual health, to fine-tune your Midos and even to guide you into deeper levels of Deveikus / conscious unity with Hashem. The vibratory patterns of the Aleph-Beis are particularly useful portals into our deeper conscious selves. Through chanting and deep listening, we can use the letters and sounds to shift our very mindset, to induce us into a state of presence and spiritual elevation.

THE POWER OF CHOICE:
A Practical Guide to Conscious Living

It is the essential premise of this book that we hold the key to unlock many of the gates that seem closed to us and keep us from living our fullest life. That key we all hold is the power to choose. The Power of Choice is the primary tool that we have at our disposal to impact the world and effect change within our own lives. We often give up this power to outside forces such as the market, media, politicians or peer pressure; or to internal forces that often function beyond our conscious control such as ego, anger, lust, greed or jealousy. Making conscious, compassionate and creative decisions is the cornerstone of living a mature and meaningful life.

MYSTIC TALES FROM THE EMEK HAMELECH

Mystic Tales of the Emek HaMelech, is a wondrous and inspiring collection of stories culled from the Emek HaMelech. Emek HaMelech, from which these stories have been taken, (as well as its author) is a bit of a mystery. But like all good mysteries, it is one worth investigating. In this spirit the present volume is being offered to the general public in the merit and memory of its saintly author, as well as in the hopes of introducing a vital voice of deeper Torah teaching and tradition to a contemporary English speaking audience

---

INNER WORLDS OF JEWISH PRAYER
A Guide to Develop and Deepen the Prayer Experience

While much attention has been paid to the poetry, history, theology and contextual meaning of the prayers, the intention of this work is to provide a guide to finding meaning and effecting transformation through the prayer experience itself.

Explore: *What happens when we pray? *How do we enter the mind-state of prayer? *Learning to incorporate the body into the prayers. *Discover techniques to enhance and deepen prayer and make it a transformative experience.

This empowering and inspiring text, demonstrates how through proper mindset, preparation and dedication, the experience of prayer can be deeply transformative and ultimately, life-altering.

WRAPPED IN MAJESTY
Tefillin - Exploring the Mystery

Tefillin, the black boxes and leather straps that are worn during prayer, are curiously powerful and mysterious. Within the inky black boxes lie untold secrets. In this profound, passionate and thought-provoking text, the multi-dimensional perspectives of Tefillin are explored and revealed. Magically weaving together all levels of Torah including the Peshat (literal observation), to Remez (allegorical), to Derush, (homiletic), to Sod (hidden) into one beautiful tapestry. Inspirational and instructive, Wrapped in Majesty: Tefillin, will make putting on the Tefillin more meaningful and inspiring.

SECRETS OF THE MIKVAH:
Waters of Transformation

A Mikvah is a pool of water used for the purpose of ritual immersion; a place where one moves from a state of Tumah; impurity, blockage and death— to a place of Teharah; purity, fluidity and life.

In SECRETS OF THE MIKVAH, Rav Pinson delves into the transformative powers of the Mikvah with his trademark all-encompassing perspective that ranges from the literal, Pshat observation and Halachic implications of the texts, to the allegorical, the philosophical, and finally, to the deep secrets of the

Mikvah as revealed by Kabbalah and Chassidus.

This insightful and inspirational text demonstrates how immersion in a Mikvah can be a transformative and life-altering practice, and includes various Kavanos—deep intentions—for all people, through various stages of life, that empower and enrich the immersion experience.

————

THE SPIRAL OF TIME:
A 12 Part Series on the Months of the Year.
The following titles from the series are now available!

THE SPIRAL OF TIME:
Unraveling the Yearly Cycle

Many centuries ago, the Sages of Israel were the foremost authority in the fields of both astronomical calculation and astrological wisdom, including the deeper interpretations of the cycles and seasons. Over time, this wisdom became hidden within the esoteric teachings of the Torah, and as a result was known only to students and scholars of the deepest depths of the tradition. More recently, the great teachers, from R. Yitzchak Luria (the Arizal) to the Baal Shem Tov, taught that as the world approaches the Era of Redemption, it is a Mitzvah / spiritual obligation to broadly reveal this wisdom.

"The Spiral of Time" is volume 1 is a series of 12 books, and serves as an introductory book to the basic concepts and nature of the Hebrew calendar and explores the special day of Rosh Chodesh.

————

THE MONTH OF SHEVAT:
ELEVATING EATING & The Holiday of Tu b'Shevat

Each month of the year radiates with a distinct Divine energy and thus unique opportunities for growth, *Tikkun* and illumination. According to the deeper teachings of the Torah, all of these distinct qualities, opportunities and natural phenomena correspond to a certain data set. That is, the nature of each month is elucidated by a specific letter of the Aleph Beis, a tribe, verse, human sense, and so forth. The month of Shevat is particularly connected to food and our relationship to bodily intake. During this month we celebrate Tu b'Shevat, the New Year of the Tree, and aspire to create a proper and physically/emotionally/spiritually healthy relationship with food.

THE MONTH OF ADAR:
Transformation Through Laughter & Holy Doubt

Each month of the year radiates with distinct Divine qualities and unique opportunities for growth and spiritual illumination. As Adar concludes the monthly cycle of the year, as well as the solar phenomena of the winter, it is an appropriate month to think about our essential identity, before moving out to meet the world come spring. This month we strive to create a healthy relationship with holy humor, unbounded joy, and a general sense of lightness of being. Through the work of Adar we transform negative, crippling doubt and uncertainties into radical wonderment and openness.

THE MONTH OF IYYAR:
EVOLVING THE SELF
& The Holiday of LAG B'OMER

The month of IYYAR is the second month of the spring, a month that connects the Redemption from Egypt in Nissan with the Revelation of Torah in Sivan. The Chai/ Eighteenth day of the Month is the day we celebrate the Rashbi (Rabbi Shimon Bar Yochai) and the revealing of the hidden aspects of the Torah. This is the 'Holiday' of Lag b'Omer. The book explores the unique quality of this special month, a month that has a Mitzvah of counting the Omer every day. In addition, the book explores the roots and significance of the mystical 'holiday' of Lag b'Omer. Including the customs & Practices of Lag b'Omer, such as, bonfires, bows & arrows, parades, Upsherin, and more.

THE MONTH OF SIVAN

The Art of Receiving - Shavuot and Matan Torah

Each month of the year radiates with a distinct quality and provides unique opportunities for personal growth and illumination.

Sivan is the third month of the lunar cycle. One is a singularity. Two is division. Three is harmony, a unity that synthesizes individuality and multiplicity, Heaven and Earth, Spirituality and Physicality. During this month we celebrate Shavuos and the giving of the Torah, the ultimate expression of the unity of the Above and Below and we aspire to connect with the Keser/Crown of Torah that Transcends and yet includes all Worlds.

Learning how to truly receive Higher wisdom in our Lower faculties is the mental, emotional, and spiritual exercise of the month.

THE MONTHS OF TAMUZ AND AV:

Embracing Brokenness -
17th of Tamuz, Tisha B'Av, & Tu B'Av

Each month and season of the year, radiates with distinct Divine qualities and unique opportunities for growth and Tikkun.

The summer month of Tamuz and Av contain the longest and hottest days of the year. The raised temperature is indicative of a corresponding spiritual heat, a time of harsher judgement and potential destruction, such as the destructions of the first and second Beis HaMikdash, which began on the 17th of Tamuz and culminated on the 9th and 10th of Av.

A few days later, on Tu b'Av, the darkness is transformed and reveals the greatest light and possibility for new life. During these summer months of Tamuz and Av we embrace our brokenness so that we can heal and transform darkness into light.

———

THE MONTH OF ELUL:
Days of Introspection and Transformation

Each month of the year radiates with a distinct quality and provides unique opportunities for growth and personal transformation. Elul, as the final month of the spring/summer season is connected to endings. Elul gives us the strength to be able to finish strong, to end well. Elul also serves as a month of preparation for the New Year/Rosh Hashanah.

We inhale our past year, ending with wisdom and then we also gain the wisdom to begin anew and exhale a positive year into being. The mental, emotional, and spiritual objective of this month is introspection and the reclaiming of our inner purity and wholeness.

———

THE MONTH OF CHESHVAN:
Navigating Transitions, Elevating the Fall

Directly on the heels of the inspiring and holiday-filled month of Tishrei, Cheshvan is a month that is quiet and devoid of holidays. In the month of Cheshvan we use the stored up energies of the previous months to self-generate our inspiration and creativity and provide ourselves with the strength to rise up after a fall. In Cheshvan we are entering into a stormier, wetter and colder season. It is a month of transition. The mental, emotional and spiritual objective of this month is to weather the transitions, learn to self-generate and stand tall. And if we do fall, we use the quality of this month to get back up and do so with more conviction, strength, wisdom and clarity.

THE MONTH OF TEVES:
Refining Relationships, Elevating the Body

The quality of Teves is generally harsh—much like its counterpart Tamuz in the summer, thus the tendency for many is to hunker down, retract, curl up and wait for the month to pass by, only to reemerge when the harshness has dissipated. Think for a moment about the 'easier' months of the year, which, like gentle waves in the ocean, carry us where we want to go. We can ride these energies easily and they can propel us forward effortlessly, we just need to go with the overall flow, so to speak. The harsher months, on the other hand, can be compared to the more powerful waves that emanate from the belly of the ocean, which come forcefully crashing down and can easily drown a person before they even realize what has happened. However, those who want to utilize the momentum of the powerful energy that is available during such times can, with caution and creativity, harness these intense waves and ride them higher and farther than other, more gentle circumstances may allow. However, harnessing the power of Tohu, the raw energy of the body, does in fact need to be approached with great care and attention.

———————

THE JEWISH WEDDING:
A Guide to the Rituals and Traditions
of the Wedding Ceremony

This guide is based on the teachings of Torah, Talmud, Medrash, Zohar, Halacha, Poskim, Kabbalah and Chassidus. By quoting these teachings, we actively draw down the 'presence' of these holy souls who revealed these teachings, thus extending blessings to the bride and groom and all in attendance at the Chupa.

www.ingramcontent.com/pod-product-compliance
Lightning Source LLC
Chambersburg PA
CBHW060411100426

42812CB00038B/3495/J